MAKING CONSTITUTIONS IN DEEPLY DIVIDED SOCIETIES

How can societies grappling over the common values and shared vision of their state draft a democratic constitution? This is the central puzzle of *Making Constitutions in Deeply Divided Societies*. While most theories discuss constitution-making in the context of a moment of revolutionary change, Hanna Lerner argues that an incrementalist approach to constitution-making can enable societies riven by deep internal disagreements to either enact a written constitution or function with an unwritten one. She illustrates the process of constitution-writing in three deeply divided societies – Israel, India and Ireland – and explores the various incrementalist strategies deployed by their drafters. These include the avoidance of clear decisions, the use of ambivalent legal language and the inclusion of contrasting provisions in the constitution. Such techniques allow the deferral of controversial choices regarding the foundational aspects of the state to future political institutions, thus enabling the constitution to reflect a reality of divided identity.

HANNA LERNER is an assistant professor in political science at Tel Aviv University and a Luce visiting fellow at the Princeton Institute of International and Regional Studies, Princeton University.

MAKING CONSTITUTIONS IN DEEPLY DIVIDED SOCIETIES

HANNA LERNER

CAMBRIDGE
UNIVERSITY PRESS

CAMBRIDGE UNIVERSITY PRESS
Cambridge, New York, Melbourne, Madrid, Cape Town,
Singapore, São Paulo, Delhi, Tokyo, Mexico City

Cambridge University Press
The Edinburgh Building, Cambridge CB2 8RU, UK

Published in the United States of America by Cambridge University Press, New York

www.cambridge.org
Information on this title: www.cambridge.org/9781107005150

First published 2011

Printed in the United Kingdom at the University Press, Cambridge

A catalogue record for this publication is available from the British Library

Library of Congress Cataloguing in Publication data
Lerner, Hanna.
Making constitutions in deeply divided societies / Hanna Lerner.
p.   cm.
ISBN 978-1-107-00515-0 (hardback)
1. Constitutional law–Israel.   2. Constitutional law–India.   3. Constitutional
law–Ireland.   I. Title.
K3165.L445 2011
342.02–dc22
2011002457

ISBN 978-1-107-00515-0 Hardback

For my parents,
RACHEL AND MICHAEL POSTAVSKI

CONTENTS

ACKNOWLEDGMENTS

My work on this book began in New York, continued in Jerusalem and Tel Aviv, and ended in Princeton. Throughout my journey I was fortunate to receive the generous aid of numerous teachers, colleagues and friends. I would like to thank, first and foremost, Jean Cohen and Alfred Stepan, my doctoral advisors at Columbia University, who encouraged me from the very first steps of this project. I was blessed by their wise guidance and continual support not only in writing this book but much beyond. I am also in debt to Andrew Arato from the New School of Social Research who gave generously of his time and expertise, challenged my thinking on constitutional issues and thus helped me refine and hone the arguments made in the book. Special thanks also granted to Nadia Urbinati and Jeremy Waldron who provided extremely helpful suggestions. I was fortunate to have met with the late Shmuel Noah Eisenstadt, who read an early version of the entire manuscript, and was generous in sharing with me his wisdom and his insightful advice. Many colleagues and friends have read selected chapters and offered their invaluable comments and suggestions which made this book a much better work. Among them I am particularly grateful to Murat Akan, Granville Austin, Richard Bourke, Niki Cunningham, Neri Horowitz, Christophe Jaffrelot, Amal Jamal, Bill Kissane, Mirjam Künkler, Menachem Lorberbaum, Bajeera McCorkle, Faina Milman-Sivan, Ohad Nachtomi, Scott Morrison, Philip Oldenburg, David Ponet, Zuleika Rodgers, Shylashri Shankar, Gila Stopler and Steven Wilkinson. My undying thanks and gratitude to Aliza Belman Inbal, who read every word of multiple drafts of this project and provided invaluable editing and moral support. At the Mandel Leadership Institute in Jerusalem I would like to thank the late Seymour Fox, Annette Hochstein and especially Varda Shiffer who in many ways is responsible for initiating the journey that resulted with this book. In the Department of Political Science at Tel Aviv University, I was fortunate to receive the support and encouragements of my colleagues, among them I particularly would like to thank Eyal Chowers, Azar Gat, Amal Jamal, Yossi Shain, and Michal

Shamir for their sage advice at critical moments of the project. At the Princeton Institute for International and Regional Studies, Princeton University, I enjoyed the most suitable environment that allowed me to work on the necessary final revisions of the manuscript. I am especially grateful to Mirjam Künkler and Amaney Jamal for their enthusiastic support. Special thanks and gratitude to Finola O`Sullivan, Richard Woodham and to the anonymous reviewers at Cambridge University Press for their useful comments that much improved the book. I would also like to thank Adam Vital and Peter Lemish for their editorial assistance, and to Yael Maisel, Noa On, Itai Pollack, and Reut Tondovsky for their devoted research assistance.

For financial support I would like to thank Columbia University, Tel Aviv University, The Mandel Foundation-Israel, the EU's Marie Curie International Reintegration Grant, Israel's Ministry of Immigration Absorption, Princeton Institute for International and Regional Studies and the Luce Foundation.

Finally, it is my family who deserves my endless thanks. They have always been the source of my strength. My parents, Rachel and Michael Postavski, to whom I dedicate this book, supported me like only family can. This book could never have been born without them. My partner for life Natan, never tired of helping me fulfill my dreams, and was with me every step of the way, across the ocean and back. Together with our daughters Adaya and Dana they are the light and joy of my life.

Some of the chapters/sections in this book are re-working of the following articles:

Hanna Lerner, "Constitution Writing in Deeply Divided Societies: The Incrementalist Approach", *Nations and Nationalism* 16:1, January 2010, pp. 68–88.

Hanna Lerner, "Entrenching the Status Quo: Religion and State in Israeli Constitutional Proposals", *Constellations* 16:3, 2009, pp. 445–461.

Hanna Lerner, "Democracy, Constitutionalism, and Identity: The Anomaly of the Israeli Case," *Constellations* 11:2, June 2004, pp. 237–257.

Hanna Lerner, "Constitutional Incrementalism and Material Entrenchment", in: *The Multicultural Challenge in Israel*, edited by Avi Sagi and Ohad Nachtomy, Academic Studies Press, 2009, pp. 3–25.

~

Introduction

Nearly 190 national constitutions are in force today. More than half of them have been written or rewritten in the past three decades.[1] Many of these constitutions begin with some version of the famous four words: "We the People of …" But the theoretical discussion of the role of that "We" in the process of constructing a constitution is surprisingly limited and narrow. The "We" issue is particularly problematic in the context of constitution-drafting in deeply divided societies. Where polities are still grappling with the very definition of their collectivity, crafting a formal democratic constitution that reflects shared norms and values is a daunting challenge. How can a constitution be created in the absence of societal consensus on the norms and values of the state? This challenge is the central question addressed in this book.

In recent years constitutions have become a leading tool for mitigating conflicts and promoting democracy in divided societies. From South Africa to Bosnia, great hopes have been placed in the potential contribution of the process of constitution-making to post-conflict peace and stability. However, under conditions of deep internal disagreement, enacting a formal constitution is a high-stakes game that can undermine political stability and derail democratization. Where intense polarization exists between competing visions of the state, drafting a constitution risks unleashing political crisis. This has recently been the case in countries such as Iraq and Afghanistan, where the debate over the constitution revealed deep divisions among the framers with regard to foundational norms and values that should underpin the state.[2] The need to better

---

[1] The total number of constitutions in force is difficult to determine. It depends on the definition of what is considered a constitution (see Chapter 1) but also on the meaning of being 'in force'. For example, among the 192 current member states in the UN, the UK, New Zealand and Israel do not have a formal written constitution, while Kosovo, which is not listed in the UN, adopted a formal constitution in 2008.
[2] See, for example, Barnett R. Rubin, "Crafting a Constitution for Afghanistan," *Journal of Democracy* 15, no. 3 (2004); J. Alexander Thier, "The Making of a Constitution in

understand the relationship between constitutions and the identity of "the people" who author them has also been raised by recent attempts to write or rewrite democratic constitutions in the context of deep disagreements over the vision of the polity on both national and supranational levels. This is the case, for example, in democratizing Muslim states such as Turkey, Indonesia and Egypt, which are grappling with the question of the appropriate relations between religious traditions and state institutions. These debates are usually discussed in constitutional terms and involve popular demands for constitutional reform and the drafting of proposed constitutions by various groups and organizations.[3] On the supranational level, the attempt to enact a constitution of the European Union and the 2005 failure to ratify it redirected attention to the foundational aspect of constitution-writing and to the importance of symbolic components of constitutions.[4]

Despite these increasing challenges, the puzzle of crafting a formal constitution under conditions of deep internal disagreement over the character of the state has received limited theoretical and comparative attention. In recent years the literature on constitution-writing has experienced a resurgence, following what Jon Elster has termed the "seventh wave of constitution-making," which since 1989 has included the adoption of new constitutions in former Communist countries in Eastern and

Afghanistan," *New York Law School Law Review* 51, no. 3 (2006); Peter Kurrild-Klitgaard, "Blood, Baath and Beyond: The Constitutional Dilemma of Iraq," *Public Choice* 119 (2004): 13–30; Yash Ghai, Mark Lattimer and Yahia Said, "Building Democracy in Iraq" (Minority Rights Group International, 2003); John McGarry *et al.*, "Iraq's Constitution of 2005: Liberal Consociation as Political Prescription," in Sujit Choudhry, ed., *Constitutional Design for Divided Societies* (Oxford and New York: Oxford University Press, 2008), 342–68. Andrew Arato, *Constitution Making Under Occupation: The Politics of Imposed Revolution in Iraq* (New York: Columbia University Press, 2009).

[3] See, for example, on Indonesia: Nadirsyah Hosen, *Shari'a and Constitutional Reform in Indonesia* (Singapore: Institute of Southeast Asian Studies, 2007). On Turkey: Ergun Özbudun and Ömer Faruk Gençkaya, *Democratization and the Politics of Constitution Making in Turkey* (Budapest: Central European University Press, 2009); Mehmet Fevzi Bilgin, "Constitution, Legitimacy and Democracy in Turkey," in Said Amir Arjomand, ed., *Constitutional Politics in the Middle East: With Special Reference to Turkey, Iraq, Iran and Afghanistan* (Oxford and Portland: Hart Publishing, 2007).

[4] The academic commentary on the relations between the emerging constitution and the European "political community" is vast, and growing. For some of the leading works see J. H. H. Weiler, *The Constitution of Europe* (Cambridge University Press, 1999); J. H. H. Weiler and Marlene Wind, eds., *European Constitutionalism Beyond the State* (Cambridge University Press, 2003); Dieter Grimm, "Integration by Constitution," *International Journal of Constitutional Law* 3, no. 2–3 (2005); Neil Walker, "Europe's Constitutional Engagement," *Ratio Juris* 18 (2005); Jürgen Habermas, "Why Europe Needs a Constitution," *New Left Review* 11 (2nd Series) (2001). See also special issue of *Constellations* 13, no. 2 (June 2006) discussing the failure to ratify the EU constitution.

Central Europe, as well as the enactment of the new constitution of South Africa.[5] However, most studies on constitution-crafting examine the topic from either an institutional or a procedural perspective, focusing either on public participation in the process of constitution-writing or on the democratic institutions that the process creates.[6] These studies tend to advocate various governmental instruments for resolving ethnic and national conflicts, and view the process of constitution-writing mainly as an opportunity to establish the institutional structure of a democratic government and regulate the balance of power.[7]

---

[5] Jon Elster, "Forces and Mechanisms in the Constitution-Making Process," *Duke Law Journal* 45, no. 364 (1995): 369.

[6] For example see Cass R. Sunstein, *Designing Democracy: What Constitutions Do* (Oxford and New York: Oxford University Press, 2001); Douglas Greenberg, Stanley N. Katz, Melanie Beth Oliviero, Steven C. Wheatley, eds., *Constitutionalism and Democracy: Transitions in the Contemporary World* (New York: Oxford University Press, 1993); Jon Elster, Claus Offe and Ulrich Klaus Preuss, *Institutional Design in Post-Communist Societies: Rebuilding the Ship at Sea, Theories of Institutional Design* (Cambridge and New York: Cambridge University Press, 1998); A. E. Dick Howard, ed., *Constitution Making in Eastern Europe* (Washington, DC: Woodrow Wilson Center Press, distributed by The Johns Hopkins University Press, 1993); Andrea R. Bonime, *The Politics of Constitution-Making: Spain's Transition to Democracy* (Boulder: Westview Press, 1987); Yash Ghai, "A Journey around Constitution: Reflections on Contemporary Constitutions," *African Law Journal* 122 (2005); Yash Ghai and Guido Galli, "Constitution Building Processes and Democratization," in *Democracy, Conflict and Human Security: Further Readings* (Stockholm: IDEA, 2006); Heinz Klug, *Constituting Democracy: Law, Globalism and South Africa's Political Reconstruction* (Cambridge University Press, 2000); Rett R. Ludwikowski, *Constitution-Making in the Region of Former Soviet Dominance* (Durham, NC: Duke University Press, 1996).

[7] For some of the recent studies see Andrew Reynolds, ed., *The Architecture of Democracy: Constitutional Design, Conflict Management, and Democracy* (New York: Oxford University Press, 2002); Arend Lijphart, "Constitutional Design in Divided Societies," *Journal of Democracy* 15, no. 2 (2004); Sujit Choudhry, ed., *Constitutional Design for Divided Societies: Integration or Accommodation* (Oxford University Press, 2008); Larry J. Diamond and Marc F. Plattner, eds., *Electoral Systems and Democracy* (Baltimore: The Johns Hopkins University Press, 2006); James A. Dunn, "The Revision of the Constitution in Belgium: A Study in the Institutionalization of Ethnic Conflict," *Political Research Quarterly* 27, no. 1 (1974). Sidney John Roderick Noel, ed., *From Power Sharing to Democracy: Post-Conflict Institutions in Ethnically Divided Societies* (Montreal: McGill-Queen's Press, 2005); Marc Weller and Stefan Wolff, eds., *Autonomy, Self-Government and Conflict Resolution: Innovative Approaches to Institutional Design in Divided Societies* (London: Routledge, 2005); Benjamin Reilly, *Democracy in Divided Societies: Electoral Engineering for Conflict Management* (Cambridge University Press, 2001). See also Vernon Bogdanor, ed., *Constitutions in Democratic Politics* (Aldershot and Brookfield: Gower, 1988); Yash Ghai, ed., *Autonomy and Ethnicity: Negotiating Competing Claims in Multi-Ethnic States* (Cambridge University Press, 2000); Robert A. Goldwin and Art Kaufman, *Constitution Makers on Constitution Making: The Experience of Eight Nations* (Washington, DC and Lanham: American Enterprise Institute for Public Policy Research, 1988).

However, constitutions also play an important role in expressing the common aspirations and norms of the nation. As such, they serve as the state's charter of identity and play a foundational role in representing the ultimate goals of the state. This foundational aspect of the constitution has been generally neglected by studies in comparative politics. Very little has been said theoretically and comparatively on the relationship between the new (or rewritten) constitution and the identity of "the people" who are supposedly its authors.[8] The political and sociological dimensions of the process of constitution-writing have been studied by very few researchers, and the symbolic, ideological and foundational aspects of the constitutions have been rarely analyzed. The few works that address these issues tend to focus on particular cases, discussing them in terms of their historical context and local political culture, and have given only limited attention to the comparative perspective.[9]

The role of constitutions in multinational, multi-religious or multi-ethnic societies and the question of whether constitutions are made by "the people" or in the name of "peoples" had been discussed in the political literature, particularly in the European and Northern American context.[10] Nevertheless, these studies rarely trace the constitutional debates

---

[8] Among the rare studies that theorize the link between constitutions and identity are Beau Breslin, *The Communitarian Constitution* (Baltimore and London: The Johns Hopkins University Press, 2004); Gary Jacobsohn, *Constitutional Identity*, (Cambridge, MA: Harvard University Press, 2010). However neither of these studies analyzes processes of constitution-drafting. See also Michel Rosenfeld, *The Identity of the Constitutional Subject: Selfhood, Citizenship, Culture and Community* (London and New York: Routledge, 2010).

[9] For example, see the collection of political-theoretic readings on the Indian constitution: Rajeev Bhargava, ed., *Politics and Ethics of the Indian Constitution* (New Delhi: Oxford University Press, 2008). See also Hosen, *Shari'a and Constitutional Reform in Indonesia*; Siri Gloppen, *South Africa: The Battle over the Constitution* (Dartmouth: Ashgate, 1997) and the essays included in Said Amir Arjomand, ed., *Constitutional Politics in the Middle East* (Oxford and Portland: Hart, 2007).

[10] For example: Stephen Tierney, *Constitutional Law and National Pluralism* (Oxford University Press, 2004); James Tully and Alain G. Gagnon, eds., *Multinational Democracies* (Cambridge University Press, 2001); Alan C. Cairns, *Constitution, Government, and Society in Canada/Selected Essays*, ed. Douglas E. Williams (Toronto: McClelland & Stewart 1988); Christopher Hughes, *The Federal Constitution of Switzerland* (London: Oxford University Press, 1954); Hanspeter Kriesi and Alexander H. Trechsel, *The Politics of Switzerland: Continuity and Change in a Consensus Democracy* (Cambridge University Press, 2008). For writings on the relation between "the people" and the making of the European constitution see note 4 above.

that led to the drafting of the constitutions, and they generally tend to analyze the existing constitutional arrangements, focusing on the institutional aspect of governmental structure.[11] The focus of attention is constitutional politics rather than the process of writing the constitution.[12] Similarly, the multiculturalism literature that concerns politics of identity tends to say very little about the dynamics of constitutional evolution. Instead, it discusses particular constitutional arrangements within an already existing constitutional order, or else it merely presents a normative argument for constitutional pluralism.[13]

This book aims at addressing this theoretical lacuna by focusing on the foundational and symbolic – rather than legalistic and institutional – aspects of constitution-making, and by examining the way in which deeply divided societies address their internal ideational polarization over the nature of the state through the drafting of a formal constitution.[14] What political role does a constitution-making process play in such polities that lack consensus regarding their fundamental commitments and ultimate goals? Is the constitutional-drafting process likely to increase

---

[11] Moreover, as I discuss in Chapter 2, the institutional arrangements advocated by many of these writings – such as federalism, special group rights or various forms of electoral rules – do not address the conflicts that characterize the sort of deeply divided societies that this book is concerned with. The literature on the institutional design in divided societies is vast. For a good review article of the different approaches to accommodating or integrating divided societies see John McGarry, Brendan O'Leary and Richard Simeon, "Integration or Accommodation? The Enduring Debate in Conflict Regulation," in Choudhry, *Constitutional Design for Divided Societies*, 41–88.

[12] One of the rare works on the creation of constitutions is Walter F. Murphy, *Constitutional Democracy: Creating and Maintaining a Just Political Order* (Baltimore: The Johns Hopkins University Press, 2007).

[13] To name just a few among the vast literature on multiculturalism: James Tully, *Strange Multiplicity: Constitutionalism in an Age of Diversity* (Cambridge and New York: Cambridge University Press, 1995); Will Kymlicka, *Multicultural Citizenship: A Liberal Theory of Minority Rights* (Oxford: Clarendon Press, 1995).

[14] To be clear, the role of ideational conflicts does not seem to have the same degree of importance in all processes of constitution-making. For example, constitution-making in former Soviet states such as Hungary and Poland mostly revolved around socio-economic ideological issues and structures of power. See, for example, Andrew Arato, *Civil Society, Constitution, and Legitimacy* (Lanham: Rowman & Littlefield, 2000). Elster *et al.*, *Institutional Design in Post-Communist Societies*; Stephen Holmes and Cass Sunstein, "The Politics of Constitutional Revision in Eastern Europe," in Stanford Levinson, ed., *Responding to Imperfection* (Princeton University Press, 1995), 275–305; Ulrich Klaus Preuss, *Constitutional Revolution: The Link between Constitutionalism and Progress* (Atlantic Highlands: Humanities Press, 1995); András Sajó, *Limiting Government: An Introduction to Constitutionalism* (Budapest: Central European University Press, 1999).

factional tensions, or can conflicts be mitigated through constitutional means? How can a constitution be drafted, and what kind of a constitution can be adopted, when there is no consensus on the foundational framework that the constitution is expected to represent? These questions are the main concern of this book.

The book, in other words, endeavors to explore the relationship between constitutions and the identity of "the people" who are deemed to have authored them. This link is by and large perceived in the existing theory through two competing paradigms: the essentialist paradigm of the "nation-state constitution" views constitutions as legal embodiments of pre-constitutional homogenous unities, which gain their legitimacy through an exercise of the people's *constituent power*. The alternative proceduralist paradigm of "the liberal constitution" strives at emptying formal constitutions from all identity elements and constructing a political collectivity on the basis of shared democratic procedures embodied in the constitution. As Chapter 1 of the book explains, both conceptions of constitutional identity require some form of pre-constitutional consensus – whether understood in "thick" terms of cultural, national or religious homogeneity, or in "thin" terms of shared liberal political culture. Neither of these types of consensus exists in deeply divided societies. Such societies are struggling over the question of who are "We the People" and what do "We" believe in, and they cannot adopt either of the two ideal-type constitutions. For this reason, the book seeks to go beyond the essentialist–proceduralist dichotomy and to delineate an alternative approach which reconciles the goal of constructing a democratic constitution with the need to address deep internal disagreements over the vision of the state as a whole.

Since the existing theory does not provide an adequate answer to the puzzle of constitution-making in the absence of a consensus on the shared norms and values that should underpin the state, this book seeks to find the answer in historical cases where similar problems were confronted. The book traces the process of constitution-writing in three deeply divided societies that faced the challenge of writing a new democratic constitution at the time of their foundation – Ireland in 1922, India in 1947–50 and Israel in 1948–50. It shows how by deferring controversial decisions regarding the character of the state, deeply divided societies can formulate a democratic formal constitution or function with a material, unwritten, constitutional arrangement. This approach, which I term *the incrementalist approach to constitution-making*, is presented in

Chapter 2. By postponing constitutional choices on foundational issues, the incrementalist approach deviated from the common perception of the moment of constitution-making as a "revolutionary moment," introducing instead elements of gradualism into the process. Moreover, in order to circumvent the potentially explosive conflicts that were present at the time of independence the incrementalist constitution embraces competing visions of the state, thus representing the identity of "the people" as it really was at the time of drafting – in other words as a *divided* identity.

The incrementalist constitutional toolbox included such strategies as avoiding clear-cut decisions, using ambiguous legal language, and inserting internally contradictory provisions into the constitution.[15] The second part of the book (Chapters 3–5) explores the way these strategies were employed in Israel, India and Ireland, tracing the political and constitutional choices made by constitutional framers in the three countries. My purpose in these chapters is not to provide a comprehensive study of the entire constitutional drafting process in these countries, and the chapters do not therefore address all controversies raised during the constitutional debates. Rather, each chapter will focus on one or two fundamental divisions which were explicitly addressed by the constitutional drafters and that were managed through a variety of constitutional incrementalist strategies.

Chapter 3 focuses on the Israeli constitutional deliberations which ultimately encountered deadlock over the conflict between secular and religious definitions of the Jewish state. This was one of the major reasons for the decision taken in 1950 by the Knesset, Israel's parliament, to refrain from writing a constitution altogether. The chapter traces the constitutional debates in 1948–50, and analyzes the material and informal constitutional arrangements that evolved in the absence of a written

---

[15] Michael Foley had theorized a similar concept of "constitution abeyances," which he describes as "keeping fundamental questions of political authority in the state of irresolution." However, Foley addresses constitutional abeyances as an often unintentional and even unconscious "working anomaly within the constitution," and rejects the view that they are instruments of conflict resolution or "a conscious form of mutual accommodation between contending parties." Michael Foley, *The Silence of Constitutions: Gaps, "Abeyances" and Political Temperament in the Maintenance of Government* (London and New York: Routledge, 1989), 9–10. For another book that discusses Foley's concept of constitutional abeyances in the context of the Canadian constitution see David M. Thomas, *Whistling Past the Graveyard: Constitutional Abeyances, Quebec, and the Future of Canada* (Toronto: Oxford University Press, 1997).

constitution in religious matters. Since the incrementalist approach to constitution-writing was achieved by an explicit decision of the framers to defer controversial choices, a direct and open discussion over these contentious issues was an important stage in the framers' realization that the dispute was intractable. For this reason, the chapter on Israel focuses on the religious–secular divide within the Jewish majority. Although the non-Jewish population of Israel has been since independence approximately 20 percent, the constitutional debates within Israeli society have until recently been an exclusively Jewish affair. The definition of Israel as a Jewish state gave clear preference to a particular ethnic-cultural group, and non-Jews were consistently excluded from these debates. The leadership of the non-Jewish minority has only recently begun voicing a demand to participate in the deliberations over the future constitution of the state. The relationship between the Arab minority within Israel and the non-written constitution will also be discussed in the chapter.

In addition to the constitution debates in the early years of the state, the chapter also explores the growing involvement of the Israeli Supreme Court in the Israeli constitution's evolution, and demonstrates how more than sixty years after independence, the Israeli constitutional debate continues to revolve around the same foundational issues that impeded the adoption of the constitution in the formative period of the state.

Chapter 4 traces the constitution-drafting in India, which began in December 1946, seven months before the partition with Pakistan. Even after partition, India has remained one of the most diverse societies in the world, and the challenges inherent in this diversity were at the heart of the three years of constitutional deliberations which followed. Although the framers of the Indian constitution made clear-cut decisions regarding the institutional structure of the Indian government, they opted for an indecisive and incrementalist approach when it came to foundational issues that touched upon the definition of Indian nationhood. The long and intense conflicts over the unification of personal law and over the national language were ultimately circumvented by the adoption of ambiguous constitutional arrangements. Thus, for example, a uniform civil code was mentioned in the constitution, but in a part of the constitution that contained non-justiciable provisions, which could not be enforced by the courts. The debate over the national language was resolved by deciding that within fifteen years the government would appoint a committee to decide the issue. Meanwhile, English would continue to be used "for all official purposes," in addition to Hindi and fourteen other official languages.

The third process of constitution-writing which is explored is that of the Irish Free State (Chapter 5), which occurred in 1922 in the midst of a civil war among the Catholic population of the twenty-six counties. More people died in this war, which lasted almost a year, than in the preceding two-and-a-half years of struggle against British rule. Despite being chronologically the first among the three countries discussed in this book to enact a democratic constitution, it is dealt with last because of its unique circumstances. Unlike the cases of Israel and India, certain provisions of the 1922 constitution of Ireland were imposed on the Irish political leadership by an external power – the British government. Nevertheless, the Irish constitution was ratified democratically by the Dáil Éireann (Irish Free State Parliament). The deep divisions over the meaning of Irish nationalism and Irish sovereignty were reflected in various conflicting provisions in the constitution, and reflected both Irish independence and political subordination to the United Kingdom. The chapter argues that a similar constitutional ambivalence is embodied in the constitutional arrangements agreed upon in the 1998 Good Friday Agreement regarding the future of Northern Ireland.

A comparative constitutional study raises particular difficulties. First, a constitution is designed for a specific society, with its unique culture and concerns. As these differ from country to country, "questions about constitutions can never be answered for all societies and states, for all times."[16] Nevertheless, comparative constitutional studies are important to the extent that they enable us to identify common challenges and possible structural ways to deal with them. Despite the vast differences between them,[17] Israel, India and Ireland all faced the similar challenge of writing a formal constitution for a newly independent state that was experiencing increasing internal polarization over its most fundamental principles and norms. The process of constitution-making in all three countries involved intense disputes over the identity of the polity: should the Jewish state be understood in secular-national or religious terms? Should the principles underpinning the Indian state be those of national uniformity or of societal diversity? What is the meaning of Irish nationalism and sovereignty? Despite the differences between them, the constitutional debates in all three cases followed a

---

[16] Ruth Gavison, "What Belongs in a Constitution?" *Constitutional Political Economy* 13 (2002): 90.

[17] The differences and similarities between the three countries in terms of political, cultural and historical background are elaborated in the introduction to Part II of the book.

common pattern which led the drafters to adopt incrementalist strategies for addressing their most pressing foundational conflicts. This
common pattern will be presented in Chapter 6. At their heart was the
acknowledgment that any unequivocal choice regarding the identity of
the state could have potentially destabilizing effects. And so the framers
in Israel, India and Ireland departed from a "revolutionary" perception
of the seminal constitution-making moment, and adopted an incrementalist constitutional approach, thus transferring the most controversial
choices regarding the foundational aspect of their constitution from
the constitutional arena to the political one. Recognizing the ingrained
nature of their societies' internal conflicts over norms and values, the
architects of the constitutional arrangements in the deeply divided societies refrained from entrenching one or another normative perspective
of the state, as any attempt to do so, they feared, might exacerbate the
conflict instead of moderate it.

Another typical concern in comparative studies, particularly those
that analyze a limited number of case studies, is that of case selection. The
constitutional drafters in Israel, India and Ireland were not the only ones
to prefer the adoption of incrementalist strategies and to defer controversial constitutional choices regarding foundational issues. Other countries
may have adopted a similar approach. For example, the 1978 constitution
of Spain used an ambiguous constitutional formulation in an attempt to
forge consensus on the "national question."[18] Article 2 represents the competing visions of Spanish national identity in that it recognizes at the same
time both the unity of the "Spanish nation" and the basic right of regional
"nationalities" to autonomy, a right that precedes the constitutional order
itself.[19] This paradoxical conception of the Spanish nation embedded in
the constitutional text was accompanied by a decision of the drafters to
determine the definite contours and scope of the institutions and mechanisms of Spanish regional autonomies outside the constitutional text –
in Title VIII. Eventually, however, the committee that was supposed to
draft that Title failed to reach consensus and agreed to disagree, thus

---

[18] For discussion of the process of constitutional framing of the ambiguous formula regard-
ing the Spanish "national question" see Enric Martínez-Herrera and Thomas Jeffrey
Miley, "The Constitution and the Politics of National Identity in Spain," *Nations and
Nationalism*, 16:4 (2010) 6–30.

[19] Article 2 of the Spanish constitution reads: "The constitution is based on the indissoluble
unity of the Spanish nation, the common and indivisible country for all Spaniards, and
recognizes and guarantees the right to self-government of the nationalities and regions
of which it is composed and solidarity amongst them all."

leaving the decision regarding the future territorial organization of the Spanish state to the process of "normal" politics. Title VIII was silent on the territorial boundaries of the different regions, and on the scope and content of the regions' "right to self-government," and did not even clarify the distinction in the kind of rights recognized and guaranteed for "nationalities" as opposed to "regions."[20]

While the Spanish constitutional-drafting, as well as other processes of constitution-writing, is relevant to the topic of the book, such analyses are not necessary for developing the theoretical framework of the incrementalist approach to constitution-writing in context of the struggle over the vision of the state. The three selected cases discussed in the book – Israel, India and Ireland – represent three different models of constitutional tools that may be included in the incrementalist toolbox: the deferral of constitution-writing (Israel), ambiguous formulations within a written constitution (India) and conflicting provisions and statements (Ireland). These various constitutional strategies result from the different circumstances under which the constitutions were adopted. Additional analysis of different processes of constitution-writing may broaden the comparative perspective but would not contribute to the main theoretical point the book is trying to make.

Moreover, the goal of the book is not merely to theorize the way in which deeply divided societies manage, despite intense internal conflicts, to formulate, either formally or informally, democratic constitutional arrangements that can withstand the test of time. My hope is that this book will also contribute to constitution-writing on the practical level. The Western constitutional imagination had generally relied on the narratives of the constitution of the United States and on the French Revolution. But recent projects of writing or rewriting democratic constitutions require expanding the range of potential models that can be used by constitutional drafters. The three deeply divided societies under discussion here – Ireland, Israel and India – rarely receive theoretical attention from constitutional or political scholars. Yet their experience – both during the process of constitution-writing and the developments that followed – may provide additional sources of constitutional inspiration that are particularly relevant to contemporary constitutional debates that involve conflicts over foundation issues relating to national identity. For example, the experience of the three countries may be relevant for democratizing Muslim

---

[20] Martínez-Herrera and Miley, "The Constitution and the Politics of National Identity in Spain."

states such as Turkey and Indonesia, where questions of religion and state are hotly debated. It may even be of relevance in established Western democracies, such as Belgium, where questions of national identity are far from resolved, as well as to the emerging constitution of the European Union.

This book explores the practical and contextual factors which led to the adoption of incrementalist strategies. By doing so, it does not ignore the potentially problematic normative and institutional implications of such an approach. In Chapter 7, the potential risks and dangers related to the adoption of an incrementalist approach to constitution-making will be discussed. Among them are the risk of compromising basic rights, potential over-rigidity of the material constitutional arrangement that evolved in the absence of a formal constitutional decision, and the risk of inter-institutional polarization between the legislature and the judiciary.

Despite these dangers, the incrementalist approach is a valid constitutional option that must be recognized and understood. Thus, while this book does not ignore the problematic aspects of incrementalist constitutions, it does attempt to contribute to the evolving field of constitution-making by broadening the constitutional imagination of individuals and institutions engaged in political reconstruction worldwide. By revisiting the role played by politics and social dynamics in the construction of national constitutions – particularly in the context of fundamental disagreements over basic principles – I hope to reconsider whether the first stage of nation-building should be seen as "the hour of the lawyers"[21] or rather creating a constitution that "brings us back to the essence of the political."[22]

---

[21] Ralf Dahrendorf, *Reflections on the Revolution in Europe* (London: Chatto and Windus, 1990), 3.

[22] Daniel J. Elazar, "Constitution-Making: The Pre-Eminent Political Act," in Keith G. Banting and Richard Simeon, eds., *The Politics of Constitutional Change in Industrial Nations: Redesigning the State* (London: Macmillan, 1985), 232.

PART I

Constitutions, democracy, identity

1

Three paradigms of democratic constitutions

What is a constitution and what are its roles?

What a "constitution" exactly means is subject to a variety of occasionally conflicting interpretations. Constitutions are generally written, but as the British example famously demonstrates, they can be unwritten. Hans Kelsen theorized this dualism in the meaning of constitutions by distinguishing between constitutions in the formal sense, i.e. written documents created by a legislative act, and constitutions in the material sense, i.e. the system of formal and informal rules that regulate the political order, and which are based on, among others, conventions, customs and judicial interpretation.[1]

Historically, constitutions in the material sense preceded constitutions in the formal sense, which are a modern concept. Aristotle, for example, defines constitution (*politeia*) as "a way of organizing the inhabitants of a city."[2] Material constitutions have sometimes been written. Indeed, as early as the sixteenth century some political leaders preferred to codify their governments' fundamental principles in a written document. Such an example is the 1579 Act of Union of the United Provinces of the Netherlands.[3] Nevertheless, such written documents are different from modern formal constitutions that contain the principles of governmental organization in a single text.

The enactment of the constitutions of US states such as Virginia in 1776 and Massachusetts in 1780, as well as the drafting of the US constitution in 1787, was the turning point to modern written constitutions. Unlike in antiquity, when the primary role of a constitution was to reflect the existing legal and political reality, the modern conception of a constitution implies a "conscious formulation by people of its fundamental

---

[1] Hans Kelsen, *General Theory of Law and State* (New York: Russell & Russell, 1961).
[2] Aristotle, *Politics*, trans. Ernest Barker (Oxford University Press, 1995), 1274b32.
[3] K. C. Wheare, *Modern Constitutions* (London: Oxford University Press, 1966), 2.

law."[4] Thomas Paine was the first thinker who clearly articulated the fundamental principle of constitutionalism, stating that the principal function of a constitution was to restrain government, and that any governmental act outside constitutional boundaries should be viewed as an expression of "power without right."[5]

During the nineteenth and twentieth centuries the practice of enacting a formal constitution became the general rule of modern politics – so much so that today the idea of a fundamental transformation of a political regime or the creation of a new one, whether by revolutionary means or otherwise, that does not involve the drafting of a new constitution is unthinkable.

This book focuses on constitutions in the modern, formal sense of documents that codify legal rules that are supreme and, to a large extent, entrenched.[6] Constitutional rules are distinct from ordinary legislation and superior to it in that they provide the legal framework for the political order.[7] They are accorded higher status since they regulate the rules of the game, and determine the procedures by which ordinary laws can be enacted. For that reason, the adoption of constitutional rules has been described as "higher lawmaking," enjoying, as it does, greater democratic legitimacy than does "normal lawmaking" which is conducted by elected representatives.[8] In addition, the superiority of constitutional rules is usually preserved through mechanisms of entrenchment, their

---

[4] Charles Howard McIlwain, *Constitutionalism, Ancient and Modern* (Ithaca, NY: Great Seal Books, 1958), 3.

[5] Thomas Paine and Gordon S. Wood, *Common Sense and Other Writings* (New York: Modern Library, 2003).

[6] As later chapters will reveal, in some areas, and under certain conditions, when a written constitution fails to be constructed, a material constitution may emerge in its place. The relationship between formal and material constitutions will be further discussed in the next chapters in the context of particular constitutional arrangements. See in particular Chapter 3 and Chapter 7.

[7] Clearly, the British constitution represents a different model. For an excellent account of contemporary British constitution and its recent changes see: Anthony King, *The British Constitution* (Oxford University Press, 2007). Among the classical accounts of the British constitution are: Walter Bagehot, *The English Constitution*, ed. R. H. S. Crossman (London: C. A. Watts, 1964); A. V. Dicey, *Introduction to the Study of the Law of the Constitution* (London: Macmillan, 1961); Ivor Jennings, *The Law and the Constitution* (University of London Press, 1959).

[8] Bruce Ackerman, *The Future of Liberal Revolution* (New Haven and London: Yale University Press, 1992), 6.

amendment requiring special and relatively more rigid procedures than those required for ordinary legislation.[9] The US constitution was the first to distinguish between ordinary legislative procedures and special procedures for amending the constitution. This distinction is based on the premise that constitutional matters, which not only determine the methods by which collective decisions will be reached but also define the common good and shared goals, require a more thorough deliberative process than do day-to-day legislative matters.[10]

Generally speaking, there are two distinct roles that constitutions are expected to play: an institutional one and a foundational one. The first function includes the establishment of the legal and political structures of governmental institutions, and the procedures of future legislation. It also includes the establishment of the legal limits of governmental power. This institutional function of constitutions, to create and define the rules according to which governments function, has not only practical but also normative implications. That is, by constraining governmental power, constitutions manifest the principles of constitutionalism. Carl Friedrich, for example, argues that constitutionalism as a normative principle implies the institutionalization of specific constraints on political authorities.[11] In other words, constitutions are expected to limit governmental power by crafting an institutional system that distributes powers between the various branches of government, and by providing a formal basis for the protection of fundamental rights.[12] According to this view, the existence of principles of constitutionalism distinguishes between

---

[9] Constitutions exhibit a great deal of variety in the level of rigidity or flexibility that they provide. For a theoretical and comparative discussion on constitutional amendment rules, see Sanford Levinson, ed., *Responding to Imperfection: The Theory and Practice of Constitutional Amendment* (Princeton University Press, 1995).

[10] Donald S. Lutz, "Toward a Theory of Constitutional Amendment," *American Political Science Review* 80, no. 2 (1994).

[11] Carl J. Friedrich, *Constitutional Government and Democracy; Theory and Practice in Europe and America*, (Boston: Ginn, 1950), 26, 123.

[12] Whether constitutionalism is compatible with democracy is a different question. For a discussion of the inherent conflict between constitutionalism and the principle of majoritarian democracy see Jon Elster and Rune Slagstad, eds., *Constitutionalism and Democracy* (Cambridge and New York: Cambridge University Press, 1988); Jon Elster, *Ulysses and the Sirens: Studies in Rationality and Irrationality* (Cambridge and New York: Cambridge University Press, 1979), 94; Jeremy Waldron, "Precommitment and Disagreement," in *Law and Disagreement* (New York: Oxford University Press, 1999).

"true constitutional systems" and those that use a constitution as "window dressing."[13]

However, in addition to establishing the structure of government and regulating the balance of power, W. F. Murphy stated that constitutions

> serve as a binding statement of a people's aspirations for themselves as a nation. A text may silhouette the sort of community its authors/subjects are or would like to become: not only their governmental structures, procedures and basic rights, but also their goals, ideals, and the moral standards by which they want others, including their own posterity, to judge the community ... If a constitutional text is not "congruent with" ideals that form or will reform its people and so express the political character they have or are willing to try to put on, it will quickly fade.[14]

For constitutions to be popularly accepted as legitimate in democratic societies, they have to express the underlying common vision of the polity. This is the second, foundational, function of a constitution. Constitutions play a key role in representing the ultimate goals and shared values that underpin the state. In short, they serve as a basic charter of the state's identity. By delineating the commonly held core societal norms and aspirations of the people, constitutions provide the citizenry with a sense of ownership and authorship, a sense that "We the People" includes me.[15]

The formal expression of the foundational role of the constitution depends on the type of national identity the constitution is expected to represent. In other words, it depends on the meaning of the phrase "we the people" that is commonly included in preambles of modern constitutions.

---

[13] Lutz, "Toward a Theory of Constitutional Amendment."

[14] Walter F. Murphy, "Constitutions, Constitutionalism and Democracy," in Douglas Greenberg, Stanley N. Katz, Melanie Beth Oliviero and Steven C. Wheatley, eds., *Constitutionalism and Democracy: Transitions in the Contemporary World* (New York and Oxford: Oxford University Press, 1993), 10. See also Daniel J. Elazar: "Constitutions ... also reflect, explicitly or implicitly, the moral principles underlying polities and regimes." Elazar, "Constitution-Making: The Pre-Eminent Political Act," in Keith G. Banting and Richard Simeon, eds., *The Politics of Constitutional Change in Industrial Nations: Redesigning the State* (London: Macmillan, 1985), 240.

[15] A distinction somewhat similar to the procedural versus foundational aspects of constitutions is made by Donald S. Lutz, who distinguishes between power elements ("found in institutions for decision-making") and cultural elements ("cultural mores and values") contained in every constitution. Donald S. Lutz, "Thinking About Constitutionalism at the Start of the Twenty-First Century," *Publius* 30, no. 4 (2000). Lutz also adds the element of justice as a key ingredient of constitutionalism. This aspect does not form part of my analysis, as my focus is on formal constitutions rather than on normative analysis of the principles of constitutionalism. I do, however, discuss the normative question in the two concluding chapters.

This "we" could refer, on the one hand, to a unified, presumably homogenous, collectivity, resting on a shared cultural, ethnic or religious background, or to a plurality of "voluntaristic" individuals, who do not share a particular collective identity but define their shared identity in political or civic terms.[16]

The duality in the meaning of "the people" is reflected in the etymological roots of the English term. In its origin the word "people" was a singular noun, emerging from old French *poblo* and classic Latin *populus*, which denoted the human community, the nation, the populace, the body of citizens exercising legislative power.[17] This meaning had been maintained in various modern languages: the Italian *popolo*, the French *peuple*, the German *volk*, and the Hebrew עַם (*am*). Nevertheless, from its earliest usage in the English language, the word "people" had both singular and an implied or actual plural sense. Since the fifteenth century, "people" understood as "the body of men, women and children comprising a particular nation, community, ethnic group, etc." had been used by English writers in both the singular and plural sense.[18]

In the context of constitution-making, this duality in the meaning of "the people" is embodied in the various possible relationships between the constitutional text and "the people" that is supposedly its author, as well as its subject. In general, there are two principal ways in which this relationship can be understood: constitutions may provide a legal framework to regulate the political authorities of a particular people, and to represent the cultural, religious or linguistic characteristics of a pre-constitutional homogenous unity. Alternatively, the "people" may come together through the drafting of the constitution itself. According to the latter view, the very act of constitution-writing creates the polity and unifies the political collectivity. The distinctions between these two ideal-type constitutions are most vividly expressed by the opposing constitutional views of Carl Schmitt and Jürgen Habermas.

"The people" precede the constitution: the essentialist "nation-state" constitution

Carl Schmitt distinguished between two understandings of the concept of constitution: the first, *Verfassung*, denotes the pre-constitutional

---

[16] The literature on nationalism and on the origin and meaning of "the people" is immense. For a brief overview of the classic readings and main debates see: John Hutchinson and Anthony Smith, eds., *Nationalism* (Oxford and New York: Oxford University Press, 1994).

[17] Oxford English Dictionary website: www.oed.com (definition: people).

[18] Oxford English Dictionary website: www.oed.com (definition: people. Sense 6b).

political oneness of the people who are the founders of the constitution and cannot be encompassed and regulated or domesticated by the written document. According to Schmitt, this is the "absolute" concept of the constitution. "it is only in the sense of an absolute concept of the constitution, more specifically, as a unity and as an entirety [that a constitution] regulates comprehensively the procedure of state will formation."[19] The second, *Verfassungsgesetz*, is constitutional law and refers to individual provisions of "organizational" type, such as those relating to the legislative process and to the government, and to other procedural rules, formal legal regulations and governmental mechanisms. Written constitutional provisions of these types, according to Schmitt, were intended to protect the interests of parliamentary majorities and of parties, which "confer the character of constitutional laws on their partisan demands."[20]

The constitution, for Schmitt, was a manifestation of a presupposed political unity of the people, since only the political will itself generates its own unity.[21] Hence "the political," understood by Schmitt as the outcome of constant distinction between friend and foe, must precede the constitutional. In his words, "[the] people [*Volk*] must be present and presupposed as political unity if it is to be the subject of constitution-making."[22] The enactment of a constitution is an incarnation of the will of the people, a confirmation of their constituent power, a power not restricted by rules, institutions or superior order. As Andreas Kalyvas observes, for Schmitt, the constitution "embodies the founding political decisions of a sovereign community concerning the form of government, the fundamental rules that regulate the exercise of political power and its circumscribed area of competence, the form of political representation, and the higher principles of and symbolic values of a political association. It denotes, in other words, the core constitutional identity of a democratic political order."[23]

---

[19] Carl Schmitt, *Constitutional Theory*, trans. Jeffrey Seitzer (Durham, NC: Duke University Press, 2008) 69.

[20] *Ibid.*, 70. See also Ulrich Klaus Preuss, "Political Order and Democracy," in *The Challenge of Carl Schmitt*, ed. Chantal Mouffe (London and New York: Verso, 1999), 158; William E. Scheuerman, *Carl Schmitt: The End of Law, Twentieth Century Political Thinkers* (Lanham: Rowman & Littlefield, 1999), 280.

[21] Schmitt, *Constitutional Theory*, 65, 75–80. See also: Carl Schmidt, *The Concept of the Political* (The University of Chicago Press, 1967).

[22] Schmitt, *Constitutional Theory* 112. See also: 125–35.

[23] Andreas Kalyvas, *Democracy and the Politics of the Extraordinary: Max Weber, Carl Schmitt and Hanna Arendt* (Cambridge University Press, 2008), 139.

Schmitt takes to the extreme the problematic aspect of Sieyes' innovative notion of the constituent power as a necessary foundation for constitutional legitimacy.[24] Sieyes applied this distinction in his attempt to ground the legitimacy of the revolutionary constitution in the sovereign power of a pre-constitutional and pre-institutional unity. Indeed, the dangers of Schmitt's essentialist interpretation of the notion of constituent power and the anti-democratic, anti-egalitarian and anti-humanistic implications of his definite subordination of any law to political will, deserve a separate critical discussion, which is beyond the scope of this chapter.[25] Nevertheless, Schmitt's emphasis on the political foundations that underlie the constitution is valuable for our discussion. Despite its potentially dangerous nationalistic implications, Schmitt's essentialist position corresponds to the view of the nation-state as a realization of homogenous political unity, since the idea of a constituent power presupposes the capacity of the people to act as a collectivity.[26] Without entering the debate over the source of national identity, whether primordial or constructed,[27] the essentialist, or nation-state constitution represents a "thick" identity of a presumably homogenous people.

---

[24] "The nation is prior to everything. It is the source of everything. Its will is always legal." Emmanuel Joseph Sieyès, *What Is the Third Estate?* (New York: Praeger, 1964), 124.

[25] For a critical discussion of Schmitt's *Verfassungslehre* see: Jürgen Habermas, "On the Relation between the Nation, Rule of Law, and Democracy," in *The Inclusion of the Other: Studies in Political Theory*, edited by Ciaran Cronin and Pablo De Greiff (Cambridge, MA: The MIT Press, 1998). For a scholarly analysis of Schmitt's work in a comparative theoretical context see Kalyvas, *Democracy and the Politics of the Extraordinary*. See also Chantal Mouffe, *On the Political* (London: Routledge, 2005). Peter C. Caldwell, *Popular Sovereignty and the Crisis of German Constitutional Law: The Theory & Practice of Weimar Constitutionalism* (Durham, NC: Duke University Press, 1997); David Dyzenhaus, *Legality and Legitimacy: Carl Schmitt, Hans Kelsen, and Hermann Heller in Weimar* (Oxford and New York: Clarendon Press and Oxford University Press, 1997); Chantal Mouffe, ed., *The Challenge of Carl Schmitt* (London and New York: Verso, 1999); Jeffrey Seitzer, *Comparative History and Legal Theory: Carl Schmitt in the First German Democracy* (Westport and London: Greenwood Press, 2001).

[26] Ulrich Preuss, "Constitutional Powermaking of the New Polity: Some Deliberations on the Relations between Constituent Power and the Constitution," in Michael Rosenfeld, ed., *Constitutionalism, Identity, Difference and Legitimacy* (Durham, NC and London: Duke University Press, 1994), 148.

[27] The debate on the origins of nationalism is voluminous. Among the leading studies see Benedict Anderson, *Imagined Communities: Reflections on the Origin and Spread of Nationalism* (London and New York: Verso, 1991); Ernest Gellner, *Nations and Nationalism* (Ithaca, NY: Cornell University Press, 1983); Anthony Smith, *The Ethnic Origins of Nations* (Oxford and New York: Blackwell, 1986).

Such a constitution gives expression to the national aspirations and shared vision of the pre- or non-constitutional unity, and reflects its singular cultural, national, religious and linguistic characteristics through symbolic features and other particularistic practices and institutions. Thus, for example, the homogenizing foundational elements of the French constitution include the national language,[28] while in other constitutions they are expressed in the recognition of an official religion. For example, Denmark, Iceland and Norway, which have strong Lutheran majorities, include in their constitutions provisions establishing the Evangelical Lutheran Church as the state's official religion.[29] Germany's special immigration laws for ethnic Germans (until 1999) was another example of such an essentialist foundational approach.

"The people" come together through the making of the constitution: the liberal-procedural constitution

An alternative perspective on the relationship between constitutions and the identity of "the people" rests on an attempt to separate the *demos* (the citizens) from the *ethnos* (the nation). According to this view, the constitution does not represent the particular identity of a culturally or ethnically homogenous people. Rather, it unites together a collectivity of individuals on the basis of a minimal consensus regarding procedures for resolving political issues. That is, the constitution establishes procedures and institutions of conflict resolution within a democratic order. Such a constitutional doctrine was elaborately proposed by the notion of *constitutional patriotism*, whose most conspicuous exponent was Jürgen Habermas.[30]

---

[28] Article 2, section 2 of the French constitution states that "The language of the Republic is French."

[29] Section 4 in the constitution of Denmark; Article 62 in the constitution of the Republic of Iceland; Article 2, section 2 in the constitution of Norway. For the full text of the constitutions see Albert P. Blaustein and Gilbert H. Flanz, eds., *Constitutions of the Countries of the World* (Dobbs Ferry: Oceana Publications, 1985 and updated annually).

[30] I am relying here on Jürgen Habermas' writings on constitutional patriotism, however the principal objective in this discussion is to present an ideal-type of liberal-procedural constitution. Thus, my presentation will focus on a procedural understanding of constitutional patriotism. As I will discuss below, Habermas himself was aware of the difficulties inherent to a pure proceduralist conception of a liberal constitutional identity. Moreover, alternative interpretations of constitutional patriotism have been discussed by other theorists. One of the most elaborate explorations of the doctrine of constitutional patriotism is Jan-Werner Muller, *Constitutional Patriotism* (Princeton University Press, 2007). See also Thomas Mertens, "Cosmopolitanism and Citizenship: Kant against Habermas," *European Journal of Philosophy* 4 (1996).

The concept of constitutional patriotism suggests political culture as a replacement for the "ethnos" as the common denominator of the polity. Only this kind of shared political identity "heightens the awareness of both the diversity and the integrity of the different forms of life coexisting in a multicultural society."[31] The focal point of this kind of political identity is the shared democratic procedures according to which the state is functioning. Constitutional patriotism wishes to replace cultural attachments that rest on shared history, language and associations with allegiance to institutions and symbols that are potentially universalistic, as the foundational basis of the constitution. Such understanding of constitutional patriotism entails loyalty to the democratic procedures of the constitution, rather than to a specific cultural community. Habermas writes:

> This idea does not refer to the substantive generality of a popular will that would owe its unity to a prior homogeneity of descent or form of life. The consensus fought for and achieved in an association of free and equal persons ultimately rests only on the unity of a *procedure* to which all consent … In a pluralistic society, the constitution expresses a formal consensus. The citizens want to regulate their living together according to principles that are in the equal interest of each and thus can meet with the justified assent of all. Such an association is structured by relations of mutual recognition in which each person can expect to be respected by all as free and equal. Each and every person should receive equal protection and equal respect in their integrity as irreplaceable individuals, as members of the political community.[32]

In the liberal-procedural constitution, the shared constitutional procedures and democratic principles provide the basis of the "thin" civic identity of the people.[33] In such constitutions, the institutional and the

---

[31] Jürgen Habermas, "Citizenship and National Identity," in *Between Facts and Norms: Contributions to a Discourse Theory of Law and Democracy* (Cambridge, MA: The MIT Press, 1996), 500. Habermas' claim is not merely normative. He believes that this idea of a self-determining political community has taken on concrete legal shape in all political systems of Western Europe and the United States. Habermas, "Citizenship and National Identity," 496. Furthermore, the possibility of such civic association underpins his support for the drafting of a European constitution and lies behind his objection to what he calls the Euroskeptic's "no-demos" thesis. Habermas, "The European Nation-State."

[32] Habermas, "Citizenship and National Identity," 496.

[33] The notion of a "thin" procedural identity is often criticized as too weak to generate and maintain a deep sense of socio-political identity which is required for maintaining a democratic order. Moreover, many commentators doubt that the commitment to liberal

foundational roles of the constitution overlap. That is, both are manifested in the same constitutional provisions. The provisions that establish the democratic structure of government and assure the protection of basic rights also represent the shared commitments of "the people" to liberal-democratic norms and values.[34]

The US constitution is generally perceived by contemporary constitutional theorists as representing the closest manifestation of this ideal-type liberal-procedural constitution. It is regarded as the constitution that unifies the American people and provides the basis for their national identity.[35] The defining narrative of the United States revolves around what Bruce Ackerman terms "constitutional self-determination":

procedures and principles is sufficient to create and maintain the trust and solidarity that are necessary in order to sustain the mutual obligations upon which the social-democratic state rests. Among the most interesting discussions of the difficulties of a liberal-procedural constitution as a basis for national identity are Craig Calhoun, "Imagining Solidarity: Cosmopolitanism, Constitutional Patriotism, and the Public Sphere," *Public Culture* 14, no. 1 (2002); Avishai Margalit and Joseph Raz, "National Self-Determination," *Journal of Philosophy* 87, no. 9 (1990); Yael Tamir, *Liberal Nationalism, Studies in Moral, Political, and Legal Philosophy* (Princeton University Press, 1995); Charles Taylor and Amy Gutmann, *Multiculturalism and "The Politics of Recognition": An Essay* (Princeton University Press, 1992); Michael Walzer, *Spheres of Justice: A Defense of Pluralism and Equality* (New York: Basic Books, 1983). This problem was addressed by some theoretical attempts to reconcile Habermas' liberal universalistic principles with a particularistic conception of political cultures. See Cecile Laborde, "From Constitutional to Civic Patriotism," *British Journal of Political Science* 32 (2002): 591–612; Maurizio Viroli, *For Love of Country: An Essay on Patriotism and Nationalism* (Oxford University Press, 1995), 169–77. Nevertheless, it seems to me that such a republican interpretation of constitutional patriotism blurs the significant differences between civic and ethnic collectivity and between procedural and substantial sources of identity. This approach evades the central question of whether the basis for national identity is pre- or post-constitutional.

[34] Other liberal constitutional theories can also be grouped together under the category of the liberal-proceduralist constitution. Clearly, John Rawls' concept of constitutional consensus fits the model. Rawls distinguishes between constitutional consensus and overlapping consensus, claiming that the former is a consensus regarding democratic procedures and principles, while the latter expresses an agreement over the basic structure of society, and therefore includes "great values." He views constitutional consensus as merely a modus vivendi, and as a step toward what he terms "overlapping consensus," which he considers as a deeper and wider form of consensus than the constitutional consensus. John Rawls, *Political Liberalism* (New York: Columbia University Press, 1996), 134. Habermas' constitutional patriotism may be seen as standing between the two Rawlsian conceptions, since he seems to value constitutional agreement on democratic procedures more than Rawls does, but at the same time believes that a formal search for deeper normative consensus is not required.

[35] This is particularly true with respect to the way the US constitution is perceived today. When written and ratified during the 1780s, the founding fathers wished to anchor the

The narrative we tell ourselves about our Constitution's roots is a deeply significant act of collective self definition; its continual re-telling plays a critical role in the ongoing construction of national identity ... In part because Americans differ so radically in other respects, our constitutional narrative constitutes us as a people ... To discover the Constitution is to discover an important part of ourselves – insofar as one recognizes oneself as an American.[36]

Thomas Grey argues that reverence of the constitution as the sole basis for the American political unity transformed the document into a symbol of the people itself. Serving as "the unifying function of civil religion," the constitution is worshiped as a sacred text.[37]

In sum, on the foundational level, the Western constitutional imagination comprises two constitutional paradigms, representing two distinct types of national identity and manifesting two different understandings of the relationship between the constitution and "the people." The first is an essentialist or nation-state constitution that reflects the existing aspirations, culture and vision of a society through a set of declarations that, among other functions, protect values of national importance (including, for instance, national language and the established religion of the state). The second is a liberal constitution that expresses the shared civic identity of the citizenry through the formalization of ground rules for democratic participation, representation and deliberation.[38]

legitimacy of the new constitution in an existing cultural and political homogeneity. John Jay, in *Federalist no. 2*, stressed the uniform features of the American people, arguing that the enactment of a federal (rather than confederal) constitution was the most appropriate for "a united people, a people descended from the same ancestors, speaking the same language, professing the same religion, attached to the same principles of government, very similar in their manners and customs" (*The Federalist Papers by Alexander Hamilton, James Madison and John Jay* (Bantam Books, 1982) 7).

[36] Bruce A. Ackerman, *We the People: Foundations* (Cambridge, MA: Belknap Press of Harvard University Press, 1991), 7–36.

[37] Thomas C. Grey, "The Constitution as Scripture," *Stanford Law Review* 37, no. 1 (1984): 18. See also: Sanford Levinson, *Constitutional Faith* (Princeton University Press, 1988); Robert N. Bellah, "Civil Religion in America" *Dendalus* 96 no. 1 (1976) 1–21.

[38] The dichotomy I am proposing between types of constitution is compatible in many ways to the distinction between civic and ethnic nationalism, as was suggested by Rogers Brubaker, *Citizenship and Nationhood in France and Germany* (Cambridge, MA: Harvard University Press, 1992); Liah Greenfeld, *Nationalism: Five Roads to Modernity* (Cambridge: Harvard University Press, 1992); Tamir, *Liberal Nationalism*. I prefer not to rely on their theoretical framework for two reasons. First, I wish to focus on constitutions more than on national identities. Second, my aim in the book is to overcome the dichotomy between "thick" essentialism and "thin" constitutional patriotism, hence I am concentrating on societies which grapple with an internal conflict between the two perceptions of nationalism.

Some constitutions may be seen as close examples of the "liberal" and the "nation-state" ideal-type constitutions. For example the US constitution is a close example of the "liberal" ideal-type while the German Basic Law is a close example of the "nation-state" ideal-type. Nevertheless, the distinction between these two paradigmatic constitutions is not intended as a strict categorization of all existing constitutions. Clearly, one may identify various additional constitutional models that provide different and more nuanced forms of relationship between "the people" and the constitutional framework. The federal Swiss constitution, for example, could itself represent a separate ideal-type, as could the unique example of the unwritten British constitution, which has been challenged by calls for greater devolution.[39]

The distinction between the nation-state and liberal paradigms of constitutions represents two different perceptions of the relationship between a constitution and the "people." Constitutions may be regarded as either creating the people or reflecting its pre-constitutional identity. While the former corresponds to the "liberal" constitutional paradigm, the latter represents the basic tenet of the "nation-state" constitutional paradigm. Most democratic constitutions embody traits of both the liberal-democratic political culture (e.g. the inclusion of a bill of rights, and democratic electoral rules) and of essential characteristics in the form of state symbols and particular cultural practices (e.g. official day of rest, official language, established religion, etc.).

However, there are societies whose constitutions do not fit this categorization. These are societies that I refer to as deeply divided societies. This is because the deep ideological rifts in these societies prevent the emergence of the pre-constitutional consensus that is necessary for the crafting of either of the two paradigms of constitutions.

Pre-constitutional consensus

Constitutions are rarely, if ever, written on a clean slate. They identify and formalize the most fundamental beliefs, norms, values and aspirations of the political collectivity. Despite the many differences between the nation-state and liberal constitutional paradigms, both are characterized by the

---

[39] Stephen Tierney, *Constitutional Law and National Pluralism* (Oxford University Press, 2004).

need for pre-constitutional societal consensus regarding shared norms and values that underpin the state. This requirement is self-evident in the case of the nation-state constitution, as this ideal-type presupposes a shared ethnic or cultural background. But in the case of the liberal ideal-type constitution this requirement seems at first glance to be in conflict with the basic concept of a liberal constitution, and hence it merits a more detailed explanation.

The liberal constitutional model is perceived by many as normatively superior to the nation-state one, as it is seen as going beyond national, ethnic and religious identity and providing a culturally neutral basis for political unity. Habermas' constitutional patriotism purports to replace cultural attachments with allegiance to the democratic procedures of the state and to institutions and symbols that are potentially of universalist appeal. In his essay "Why Europe Needs a Constitution" Habermas writes:

> A nation of citizens must not be confused with a community of fate shaped by common descent, language and history. This confusion fails to capture the voluntaristic character of a civic nation, the collective identity of which exists neither independent of nor prior to the democratic process from which it springs.[40]

Habermas believes that the civic (as opposed to the ethnic) conception of the nation "reflects the fact that democratic citizenship establishes an abstract, legally mediated solidarity between strangers."[41] However, although these pre-constitutional "strangers" do not in fact share their cultural or ethnic background, they do share some common norms and values that underpin the desire of the individual members of the "voluntaristic" (as Habermas puts it) group to unify and establish a common polity. The constitution succeeds in evoking a new civic identity in what was previously a multitude of individuals because all these individuals held certain ideas in common regarding their future life together. As W. F. Murphy claims, "the myth of a people's forming themselves into a nation presents a problem not unlike that between chicken and egg. To agree in their collective name to a political

---

[40] Jürgen Habermas, "Why Europe Needs a Constitution," *New Left Review* 11 (2nd Series) (2001), 15.
[41] *Ibid.*

covenant, individuals must have already had some meaningful corporate identity *as a people*."[42]

The adoption of a liberal constitution, therefore, requires a minimal degree of societal consensus that can be understood in terms of shared political culture. The act of constitution-drafting does indeed "constitute" a new political collectivity, in the sense that it creates a political unity that did not exist before the writing of the constitution. However, this political unity cannot be constituted unless certain shared commitments to the fundamental principles of political liberalism already exist. In other words, constitutional patriotism can be realized only if all members of society accept the separation between their own particular identities and the shared civic and proceduralist identity of the state. In such societies, members hold what Alfred Stepan terms "multiple and compatible identities."[43] Only when the shared public civic identity, embodied in the constitution, is decoupled from the private identities (religious, ethnic or cultural) of the citizens, can the new civic identity facilitate the integration of the multitude of individuals into a united political collectivity.

This precondition to the success of a liberal constitution was acknowledged by Habermas in a later translation of his well-known article "Citizenship and National Identity":

> The original thesis stands: democratic citizenship need not be rooted in the national identity of a people. However, regardless of the diversity of different cultural forms of life, it does require that every citizen be socialized into a common political culture.[44]

To conclude, a societal consensus regarding shared norms and values that underpin the state is a precondition for the success of both a nation-state constitution and a liberal constitution. The former presupposes a shared ethnic or cultural background, while the latter requires the pre-existence of common commitments to liberal political culture. In both paradigms, however, the shared norms and values become entrenched through the constitution. The foundational role of the constitution can thus be understood in terms of solidifying rather than inventing a new political entity. Thus, going back to the foundational function of the constitution, one

---

[42] Murphy, "Constitutions, Constitutionalism and Democracy," 9.

[43] Alfred Stepan, "Religion, Democracy, and the 'Twin Tolerations'," *Journal of Democracy* 11, no. 4 (2000).

[44] Habermas, "Citizenship and National Identity," 500. Interestingly, these two sentences are missing in an earlier translation of this paper, included in Ronald Beiner, ed., *Theorizing Citizenship* (Albany: State University of New York Press, 1995).

would expect a constitution to reflect either a "thick" ethnic, cultural or national identity, or else a "thin" civic identity which is based on shared liberal norms and democratic procedures.

However, some societies lack the consensus that is necessary for the enactment of a constitution that has legitimacy in the eyes of society as a whole. These societies lack either cultural homogeneity that would enable them to agree on the symbolic elements of a nation-state constitution, or else popular support for the underlying principles of a liberal-proce-duralist constitution. These societies, referred to in this book as "deeply divided," are characterized by intense internal disagreements over the vision of the state, and require a third paradigm of a constitution.

2

The incrementalist approach to constitution-making

The term "deeply divided societies" is commonly used by students of conflict resolution and institutional design. Most definitions of the term tend to focus on the intensity and comprehensiveness of societal conflicts – in other words, to its volume – without paying particular attention to its quality – to the nature of the schism. Consequently, distinctions are not typically made between various types of deeply divided society: whether the society in question is segmented along ethnic, religious or economic lines, or whether the division between groups is based on any other type of identity "with high political salience, sustained over a substantial period of time and a wide variety of issues."[1] But the nature of the schism is relevant in the context of drafting a constitution. Constitution-writing is an attempt to identify and to articulate the fundamental norms and values that are shared by "the people" in whose name and for whom the constitution is drafted. In the context of a struggle over the character of the state not all types of conflict have the same effect. Not all types of conflict can be addressed by the same constitutional tools.

This chapter begins by identifying and describing deeply divided societies as the term will be used in this book. It then reviews the various constitutional solutions commonly proposed for mitigating conflicts in multicultural, multinational or multilingual societies. It will discuss the limitations of these solutions when applied to deeply divided societies of the type discussed in the book. The last section of the chapter provides an initial outline of an alternative approach that addresses the problems faced by deeply divided societies when they draft constitutions.

---

[1] Ian Lustick, "Stability in Deeply Divided Societies: Consociationalism Versus Control," *World Politics* 31, no. 3 (1979): 325. A somewhat similar definition is used by Eric A. Nordlinger, *Conflict Regulation in Divided Societies* (Cambridge, MA: Center for International Affairs Harvard University, 1972), 9. See also: Arend Lijphart, "Majority Rule Versus Democracy in Deeply Divided Societies," *Politikon* 4, no. 2 (1977).

Deeply divided societies

Definitions are a risky business. As Ludwig Wittgenstein noted, clear definitions are difficult to achieve.[2] Moreover, the difficulty of defining political concepts and the intra-class variations allowed by any type of classification are inherent problems in comparative political research.[3] Nevertheless, a comparative discussion of constitution-writing in deeply divided societies cannot start without some elaboration of the types of society this category comprises. This elaboration will also help to explain, at a later stage, the selection of countries included in this study, and will help identify additional cases of divided societies, where the adoption of a similar constitutional approach may be relevant.[4]

The deeply divided societies that the book explores are characterized by conflicts between groups that have competing visions of their state. The conflict is between clashing societal norms and values, most notably regarding questions of national or religious identity. These competing perspectives often also clash with respect to the adoption or rejection of the principle of political liberalism.[5] That is, the tension is between those who distinguish between private identity and public shared civic identity and those who reject this distinction. Such conflicts usually cannot be resolved by redistributing power or resources. Examples of such divisions are those between secular and religious Jews in Israel and between nationalist and moderate Hindus in India.

---

[2] Ludwig Wittgenstein, *Philosophical Investigations*, trans. G. E. M. Anscombe (New York: Macmillan, 1968).

[3] Giovanni Sartori, "Comparing and Miscomparing," *Journal of Theoretical Politics* 3, no. 3 (1991): 246.

[4] The problem of creating a clearly defined category of "deeply divided societies" stems also from the fact that whether a certain society at a particular historical moment should be considered "deeply divided" depends not only on the definition of the category but also on one's understanding and interpretation of the social and political conditions that existed at the time. For example, whether, and to what extent, the United States may be considered to have been deeply divided at time its constitution was drafted is subject to historical debate. See, for example, Bernard Bailyn, *The Ideological Origins of the American Revolution* (Cambridge, MA and London: The Belknap Press of Harvard University Press, 1992), 321–79; Walter A. McDougall, *Freedom Just around the Corner: A New American History 1585–1828* (New York: HarperCollins, 2004), 280–320; Herbert J. Storing, "Slavery and the Moral Foundation of the American Revolution," in Robert H. Horowitz, ed., *The Moral Foundation of the American Republic* (Charlottesville: University Press of Virginia, 1979); Gordon S. Wood, *The Creation of the American Republic, 1776–1787* (New York: Norton, 1972), ch. 12.

[5] John Rawls, *Political Liberalism* (New York: Columbia University Press, 1996), 134.

These are the kind of conflicts that Albert Hirschman termed "either–or" or "non-divisible", and they are typically characterized by an absolute unwillingness to compromise on the issues upon which the conflict is based, as opposed to the "divisible" or "more-or-less" conflicts, which are easier to settle, because the warring parties can agree to "split the difference" or compromise.[6] When such deeply divided societies come to the task of drafting a constitution, the constitution's foundational aspects typically attract more political attention than its procedural ones, and the lack of shared norms becomes one of the central obstacles to the writing of the constitution.

In such deeply divided societies, the schism between the conflicting sets of values – for example between the liberal and illiberal camps – does not necessarily overlap with other religious, ethnic or national fault lines that characterize these societies. Rather, in many cases, the two types of division cut across each other. In Israel, for example, one of the most intense disputes over the principles of political liberalism exists between secular and Orthodox Jews. That is, the Jewish majority population, which is in tension with the minority Palestinian population, is deeply divided within itself between religious and secular visions of a Jewish state. And it is this division that is widely considered as one of the principal obstacles to drafting a constitution. Similarly, the controversy over the meaning of India's secularism does not correlate with the religious and ethnic divisions in India. Hindus, as well as Muslims, hold competing perspectives regarding the relations between religion and state.

The conflict over liberal political values plays a central role in the type of deeply divided societies discussed in this book. Unlike multinational societies such as Belgium or Canada, in which the fundamental principles of political liberalism are shared, by and large, by the entire society, in the deeply divided societies under consideration, at least one of the competing groups is hostile to basic liberal principles.[7] The illiberal group may be

---

[6] Albert O. Hirschman, "Social Conflicts as Pillars of Democratic Market Society," *Political Theory* 22, no. 2 (1994): 203.

[7] A similar distinction has been made by Yael Tamir, who distinguished between "thin" and "thick" multiculturalism. For Tamir, "thin" multiculturalism relates to two or more liberal cultural communities within one state, such as the English- and French-speaking communities in Canada, while "thick" multiculturalism involves cultures at least one of which is illiberal. While the former "leads to a particular type of interest-group politics, the latter leads to a *modus vivendi*, which is based on two, very different, points of view: a liberal one which emphasizes respect for different ways of life, and an illiberal one which seeks to secure its own existence in the midst of a liberal society." Yael Tamir, "Two Concepts of Multiculturalism," *Journal of Philosophy of Education* 29, no. 2 (1995): 161.

in the minority, as in the case of Orthodox Jews in Israel, but it may also be the majority, as is the case in Turkey. In either case, however, what is important is that each of the camps in deeply divided societies – whether liberal or illiberal, whether in the majority or the minority – wishes to impose its political philosophy on the state as a whole. Each side wants the constitution to express its aspirations and goals. The Israeli case provides, again, an interesting illustration. Since before political independence, Orthodox Jews have tried to influence the fundamental values and norms of the state, unlike religious minorities in most Western democracies, who wish to maintain their cultural autonomy through a set of special group rights.[8]

Constitution-drafting as a high-stakes moment

If the foundational role of a constitution is to reflect the state's ideational consensus, how is this role fulfilled in deeply divided societies? And what is the effect of the process of constitution-making on ideologically polarized societies – does it exacerbate internal conflicts, mitigate them, or have no substantial effect on their intensity?

The process of constitutional design creates risks that may threaten the fragile stability of deeply divided societies. The act of writing a constitution brings these conflicts into the high-stakes arena of entrenched law, and places additional pressures on the political system.

Under conditions of intense internal disagreements, the constitutional debates risk turning into a political battleground, emphasizing the differences between the various positions rather than bridging them. Conflicts over foundational issues may be manageable or even concealed when a constitution is already functioning and shared vision is taken for granted. However, at time of constitutional-drafting, foundational disagreements may be inflamed. Instead of being a vehicle for compromise, the constitutional debate can become a source of escalating tensions. In

---

Tamir's "thick" multiculturalism is not fully compatible with of the concept of deeply divided societies as discussed in this book, because it assumes a liberal setting in which the tensions are expressed. That is, both of Tamir's concepts of multiculturalism refer to societies in which the liberal group is the dominant majority, whereas in deeply divided societies the majority is not necessarily liberal in its views.

[8] Asher Cohen and Bernard Susser, *Israel and the Politics of Jewish Identity: The Secular-Religious Impasse* (Baltimore: The Johns Hopkins University Press, 2000), 20. For an excellent scholarly study of the Christian Democratic parties in Europe see Stathis N. Kalyvas, *The Rise of Christian Democracy in Europe* (Ithaca, NY: Cornell University Press, 1996).

the worst-case scenario, the intensification of the ideational conflict may lead to outbreaks of violence, to civil war, or even the partition of the territory.

A good example of this is the failed attempt to craft a constitution for the united India. In December 1946 the All India Constituent Assembly began writing a constitution for the soon-to-be-independent state. From the very beginning, the drafting process reflected a conflict between the two leading parties in India, which held opposing views of Indian national identity: between the mostly Hindu Congress Party, which envisioned a centralized federal India based on a pluralistic conception of national identity, and the Muslim League, which perceived nationalism in homogenizing terms and viewed Hindu dominance in a majoritarian democratic system as a threat.[9] As discussed in Chapter 4, the tripartite negotiations between the Congress, the League and the British government regarding the structure of the Constituent Assembly show how the parties imported their political disputes into the constitutional debate over the composition and procedures of the Assembly, and used legal language to push through their ideological agendas, rather than to serve as a vehicle for compromise. Eventually, in June 1947, after seven months of intense negotiations accompanied by violent riots, the subcontinent was partitioned into two countries: India and Pakistan.

But do processes of constitution-writing necessarily exacerbate societal polarization, or could they mitigate tensions and prevent sectarian violence?

Deliberativist constitutional theorists would argue that one cannot expect constitutions to settle fundamental societal controversies. This view is shared by many liberal political theorists, most notably John Rawls and Jürgen Habermas. One of the clearer statements of this liberal preference for a "thin" constitution was presented by the Canadian legal theorist Jeremy Webber. "Constitutions," he argues, "are not primarily a mode of expressing the will of a unified people today. Rather, they establish a framework for the construction and reconstruction of the people's will long into the future."[10] Instead of enshrining the shared values of the nation, constitutions create a "feeling of commonality" through a public

---

[9] Indeed, there were Congress Party members who advocated Hindu nationalism, yet Nehru's approach was more pluralistic. See Sunil Khilnani, *The Idea of India* (New York: Farrar, Straus and Giroux, 1999).

[10] Jeremy Webber, "Constitutional Reticence," *Australian Journal of Legal Philosophy* 25 (2000): 131.

"conversation,"[11] by ensuring the participation of all members of society in public debates. Emphasizing the procedural role of the constitution, Webber calls for "[constitutional] reticence in the entrenchment of ostensibly common values and beliefs."[12] Constitutions, he contends, should "focus upon process rather than substance."[13] Constitution-drafting is essentially based, according to Webber, on a modus vivendi: "Perhaps we do not agree to a definite set of values," he writes, "but nevertheless consent to a process for resolving our differences."[14]

Webber's desire to rid constitutional debates of contentious substantive dispute is attractive. Indeed, it is difficult to object to the idealism that encourages "communities [to] be open to their members holding a broad range of beliefs, and to revising those beliefs through discussion over time," and which holds that constitutions should reflect such openness.[15] However, this ideal is often at odds with political reality. Like other constitutional proceduralists, Webber's universe is limited to multicultural societies that adhere to the basic principles of political liberalism. He admits to viewing liberalism as a tradition that not only enables public participation and deliberation, but also establishes a sense of commonality and unity.[16] Nevertheless, he opposes the introduction of illiberal elements into the constitutional discussion because of their tendency to distort rational arguments. This is one of his reasons for recommending that reference to fundamental controversies be excluded from all constitutional debate.[17]

Like other multicultural theorists who write about constitutions,[18] Webber prefers to isolate the domain of constitutional deliberation from

---

[11] *Ibid.*, 132. See also Jeremy Webber, *Reimagining Canada: Language, Culture, Community, and the Canadian Constitution* (Kingston and Buffalo: McGill University Press, 1994).

[12] Webber, "Constitutional Reticence," 134.

[13] *Ibid.*, 144.

[14] *Ibid.*, 146. Even the consent to procedures is perceived by Webber in minimalist terms, as merely provisional. As he explains, he does not assume the "deliberate acceptance by each citizen [of the constitutional procedures]. Rather than agree, it is more accurate to say that we defer to the processes: they are there when we arrive, we proceed to work through them, and we naturally hesitate before incurring the high costs of stepping outside them into revolutionary upheaval … we work within them, but we may simultaneously criticize and seek to change them." Webber, "Constitutional Reticence," 146–7.

[15] Webber, "Constitutional Reticence," 153.

[16] *Ibid.*, 146.   [17] *Ibid.*, 132.

[18] There are not many. Theorists of multiculturalism rarely address the question of constitution-making, and most of those who do focus on Canada, Australia and the United States. Although these societies are multicultural or multinational, they are not deeply divided. The central constitutional dispute in such societies is over special group rights, not about the overall ethical framework of the state.

any illiberal viewpoints that might undermine the harmony of its participants. In pluralistic societies, constitutions could perhaps function as neutral mechanisms of conflict resolution. However, this is extremely difficult in deeply divided societies where there is no consensus regarding constitutional principles (liberal or otherwise).

Webber believes that his theory of constitutional reticence is applicable to all societies, because all types of political disagreement are compatible with democratic systems. By simplifying and overgeneralizing the concept of disagreement, Webber does not make allowance for the various levels of intensity of political controversies and societal rifts. Not all disagreements can be resolved by the same means. In deeply divided societies, ideational disputes that touch upon citizens' deepest beliefs and commitments cannot be taken off the political agenda.[19]

Are deeply divided societies doomed to remain without a constitution until they resolve their internal conflicts? On the one hand, these societies cannot adopt a nation-state constitution, because of their sectarian divisions. On the other hand, they cannot draft a liberal-proceduralist constitution, because there is no consensus on principles of political liberalism. How can deeply divided societies resolve this problem?

Institutional design in multi-ethnic and multinational societies

The only alternative to partition, which is usually an unwelcome and impractical solution,[20] is either to impose the views of one group on society as whole or else to craft some form of compromise. The former solution was adopted, for example, by the framers of the modern, secular Turkish constitution in 1924. The key question faced by the reformists, headed by Mustafa Kemal, was the role of religion and religious authorities in the modern Turkish republic. Atatürk promoted the separation of religion and politics in an attempt to transfer religion from the political to the private sphere.[21] Nevertheless, while the Kemalist era is frequently

---

[19] Rawls, *Political Liberalism*, 151.

[20] Donald L. Horowitz, *Ethnic Groups in Conflict* (Berkeley: University of California Press, 1985), ch. 6.

[21] On the similarities and differences between Turkish *Laikik* and French *Leïcité* see Murat Akan, "The Politics of Secularization in Turkey and France: Beyond Orientalism and Occidentalism" (PhD thesis, Columbia University, 2005), 159. Ahmet T. Kuru, *Secularism and State Policies toward Religion: The United States, France, and Turkey* (New York: Cambridge University Press, 2009).

referred to as a model for Islamic political liberalization, it is important to remember that the radical reforms embraced by Atatürk came at a cost. As there was no open debate, not only was the process of drafting the constitution inherently undemocratic but also the political system it originally established.[22] It was only after World War II that a multi-party era began and a greater degree of freedom of expression was allowed. For the first time religious leaders began to express more openly their hostility to secularism and their demand for an Islamic restoration. Even so, the Turkish constitution was rewritten twice, first in 1961 and then in 1982, in both cases following a *coup d'état*, in a process that was largely controlled by the military.[23]

In contrast to the pseudo-democratic constitutional measures employed in Turkey,[24] scholars of institutional design in multi-ethnic, multicultural and multinational conflicts have tried to identify democratic solutions to mitigate identity conflicts. This body of research has produced a large range of alternative institutional mechanisms for enhancing democracy and stability in divided and post-conflict societies that remain polarized along religious, ethnic or linguistic lines. These include such arrangements as federalism, devolution, consociationalism, power-sharing, a variety of electoral systems and the granting of special group rights. While these mechanisms may be useful tools in mitigating conflicts between identity groups, they are applicable only under particular geographical or societal circumstances, and do not address the intricate conditions of ideational conflicts in the deeply divided societies under discussion.

Federal solutions, for example, may be effective when the various ethnic, national or linguistic groups are territorially concentrated, as is the case in Belgium, Switzerland or Canada, but they are less useful when the populations in question are geographically dispersed.[25] Political

---

[22] Eric Zurcher, *Turkey: Modern History* (London: I. B. Tauris, 2005), ch. 10

[23] Akan, "The Politics of Secularization in Turkey and France," chs. 9 and 10.

[24] Merhen Kamrava, "Pseudo-Democratic Politics and Populist Possibilities: The Rise and Demise of Turkey's Refah Party," *British Journal of Middle Eastern Studies* 25, no. 2 (1998): 279.

[25] Alfred Stepan, "Toward a New Comparative Politics of Federalism, (Multi)Nationalism, and Democracy: Beyond Rikerian Federalism," in *Arguing Comparative Politics* (Oxford University Press, 2001); Willian Safran and Ramon Maiz Suarez, eds., *Identity and Territorial Autonomy in Plural Societies* (London: Routledge, 2000); George Alan Tarr, Robert Forrest Williams and Joseph Marko, eds., *Federalism, Subnational Constitutions and Minority Rights* (Santa Barbara: Greenwood Publishing Group, 2004); Ute Wachendorfer-Schmidt, ed., *Federalism and Political Performance* (London: Routledge,

scientists who advocate consociational solutions, most notably Arend Lijphart, focus on institutional mechanisms of power-sharing such as coalition governments and veto rights to address conflicts between ethnic and national groups.[26] However, these proposals do not resolve disagreements over the normative principles that are to apply to the entire state, and that may cut across ethnic or other lines, such as issues of church and state.[27] In contrast to the accommodationist approach taken by theories of consociationalism and power-sharing, a more integrational approach to conflict resolution in divided societies is represented by political scientists who focus on the design of electoral rules as the solution for ethnic conflicts.[28] But electoral rules are not an appropriate tool to address conflicts between competing perspectives on the character of the state, where the conflicting camps wish to imprint their vision in state symbols and national emblems – for example, when the conflict is over the wording of the constitution, whether it should include a reference to God. Finally, various theorists of multiculturalism have advocated for special group rights and formal recognition of the claims of national, religious or ethnic minorities.[29] While these arrangements may indeed satisfy the demands of minority groups in liberal multicultural or multinational countries

2000); Yash Ghai, ed., *Autonomy and Ethnicity: Negotiating Competing Claims in Multi-Ethnic States* (Cambridge University Press, 2000).

[26] Arend Lijphart, *The Politics of Accommodation: Pluralism and Democracy in the Netherlands* (Berkeley: University of California Press, 1968); Lijphart, "Majority Rule Versus Democracy in Deeply Divided Societies."

[27] This is notable, for example, in Lijphart's recent article "Constitutional Design in Divided Societies," which lists a number of institutional recommendations regarding electoral systems and the structure of the executive and legislative branches, yet ignores issues related to the normative and symbolic elements of the constitution. Lijphart, "Constitutional Design in Divided Societies," *Journal of Democracy* 15, no. 2 (2004). For more recent discussion on the mechanism of power-sharing for addressing ethnic conflicts see Ian O'Flynn, David Russle and Donald Horowitz, eds., *Power Sharing: New Challenges for Divided Societies* (London: Pluto Press, 2005); Philip G. Roeder and Donald S. Rothcild, eds., *Sustainable Peace: Power and Democracy after Civil Wars* (Ithaca, NY: Cornell University Press, 2005); Sidney John Roderick Noel, ed., *From Power Sharing to Democracy: Post-Conflict Institutions in Ethnically Divided Societies* (Montreal: McGill-Queen's Press, 2005).

[28] Horowitz, *Ethnic Groups in Conflict*; Steven Wilkinson, *Votes and Violence: Electoral Competition and Ethnic Violence in India* (Cambridge and New York: Cambridge University Press, 2004); Benjamin Reilly, *Democracy in Divided Societies: Electoral Engineering for Conflict Management* (Cambridge University Press, 2001).

[29] For example: Will Kymlicka, *Multicultural Citizenship: A Liberal Theory of Minority Rights* (Oxford: Clarendon Press, 1995); James Tully, *Strange Multiplicity: Constitutionalism in an Age of Diversity* (Cambridge and New York: Cambridge University Press, 1995).

such as Canada and the United States, they are less relevant to countries in which the core conflict over the character of the state is between liberal and illiberal visions.[30] This, for example, is the case in Muslim democratizing countries such as Turkey and Indonesia, where conflicts revolve around the appropriate relationship between traditional religious law and the secular institutions of the modern state.

The incrementalist approach to constitution-making

The drafting of a new constitution under conditions of deep disagreement over the vision of the state thus requires an innovative approach. Under such delicate conditions, the enactment of rigid and supreme constitutional arrangements, which pose constraints on future generations, is perceived as forcing unequivocal choices between competing systems of norms and identities.

This seemingly constitutional impasse may be resolved by reconceptualizing the moment of constitution-making. Instead of perceiving it as a moment of revolutionary transformation, elements of gradualism may be introduced into the constitution-making process. Instead of viewing the moment of enacting a constitution as one that has a profound effect on the identity of the nation, it may be seen as one stage in a long-term evolutionary process of collective redefinition. Instead of perceiving it in terms of formal codification of clear and unequivocal decisions, it may be viewed as an opportunity for formulating ambiguous and opaque provisions, which in fact embody a decision to defer controversial choices on foundational issues to the future.

I will term this constitutional view as the *incrementalist* approach to constitution-writing. It represents an approach rather than a strict model since it may be manifested through various constitutional strategies, such as avoidance decision-making, using ambiguous and vague legal language and including contradictory provisions in the constitution. All constitutional strategies included in the incrementalist toolbox are intended to defer to the future controversial choices regarding the foundational aspect of the constitution in order to permit some form of agreement on a constitution to be reached. The incrementalist approach does not mean that decisions regarding the structure of governmental institutions are deferred to the future. Rather, decisions on the institutions of government and regulation of power are clear, and they allow for the democratic

---

[30] Tamir, "Two Concepts of Multiculturalism."

order to function. By contrast, on controversial foundational issues such as church–state relations and the definition of national identity, an incrementalist approach means that clear-cut decisions are avoided in order to circumvent overt conflict.[31] Instead of making unequivocal choices, the drafters transfer such controversial decisions from the constitutional to the political arena.

Naturally, the incrementalist strategy used by drafters of constitutions will differ depending on the circumstances surrounding the constitution-writing project in the specific country. In the case of Israel, for example, the inability to reach an agreement over the religious or secular character of the state was one of the leading causes for the decision to postpone the drafting of the constitution altogether. In India, a constitution was drafted, but it included provisions that explicitly deferred decisions on controversial issues such as the national language and the unification and secularization of personal law. In Ireland, it was not even possible to agree to defer decisions, as all parties that were involved with the writing of the constitutions, namely the Irish and the British, insisted on the inclusion of conflicting constitutional provisions and statements. As a result, the Irish constitution is an ambivalent document that incorporates contradictory clauses, which lend themselves to mutually inconsistent interpretations. But despite the range of incrementalist strategies that the three case studies exhibit, they all embody four principles that underpin

---

[31] Cass Sunstein's notion of "incompletely theorized agreements" in the constitutional context follows a similar logic. According to Sunstein, under conditions of unbridgeable intractable disagreements, constitution-making becomes possible if people agree on certain practices rather than on abstract principles or grounds for justifying these practices. Alternatively, incompletely theorized agreements may be incompletely specified in the sense that people who agree on abstract principles may not necessarily agree on what those principles entail in practice. Sunstein, *Designing Democracy: What Constitutions Do* (Oxford and New York: Oxford University Press, 2001), 50–6. While Sunstein praises the practical quality of incompletely theorized agreements, he provides very few examples, and says little on how these types of agreements are achieved. Moreover, the difference between the two types of incompletely theorized agreements – those that agree on the practicalities and those that agree on general principles – is not well theorized by Sunstein. In deeply divided societies that grapple with conflicting visions of the state, the disagreement is often on both the abstract and the practical level, and it is difficult to distinguish between the two. As another comparative constitutional scholar has noted, referring to the difference between American and Israeli constitution-writing, "it is one thing to compromise principle in the face of political exigency; quite another to achieve a viable constitutional result in the face of competing, potentially contradictory, visions." Gary Jacobsohn, *Apple of Gold: Constitutionalism in Israel and the United States* (Princeton University Press, 1993), 105.

the incrementalist approach to constitution-making: non-majoritarianism; a non-revolutionary approach; representation of the ideological disagreements; and transferring the problems from the constitutional to the political sphere. All four principles deviate from the commonly held perception of the constitution-making moment.

Non-majoritarianism

Majoritarian decision-making is a core democratic principle.[32] However, it is of limited value in deeply divided societies when at issue is the need to resolve disputes over fundamental norms and the ultimate goals of the state. In such situations, a consensual approach is more effective than majoritarianism. There are two basic reasons for this. Imposing the wishes of the majority on a minority group risks exacerbating the conflict and might destabilize the democratic order. Furthermore, in order for a constitution to be widely accepted as legitimate it needs to be based on broad popular support. Both types of arguments were made during the constitutional debates in India and in Israel.[33] The case of Ireland was somewhat different, as the debate over majoritarianism spilled over to the debate over the Anglo-Irish Treaty.[34]

The underlying perception, which is a common thread among constitution-drafters in deeply divided societies, is that democracy cannot survive if based solely on majority rule, and that decisions that define the collectivity should be based on as broad a consensus as possible. And to the extent that a broad consensus does not exist at the time of the drafting of the constitution, then this is an argument in favor of postponing decisions until such time as the relevant issues can be formulated in a manner that is widely acceptable.

Non-revolutionary approach to constitution-making

Constitution-making is commonly associated with revolution in two ways. First, since the end of the eighteenth century, successful revolutions

---

[32] Arend Lijphart, *Patterns of Democracy: Government Forms and Performance in Thirty-Six Countries* (New Haven: Yale University Press, 1999); Arend Lijphart, "Non-Majoritarian Democracy: A Comparison of Federal and Consociational Theories," *Publius, Federalism and Consociationalism: A Symposium* 15, no. 2 (1985).

[33] Israel's *Knesset Records* 1950: 812, 1267. Indian Constituent Assembly Debate [*CAD*], vol. IX: 1315, vol. VII: 543.

[34] Richard Bourke, *Peace in Ireland: The War of Ideas* (London: Pimlico, 2003).

have led to the establishment of written constitutions that incorporate the substantive achievements of the revolution.[35] Second, drafting a new constitution is itself an opportunity for radical societal change. This view was expressed in recent decades by constitutional theorists who called for a "clean break with the past" and a "speedy action" in the construction of liberal societies in Eastern Europe.[36] It is inspired to a large extent by the American experience, where a written constitution was the final legitimation of the Revolution, a revolution that gave birth to a new people.[37]

However, in face of an intractable struggle between competing definitions of nationhood or between contradicting visions of the state, the incrementalist approach rejects the revolutionary understanding of constitution-drafting, preferring to leave the future unfettered by principled constraints. It rests on the understanding that a consensus on the definition of the state's identity, which is required for the adoption of viable constitutional principles, cannot be achieved by radical transformation but rather through an evolutionary process of gradual social and political change.

This approach is closer to the Burkean gradualist perception of constitutional change, embedded in what Gerald Chapman terms his "practical imagination."[38] Constitutions, Burke believed, should not be developed in a radical and revolutionary way but rather in an incremental fashion. The common-law tradition, which Burke vigorously defended, considered constitutions to be the result of slow accumulation of concrete decisions built up by courts and other practical decision-makers over decades, generations, even centuries. A constitution, Burke contended, is "made by what is ten times better than choice, it is made by the peculiar circumstances, occasions, tempers, dispositions, and moral, civil, and social habitudes of the people, which disclose themselves only in a long space of time."[39]

The Burkean adherence to gradual emergence of national consensus on foundational issues and to the importance of context as a fundamental

---

[35] Hanna Arendt, *On Revolution* (New York: Viking Press, 1965).

[36] Bruce Ackerman, *The Future of Liberal Revolution* (New Haven and London: Yale University Press, 1992), 46–68.

[37] Jacobsohn, *Apple of Gold*, 109.

[38] Gerald W. Chapman, *Edmund Burke: The Practical Imagination* (Cambridge, MA: Harvard University Press, 1967).

[39] Edmund Burke, "Speech on the Reform of Representation in the House of Commons. June 1784." In: *Thoughts in the Present Discontent and Speeches* (Middlesex: The Echo Library, 2006) 78.

element shaping legitimate political reform,[40] accompanied by the belief
that disagreements may be resolved in an evolutionary rather than a revolutionary way – these are all part of the political spirit which underpins the
incrementalist approach to constitution-making in divided societies. The
introduction of a long-term perspective into the equation of constitution-
making allows deeply divided societies to defer controversial decisions
regarding the foundational elements of the constitution to the future.
This circumvention of potentially explosive conflicts allows for conflicted
societies to focus on the establishment of democratic institutions, within
whose framework future deliberation regarding the foundational issues
can take place.

We the divided people: representing the existing disagreements

Constitutional incrementalism should not be seen as merely an evasion
of making decisions regarding societal and political problems forced by
complicated reality. The various strategies included under the incrementalist approach of constitution-making are not equated with the liberal
bracketing doctrine of "taking [controversial issues] off the agenda,"
to use Rawls' terminology,[41] or what is known in the legal language as
"gag rules."[42] The incrementalist constitution differs from the liberal-
deliberative approach, which ultimately seeks to empty the constitution
from disputed elements and construct a legitimate constitution based
on common procedures and democratic principles. This "bracketing"
paradigm is shared, in various nuances, by Habermas' *constitutional
patriotism*, by Rawls' notion of *overlapping consensus*, as well as by
Jeremy Webber's suggestion for *constitutional reticence* with regard to
all divisive questions.[43]

---

[40] In truth, an element of Burkeanism exists in any modern constitutional structure.
Constitutional amendments, as well as the Supreme Court's changing constitutional
interpretation, are two examples of gradual constitutional reform, grounded in contextual Burkean principles. My argument focuses on the moment of constitution-making in
which a polity is being formed. Even in this particular moment, I argue, under certain
conditions, a Burkean contextualist approach may fit better than a radical revolutionary
rational constitutional design.

[41] Rawls, *Political Liberalism*, 151.

[42] Stephen Holmes, "Gag Rules or the Politics of Omission," in Jon Elster and Rune
Slagstad, eds., *Constitutionalism and Democracy* (Cambridge and New York: Cambridge
University Press, 1988).

[43] The nuance differences between the theories are discussed in Chapter 1.

This liberal constitutional doctrine is difficult to implement in societies still struggling over the definition of their collectivity and over their most fundamental commitments and beliefs. The liberal demand to differentiate between private identities and beliefs of the citizens and their public commonalities of shared democratic procedures cannot be met if the members of society define themselves in terms of their conflicting visions regarding the state as a whole. The core of the division in deeply divided societies is between rival perceptions of the collectivity in its entirety, between competing visions of the state as a whole. These issues could not be bracketed during the writing of a constitution, which symbolizes the climax of a process of national renewal.

Instead of bracketing the disputes over the credo and shared ethos of the state, the incrementalist constitution addresses them directly. The framers do not close their eyes to the tensions. Instead, they choose to embrace the competing positions. The third principle of the incrementalist approach thus refers to the inclusion, in the constitution, of all the competing and mutually contradictory positions of the various factions. Instead of providing clear-cut decisions, the constitution embraces the conflicting visions of the state by including vague and even contradictory provisions.

Thus, the incrementalist constitution goes beyond the commonly held dualism between the two ideal-types of constitutional identity. As elaborated in Chapter 1, the Western constitutional imagination consists of two principal paradigms regarding the relationship between constitutions and the identity of "the people." In the nation-state constitution, "we the people" represents the national or cultural commonalities of a presumably homogeneous population. By contrast, the liberal constitution expresses the shared commitment of "we the citizenry" to the underlying principles of political liberalism. The incrementalist constitution adopted by a deeply divided society thus represents a third option: it reflects the identity of "the people" as it really was at the time of constitution-drafting, that is, a *divided people*.

Where there are no shared norms or values, the accommodational, incrementalist constitution represents the very minimal common denominator that can guarantee popular support in the government: "we the divided people" agree that the polity is polarized, and that these are the core issues around which the disagreements revolve.

Transferring decisions to the political sphere

By refraining from making decisions that require choosing from among the competing visions of the state, incrementalist constitutional arrangements transfer such decisions to the political realm. Recognizing that decisions with respect to sensitive societal issues require long-term public and political debate, the incrementalist strategy channels the debate over these issues to the arena of ordinary parliamentary politics. Contentious foundational issues are thus transferred from the constitutional sphere of "high lawmaking" to the political sphere of "normal lawmaking," to use Bruce Ackerman's distinction.[44]

This transfer is based on the assumption that the domain of ordinary legislation allows for greater flexibility in accommodating the demands of the conflicting camps, and more room for innovative and nuanced solutions to intricate and complex ideational tensions. Since ordinary legislation usually does not require the special amendment procedures for altering the entrenched constitutional arrangements, it may be viewed as more compatible with the evolutionary perception of constitutional formation. However, whether the transfer of foundational issues from the constitutional to the political sphere truly provides for greater flexibility is questionable. The deferral of controversial choices may allow for the emergence of a material, unwritten, constitutional arrangements, which could in practice become more rigid than a formal one, since they lack a formal mechanism of amendment.[45]

The expectation that the political system will address the foundational issue that had been left undecided by the drafters of the constitution is one of the important elements that distinguish between the incrementalist approach to constitution-making and similar constitutional concepts such as Michael Foley's "constitutional abeyances." Abeyances are ways "of accommodating the absence of a definitive constitutional settlement and of providing the means of adjusting to the issues left unresolved in the fabric of the constitution."[46] Foley regards constitutional abeyances as often unintentional, even unconscious "working anomal[ies] within the constitution," and rejects the view that they are "constitutional 'deals' by which particular issues are attended to through a conscious form of mutual accommodation between contending parties."[47] By contrast, incrementalist constitutional strategies are adopted by the framers in

---

[44] Bruce Ackerman, *We the People: Foundations* (Cambridge, MA: Belknap Press of Harvard University Press, 1991), ch. 1.

[45] See Chapter 7 for an elaborated discussion of the problem of potential rigidity of the incrementalist constitution.

[46] Michael Foley, *The Silence of Constitutions: Gaps, "Abeyances" and Political Temperament in the Maintenance of Government* (London and New York: Routledge, 1989), 10.

[47] *Ibid.*

deeply divided societies precisely in order to avoid direct conflict and to allow for the resolution of the tension at some time in the future.

The way in which incrementalist constitutional tools have been used in practice is explored in the next part of the book. The following three chapters examine how the incrementalist approach to constitution-making was embraced by three deeply divided societies that wrote their constitutions under conditions of intense struggle over the character of the state: Ireland in 1922, Israel between 1948 and 1950, and India between 1946 and 1950.

PART II

Varieties of constitutional incrementalism

The next three chapters will trace the constitutional debates in three deeply divided societies, Israel, India and Ireland, all of which, at independence, adopted various incrementalist constitutional strategies to address their internal foundational conflicts. The differences between the three countries – in terms of geographic size, population, culture and religious composition, as well as in the circumstances under which their constitutional debates occurred – are dramatic. At independence in 1947, India had a population of 250 million, of which roughly 75 percent were Hindu and nearly 20 percent were Muslim, with the remainder comprised a variety of religious minorities, including Sikhs, Christians, Buddhists, Jains and Parsis. Hundreds of different languages and dialects are spoken in India, a country of numerous ethnic groups, cultural traditions, tribes, sects and castes. In addition, India faced the challenge of incorporating into the newly established polity 562 princely states, which were not part of British India. By contrast, Israel had a population of only 600,000 Jews at independence in 1948. Despite the presence of a sizable Palestinian minority numbering around 150,000, and composed mainly of Muslims with smaller communities of Christians, Druze and Bedouins, as far as the constitutional debate was concerned, the main divide was between the religious-Orthodox and the secular Jewish populations. Finally, the Irish Free State was established in 1922 in the twenty-six counties of Ireland and had a population of two million, 95 percent of which was Catholic, with a small Protestant minority. While Israel and India deliberated their constitutions as sovereign states, in Ireland, the question of the degree of independence of the Free State from British rule was one of the central questions debated during the constitution-writing process.

Despite these considerable differences, the three cases share several important common features. First, all three countries were, in S. N. Eisenstadt's terms, new democracies in ancient civilizations.[1] These

---

[1] S. N. Eisenstadt, *Paradoxes of Democracy: Fragility, Continuity, and Change* (Washington, DC and Baltimore: Woodrow Wilson Center Press and The Johns Hopkins University Press, 1999), 51.

countries were not artificially created by colonial border-sketching, as was the case in many states in Africa, Latin America and Eastern Europe. Their societies emerged from cultural traditions that were hundreds, if not thousands, of years old. In addition, since all three countries underwent a period of British rule, all three emerging political systems were based to a varying degree on the Westminster parliamentary tradition. Furthermore, all three countries experienced territorial partition at the time of independence.[2]

Most importantly for present purposes, in all three societies independence brought to the fore significant internal tensions. In all three cases, the success of the national struggle for political self-determination revealed the polarization between rival visions of the independent state. In Israel, the dispute between the religious and secular definitions of Jewish identity was the chief factor that prevented the adoption of a constitution. In India, the clash between two paradigms of nationalism – an exclusivist view of national identity in monolithic terms (either Hindu or Muslim) and an inclusivist view which accepted India's plurality – led to the partition of the country in the first phase of constitution-making. After the creation of Pakistan, the disagreement over the national and religious identity of India continued to stir the Constituent Assembly. Two particular areas of dispute were the question of unification of family law of the different religious communities and the status of Hindi as a national language. In Ireland, the constitution-drafting process was part of the struggle for independence from Britain, and revealed a deep division within the Irish Catholic society, between culturalist-moralist and political-pragmatic perceptions of Irish nationalism. In other words, in all three cases, the foundational aspect of the constitution was the center around which the constitutional debates revolved. What "we the people" meant was thus the primary question that the drafters in all three countries needed to address.

Despite the intensity of these internal struggles, which in two cases led to the outbreak of violence – partition in India and civil war in Ireland – and in the case of Israel threatened the stability of the newly independent state, all three countries managed to establish a solid democratic polity which has withstood the test of time. This was partly achieved by

---

[2] See, for example, T. G. Fraser, *Partition in Ireland, India and Palestine: Theory and Practice* (London: Macmillan, 1984); Nicholas Mansergh, "The Prelude to Partition: Concepts and Aims in Ireland and India," in Diana Mansergh, ed., *Nationalism and Independence: Selected Irish Papers* (Cork University Press, 1997).

the adoption of incrementalist constitutional strategies that enabled the deferral of controversial choices regarding foundational issues to the future.

Finally, it is interesting to note that not only were political leaders in the three countries aware that they had in common their struggle against British rule,[3] but also that they were influenced by each other in their approach to constitution-writing. This is most evident in the way the Indian framers used the Irish constitution as one of their central sources of inspiration for their own drafting. Ireland was one of three countries to which B. N. Rau, the constitutional advisor of the Indian Constituent Assembly, traveled to research possible constitutional arrangements in preparation for the drafting of the Indian constitution. In addition, key decisions of the Indian Constituent Assembly regarding various symbolic and foundational issues, such as national language and the unification of personal law, were influenced by the Irish constitutional experience. Thus, for example, during the debates over national language, Nehru cited Irish Prime Minister Eamon de Valera's advice in order to persuade the Constituent Assembly to write the Indian constitution in English rather than in Hindu. According to Nehru, de Valera regretted drafting the 1937 constitution in Gaelic and admitted to him that the Irish had found Gaelic "hard going" and were reverting more and more to English.[4] More

[3] For example, Eamon de Valera, the president of the Irish Dáil Éireann (Irish Parliament), celebrated the Indian–Irish brotherhood during a speech delivered on February 28, 1920 at the India Freedom Dinner of the Friends of Freedom for India in New York: "we in Ireland and you of India must each of us endeavor, both as separate peoples and in combination, to rid ourselves of the vampire that is fattening on our blood ... Our cause is a common cause. We swear friendship tonight." Eamon de Valera, *India and Ireland* (New York: Friends of Freedom for India, 1920). For more on the relations between Indian and Irish leaders, see Sarmila Bose and Eilis Ward, "'India's Cause Is Ireland's Cause': Elite Links and Nationalist Politics," in Michael Holmes and Denis Holmes, eds., *Ireland and India: Connections, Comparisons, Contrasts* (The Irish-Indian Business and Economic Association, and the Department of Government and Society, University of Limerick, 1997). By contrast, the relationship between Indian and Irish leaders and the Israeli ones may not have been as warm; nevertheless, the Jewish population in Palestine followed the Indian, as well as the Irish, struggle for independence with great admiration. Thus, for example, Nehru's autobiography was was translated to Hebrew and published in Israel in 1942. Jawaharlal Nehru, *An Autobiography*, trans. H. Glikshtein (Merchavia, Palestine: Hakibutz Haartzi, Hashomer Hatzair, 1942). Further, the Jewish militaristic undergrounds of the Irgun and Lechi tried to imitate the Irish urban guerilla methods, developed by Michael Collins, against the British. Joseph Heller, *The Stern Gang: Ideology, Politics, and Terror, 1940–1949* (London and Portland: Frank Cass, 1995).

[4] Granville Austin, *The Indian Constitution: Cornerstone of a Nation* (Oxford and New York: Oxford University Press, 1999), 286.

importantly, the Indian Constituent Assembly imported from Ireland one of the incrementalist tools it used in order to defer decisions regarding the uniform civil code: the idea of non-justiciable constitutional provisions (that is, provisions that cannot be enforced by court) first appear in the 1937 Irish constitution.[5]

[5] For more details on this see Chapter 4.

3

Informal consociationalism in Israel

> We are an ancient people, who have lived thousands of years with no
> constitution – can we not continue to live without a constitution? ... The
> debate over the fundamental constitution will last many years, and will
> involve the entire state of Israel and the Diaspora ... Rather than concern-
> ing themselves with what needs to be done, Jews around the world dispute
> the constitution.
>
> David Ben-Gurion, 1949[6]

The State of Israel was established in 1948 as a democratic state for the
Jewish people. Although in the pre-state period the leaders of the Yishuv
(the Jewish community in Mandatory Palestine[7]) had begun discussions
about the formation of a constitution, Israel has never adopted a formal
constitution. From the beginning, the debate over the constitution concerned not only the content of the constitution but also the appropriate
method of adopting it. The debate reflected the profound ideational divide over foundational issues, particularly the deep disagreement between
a religious and a secular vision of Israel as a Jewish state.

The inability of the framers of the constitution to reach a consensus
regarding the appropriate relationship between Jewish religious law and
the institutions of the modern state led them to deploy a strategy of avoidance and to postpone the drafting of a written constitution. Despite an
overwhelming secular majority in the first Knesset (Israel's parliament),
the political leadership of the country preferred not to make controversial
decisions regarding the foundational aspects of the constitution, adopting

---

[6] David Ben-Gurion, during discussions on the Israeli constitution in Mapai (the Israel
Labor Party), 1949, cited in Giora Goldberg, "'When Trees Are Planted There Is No Need
for Constitution': On State Building and Constitution Making," *State, Government and
International Relations* 38 (1993): 37 (Hebrew).
[7] For an excellent study of the Israeli Yishuv see: Dan Horowitz and Moshe Lissak, *Origins
of the Israeli Polity: Palestine under the Mandate* (Chicago and London: University of
Chicago Press, 1978).

51

an incrementalist approach instead. This approach is still embraced by Israeli political leaders today. As the religious-secular conflict remains unresolved, the Knesset continues to avoid drafting a formal constitution.

This chapter focuses on two critical moments in the constitutional development of Israel, the analysis of which will help explain the significance of the fact that Israel has no written constitution. The first is the 1950 decision of the first Knesset not to draft a comprehensive constitution. By adopting instead an incrementalist approach, this decision enabled the emergence of informal consociational arrangements in the religious sphere. The second critical moment is the 1992 enactment of two Basic Laws on human rights and their interpretation by the Supreme Court as a "constitutional revolution." The revolutionary rhetoric of the Court was perceived as an attempt to break away from the informal, consociational arrangements in religious affairs that had emerged over the years.

A careful study of these two developments reveals that the dispute over the role of the constitution is echoed in contemporary debates over the future of Israel's constitution. As in 1950, the Israeli Knesset is still divided today over the most fundamental norms and shared values that should serve as the foundations of the state. As in 1950, the Knesset's 2006 debate on the future of Israel's constitution ended with the adoption of the same incrementalist approach to constitution-making.

This chapter will mainly focus on the constitutional debates that took place within the Jewish majority. Although the non-Jewish population of Israel has consistently stood at approximately 20 percent,[8] deliberations over the constitution have remained exclusively internal to the Jewish population. The non-Jewish citizenry enjoys formal equal rights yet is consistently excluded from Israeli nationhood, which is understood in terms of its Jewish identity. This exclusion is reflected in legislation and in national emblems and state ceremonies.[9] Thus, during the formative years of the state, the non-Jewish population was by and large excluded from the discussions over the constitution. In addition, some cite the wish to

---

[8] According to the 2005 Report of Israel's Central Bureau of Statistics, in 2004 76.4 percent of the population was Jewish, 16 percent Muslim, 2.1 percent Christian, 1.6 percent Druze and 3.85 percent unclassified religiously (these are mostly immigrants from the former Soviet bloc, who are not recognized as Jews by the rabbinical institutions).

[9] David Kretzmer, *The Legal Status of the Arabs in Israel* (Boulder: Westview, 1990); Baruch Kimerling, "Religion, Nationality and Democracy in Israel," *Zemanim* 50 (1994) (Hebrew); Sammy Smooha, "Minority Status in an Ethnic Democracy: The Status of the Arab Minority in Israel," *Ethnic and Racial Studies* 13 (1990); Yoav Peled, "Ethnic Democracy and the Legal Construction of Citizenship: Arab Citizens of the Jewish State," *American Political Science Review* 86, no. 2 (1992): 434–5.

limit the civic rights of the Palestinian minority in Israel as one of the reasons the Knesset avoided enacting in 1950 a constitution that contained a comprehensive bill of rights.[10]

In recent years, the Israeli Palestinian minority has increasingly demanded a voice in the redefinition of the identity of the State of Israel, calling for the transformation of the state from its definition as "Jewish and democratic" to a liberal-democratic state in which the Palestinians would be recognized as a national minority.[11] This position was advocated in a series of constitutional proposals, published during 2005 by leading Arab Israeli intellectuals and NGOs.[12] The role played by Israeli Arabs in the constitutional debate in Israel and the question of what the effect of the incrementalist constitutional approach was on minority rights in Israel will also be addressed in this chapter.

Refraining from drafting a constitution in the formative stage

On November 29, 1947, the United Nations General Assembly passed a resolution calling for the termination of the British Mandate over Palestine and its partition into a Jewish state, an Arab state and an international government over the city of Jerusalem. Under the UN decision, two months after the departure of the British forces from the country (planned for October 1, 1948) the independent states were to elect constituent assemblies which would draft democratic constitutions. The British government, in reaction, decided to withdraw from Palestine earlier than planned, and announced that it would terminate the Mandate on May 15, 1948. In order to avoid a political and legal vacuum, the leadership of the Yishuv (the Jewish community in Palestine) decided to establish a Provisional Council and to declare the establishment of the State of Israel in accordance with the UN's partition plan. The following day,

---

[10] Yonathan Shapira, *Politicians as a Hegemonic Class: The Case of Israel* (Tel Aviv: Sifriat Poalim, 1996), 33 (Hebrew).

[11] Amal Jamal, "Strategies of Minority Struggle for Equality in Ethnic States: Arab Politics in Israel," *Citizenship Studies* 11, no. 3 (July 2007): 263–82; Gershon Shafir and Yoav Peled, *Being Israeli: The Dynamics of Multiple Citizenship* (Cambridge University Press, 2002).

[12] The three documents include: the "Future Vision" of the National Committee for the Heads of Arab Local Authorities in Israel; the "Haifa Document," published in the framework of Mada Al-Carmel, The Arab Center for Applied Social Research; and the "Democratic Constitution" published by Adalah, The Legal Center for Arab Minority Rights in Israel.

its territory was attacked by the military forces of Egypt, Jordan, Syria, Lebanon and Iraq. The war lasted for over eighteen months.

The Declaration of the Establishment of the State of Israel (henceforth the Declaration of Independence) presented the legal, historical, moral and ideological grounds for the establishment of the new state (Paragraphs 1–11), and defined its essential characteristics and central institutions (Paragraphs 13–19). The document was signed by representatives of all the major parties and communities in the Yishuv, from the Orthodox Agudat Israel to the Israeli Communist Party. The wording of the Declaration represented a compromise between religious and secular worldviews regarding the character of the Jewish state. The compromise was facilitated by the use of ambiguous terminology that could be interpreted in a variety of ways. For example, one of the controversies among the drafters of the document concerned the question of whether it should mention the "God of Israel." While the religious representatives demanded to thank the Holy One for the renewal of Jewish sovereignty in the Land of Israel after two millennia of exile, for the secular founders, many of whom were socialists and atheists, any mention of God was considered an affront to their most cherished beliefs.[13] The vague formulation that was agreed upon eventually stated that Israel's independence was born from "trust in the Rock of Israel." The word "trust" ("bitachon") could be understood to mean either "security" or "faith." Similarly, "Rock of Israel" could be taken as a reference to God or as a secular, somewhat poetic phrase connoting Jewish resolve and survival.[14]

The legal status of the Declaration of Independence is debatable. Like all declarations of independence, it is essentially a celebratory and hortatory statement without legal effect, made by individuals who had as yet no formal legal standing in the new legal entity that was the State of Israel. Over the years, however, the Supreme Court has used the Declaration of Independence on numerous occasions as the interpretive basis for substantive rulings. Among them, for example, are those concerning administrative detentions, freedom of speech, freedom of religion and the definition of "who is a Jew?". It was only with the enactment in 1992 of Basic Law: Freedom of Occupation that Israeli law first gave legal effect to the Declaration.[15]

---

[13] Asher Cohen and Bernard Susser, *Israel and the Politics of Jewish Identity: The Secular-Religious Impasse* (Baltimore: The Johns Hopkins University Press, 2000), xi.

[14] *Ibid.*

[15] This was the first time that the term "Declaration of the Establishment of the State of Israel" appeared in Knesset legislation.

In line with the UN resolution, the operative section of the Declaration of Independence (Paragraph 12) states that the constitution of the State of Israel would be adopted by an elected Constituent Assembly. The elections for the Assembly were planned for October 1, 1948, but were later postponed by three months, because of the outbreak of the War of Independence. In the meantime, the Provisional Council continued to function, and in July 1948 it appointed a Constitutional Committee, chaired by Zerach Vahrhaftig of the Religious Zionist Party.[16] Until the February 1949 elections for the Constituent Assembly, the committee held twenty meetings. It was during these deliberations that the question of the content of the constitution was replaced by the question of the very need for a written constitution in the first place.

A constitutional proposal, drafted by Dr. Leo Kohn, an advisor to the Ministry of Foreign Affairs in the Jewish Agency, served as the basis for the Committee's discussions.[17] In addition, various individuals, groups and representatives of local government submitted to the Committee several constitutional drafts, documents and suggestions. The drafts varied in their prescriptions for the appropriate relations between religion and state, from a completely secular and liberal constitution (Dr. Werner Frauschteter's proposal) to a theocratic formulation which suggested democratic representation based on separate electorates for men and women (Dr. Zeev Falk's draft).[18] Vahrhaftig, the chair of the Committee, described in his report the broad agreement among Committee members with regard to institutional and governmental issues. By contrast, the Committee was bitterly divided over the question of state–religion relations. The tensions around this issue led Vahrhaftig to the conclusion that the differences of views on this subject were impossible to bridge,

---

[16] The Constitutional Committee comprised two members of Mapai, and one representative of each of Agudat Israel, Mapam (United Workers' Party), the Israeli Communist Party, the General Zionists and the Progressive Party (Liberals).

[17] Amihai Radzyner, "A Constitution for Israel: The Design of the Leo Kohn Proposal, 1948," *Israeli Studies* 54, no. 1 (2010): 1–24.

[18] Dr. Werner Frauschteter's draft was in Hebrew and was seventy-nine articles long; a proposal by Zeev Flack comprised thirty-six articles. An additional two drafts were those of Dr. Itamar Freund, which were written in German and consisted of 195 articles; and the proposal of Dr. Shmuel Rolvent, which was written in English, comprised 145 articles, and came with a warm letter from Laski, his teacher at London School of Economics. For details on these as well as on several additional documents and constitutional proposals which were submitted to the Committee, see: Zerach Vahrhaftig, *A Constitution for Israel: Religion and State* (Jerusalem: Mesilot, 1988), ch. 3 (Hebrew).

and that consequently the drafting of the entire constitution should be postponed.[19]

Despite the provisions of the Declaration of Independence and the terms under which the Constituent Assembly was elected, two days after its first session, it enacted a Transition Law, and transformed itself into the first Knesset (parliament). The first elected legislature now combined the authority of the Constituent Assembly with the powers of the Provisional Council.[20]

The Transition Law led to uncertainty with respect to the constitution. The law did not explicitly acknowledge the first Knesset's duty to enact a constitution, nor did it limit the time period for its drafting. In fact, the question of the constituent authority of the Knesset was still being debated half a century after Israel's establishment. The approach formalized in a Supreme Court ruling in 1995 (*United Mizrahi Bank* v. *Migdal*) was that both constituent powers and ordinary legislative powers are vested in the Knesset, and consequently, the Basic Laws are superior to ordinary legislation.[21] The Knesset, according to this doctrine, has a double role, similar to other legislatures in the world (such as Germany, Austria, India) that engage in constitutional amendment.[22] Nevertheless, there are two important differences that distinguish Israel from other countries with dual legislative authority. First, in all other cases the legislature was established under the constitution which granted it, among other powers, the power to amend the constitution. Second, Israeli constitutional law does not provide the procedures by which constitutional legislation is to be passed.[23]

---

[19]   *Ibid.*, chs. 3–6.

[20]   For the text of the Transition Law see *Knesset Record* 1 (1949): 52.

[21]   CA 6821/93, *United Mizrahi Bank Ltd.* v. *Migdal Cooperative Village*, PD 49(4) 221. In a minority opinion, Justice Michael Cheshin argued that the Transition Law altered the authority of the Constituent Assembly and changed it to a regular legislator. According to Cheshin, the instruction to adopt a constitution was irrevocable, directed only to the Constituent Assembly, which had no authority to pass it to any other bodies, namely to the following Knesset.

[22]   Former Chief Justice Aharon Barak described the Knesset as wearing "two hats ... first, a hat of constituent authority, and second, a hat of legislative authority". Aharon Barak, "The Constitutional Revolution: Protected Human Rights," *Mishpat Umimshal: Law and Government in Israel* 1, no. 1 (1992): 16 (Hebrew).

[23]   Amnon Rubinstein and Barak Medina, *Constitutional Law of the State of Israel*, 5th edn. (Tel Aviv: Schocken, 1997), vol. I, 368 (Hebrew). Rubinstein, who authored the most comprehensive study of Israeli constitutional law, claims that the deviation of the elected Constituent Assembly from the explicit instructions of the Declaration of Independence is the source of all the complicated developments that led eventually to the absence of a constitution in the ensuing years (p. 5).

Table 3.1 *Party Composition of the Constitution Assembly/First Knesset*

Name of Party	Number of MKs	Included in the coalition/opposition
MAPAI (Eretz Israel workers' party)	46	Coalition
Mapam (united workers party)	19	Opposition
United Religious Front*	16	Coalition
Herut	14	Opposition
General Zionists (Liberal Party)	7	Opposition
Progressive Party (independent liberals)	5	Coalition
Sephardim and Oriental Communities	4	Coalition
Maki (Israeli Communist Party)	4	Opposition
Democratic List of Nazareth	2	Coalition
WIZO	1	Opposition
Fighters List	1	Opposition
Yemenite Association	1	Opposition
TOTAL	120	

Source: www.knesset.gov.il/history/eng/eng_hist1_s.htm
* Includes four parties: Mizrahi, Hapoel HaMizrahi, Agudat Yisrael and Poalei Agudat Yisrael.

One of the leading supporters of the Transition Law, and one of the fiercest opponents of the project of drafting a constitution, was David Ben-Gurion, Israel's first prime minister.[24] He began to express public opposition to the enactment of a formal constitution in February 1949, although some argue that his stance was apparent even before independence.[25] Already in 1930 Ben-Gurion wrote that "if a sovereign Jewish state would be established, it would draft its constitution independently" yet he added that this constitution would be enacted "only after peace and public security would be obtained."[26]

Despite the large majority of the secular camp in the Knesset (only sixteen members, out of 120 Knesset members, represented the religious parties – see Table 3.1), in June 1950, eighteen months after it was elected as a Constituent Assembly, the Knesset decided not to draft a constitution in a single document. Following a heated debate, a compromise resolution

---

[24] On Ben-Gurion's view see more below.
[25] Neri Horowitz, "The Haredim (Ultra-Orthodox) and the Supreme Court: Breaking the Tools in Historical Perspective," *Kivunim Hadashim* 5 (2001): 38 (Hebrew).
[26] Goldberg, "When Trees Are Planted There Is No Need for Constitution," 29, 35.

was passed, named after its sponsor, Haim Harari, the chair of the Knesset Committee.[27] The resolution stated as follows:

> The first Knesset charges the Constitutional, Law and Justice Committee with preparing a proposed constitution for the state. The constitution will be composed of individual chapters, in such a manner that each of them shall constitute a Basic Law in itself. The individual chapters shall be brought before the Knesset as the Committee completes them, and all the chapters together will form the state constitution.[28]

Numerous arguments were raised during the Knesset debate for and against the drafting of a constitution. The reasoning has been the subject of considerable scholarly debate.[29] What is clear is that underlying this debate over the future of the constitution was the recognition, shared by the representatives of all political parties, of the profound ideological rift in Israeli society between the secular and the religious visions of the state.[30]

"What is the State of Israel?"

The secular–religious conflict in Israel differs in its intensity from religious conflicts in other Western democracies. Rather than focusing on issues of allocation of power and resources among various groups – Christian

---

[27] Of 119 Knesset members (one had passed away), fifty voted in favor, thirty-eight against, three were absent from the vote and sixteen abstained, *Knesset Record* 5 (1950): 1722. An opposition bill, supported by the right-wing Herut Party led by Menachem Begin, the socialist United Workers Party and the Communists, demanding that the Constitutional Committee present a draft constitution to the Knesset was rejected.

[28] *Knesset Record* 5 (1950): 1743.

[29] See for example: Shapira, *Politicians as a Hegemonic Class*; Philippa Strum, "The Road Not Taken: Constitutional Non-Decision Making in 1948–1950 and Its Impact on Civil Liberties in the Israeli Political Culture," in S. Ilan Troen and Noah Lucas, eds., *Israel: The First Decade of Independence* (Albany: State University of New York Press, 1995), 83–104; Goldberg, "When Trees Are Planted There Is No Need for Constitution."

[30] As Gary Jacobsohn compellingly observed, the need to reconcile between competing visions of the state was not only the major challenge which explains the avoidance of the Israeli founders from drafting a constitution, but also provides the core explanation for the difference between the American and the Israeli experience of constitution-drafting. For the American founders, he argued, a written constitution was needed to affirm their existence as a nation: "Where the definition of nationhood is straightforwardly understood in terms of a set of political ideals, binding the future through constitutional mandate becomes an intrinsic part of the self-understanding of the policy." By contrast, Israeli founders were still struggling over the very definition of their nationhood. Jacobsohn, *Apple of Gold: Constitutionalism in Israel and the United States* (Princeton University Press, 1993) 105.

Democratic parties in Europe, for example, are concerned primarily with preserving the interests of their religious institutions and education systems[31] – the religious parties in Israel are also interested in leaving the imprint of religious Judaism on the state's institutions, legislature and judicial system. What is at stake is "a struggle over the ultimate values rather than distributive justice, over the whole rather than the parts."[32]

The internal debate over Jewish identity in the modern world dates back to late eighteenth-century Europe. Religious Orthodoxy and the Zionist national movement represented opposite reactions to modernism. The emergence of Jewish nationalism in the form of the Zionist movement posed new and powerful challenges to Orthodox Jews by providing a secular, modern and nationalist alternative to traditional Judaism. The return to Zion was intended to create a new Jewish identity defined in political-territorial rather than in religious-communal terms.[33] Most ultra-Orthodox Jews rejected Zionism for its atheist approach generally, and also because the Zionist principle of self-emancipation violated religious doctrine, according to which only God could redeem the Jewish people and return them to the land of Israel. Between the secular Zionists and the ultra-Orthodox stood the religious Zionists, who viewed the foundation of the state as the beginning of redemption. For them, the political-territorial aspect of Jewish identity was a supplemental component to the traditional national-religious definition of Jewish identity.[34]

After World War II, as the possibility of an independent Jewish state became increasingly more real, the religious–secular struggle over the prospective legal system of the new state intensified. The leaders of the Orthodox Agudat Israel Party demanded that the legal system be based on the Halacha (Jewish religious law). As Y. M. Levin, leader of Agudat Israel, stated in a meeting with the heads of the Jewish Agency, the de facto pre-state government: "A Jewish state that is not governed by the Halacha after two thousand years of Exile is a desecration of God, [it is] the shunting aside of the Torah, a rebellion against the Kingdom of God in its very land itself, and is untenable."[35]

---

[31] Stathis N. Kalyvas, *The Rise of Christian Democracy in Europe* (Ithaca, NY: Cornell University Press, 1996).

[32] Cohen and Susser, *Israel and the Politics of Jewish Identity*, 20–21.

[33] Dan Horowitz and Moshe Lissak, *Trouble in Utopia: The Overburdened Polity of Israel* (Albany: State University of New York Press, 1989), 139.

[34] *Ibid.*

[35] Cited in Menachem Friedman, "These are the Chronicles of the Status-Quo: Religion and State in Israel," in Uri Dromi, ed., *Brethren Dwelling Together. Orthodoxy and*

The Halacha is a comprehensive, self-contained legal system. As such, it could theoretically have been an alternative to the civil legal system of the state. From the perspective of an Orthodox Jew, Halachic law takes precedence over the law of the state.[36] Consequently, the fundamental issue in terms of the relationship between religion and state was not simply whether to grant the Jewish religion and its institutions official recognition and legal status (as is often the issue in other countries where church–state questions are debated), but the thornier issue of legal precedence between the laws of the state and Halachic law. This problem was clearly expressed during the Knesset deliberations over the constitution, by MK Meir Levonstein of Agudat Israel who declared: "There is no place in Israel for any constitution created by men. If it contradicts the Torah – it is inadmissible, and if it is concurrent with the Torah – it is redundant."[37]

It was thus not only a question of symbolism or of granting cultural and educational autonomy to particular communities, but also, in the most fundamental way, a debate over the norms and values of the state. And in 1949, when the issue of the constitution first appeared on the agenda of the Knesset, it was clear to all that the central problem which divided them with regard to the content of the future constitution was, in the words of one MK, "one cardinal question: what is the State of Israel?"[38]

The Knesset debates: February–June 1950

The first Knesset decided not to appoint a separate constitutional committee, but to grant the Committee of Law and Justice the authority to present a draft constitution. Nachum Nir, a Member of Knesset from Mapam (United Workers' Party) and a fervent supporter of a written constitution, was elected as the first chair of the Committee, which since that time has been called the Constitution, Law and Justice Committee. From the beginning, the discussions of the committee did not focus on the content of the future constitution, but rather on the question of whether a written constitution should be adopted at all.[39]

Non-Orthodoxy in Israel: Positions, Propositions and Accords (Jerusalem: Israel Democracy Institute, 2005), 72 (Hebrew).

[36] Horowitz and Lissak, *Trouble in Utopia*, 59–60, 138.

[37] *Knesset Record* 4 (1950): 744.

[38] Avraham Goldrat, United Religious Front, *Knesset Record* 5 (1950): 1315.

[39] As reported by Nir to the Knesset in its first debate on the constitution. *Knesset Record* 4 (1950): 714.

Two important decisions regarding the future constitution were made by the leadership of the Mapai party and by the first government in parallel with the work of the Constitution, Law and Justice Committee, and before the Knesset began official discussion of the issue. The Mapai leadership debated, intensely, the question of what should be the party's official position in the Constitutional Committee discussion. In the end, the party leadership decided, by marginal majority, to instruct their representatives on the Committee to announce that "time has not come yet to start drafting a constitution and that the Committee should discuss the Basic Laws to be proposed by the government."[40] The government discussed the constitution question six months later and, despite the objection of the Minister of Justice, Pinchas Rosen, decided that "the government does not see the need at this time to enact a constitution, but rather basic laws which are required for their own purpose."[41]

On February 1950, one year after its establishment, the Knesset finally began its formal deliberations on the constitution. Although only nine sessions were devoted to the issue, these debates revealed the core arguments on either side. The polarization between the secular and the religious camps was evident to everyone. The position of the religious representatives, who claimed that they represented "loyal Judaism," was that a Jewish state should have Jewish laws. In the words of Minister of Welfare Yitzhak Meir Levin: "the goal of religious Jewry is that only the law of the Torah will be established in all areas of life in the state."[42] The secular parties, led by Prime Minister Ben-Gurion, vehemently objected to the religious representatives' aspiration to establish "a theocratic state."[43] Many of them shared the position of Mapai member Efraim Tavori, who declared: "As a socialist and as an atheist I am unable under any circumstances to sign on to a program which contains a religious formulation."[44]

---

[40] *Meeting of Mapai Party in the Knesset and Party Secretariat*, 14 June 1949, Tel Aviv (Protocol at The Moshe Sharett Israel Labor Party Archives, Beit Berl). Twelve members supported this decision, while ten members supported a competing proposal to instruct the constitutional committee to begin drafting a formal constitution. Almost a year later, only eight Mapai Knesset members still expressed their support in an immediate constitution-drafting. Among them was Moshe Sharet, who later became Israel's second Prime Minister. *Meeting of Mapai Party in the Knesset and Party Secretariat*, 14 May 1950.

[41] *Government Meeting Minutes*, 13 December 1949 (Israel State Archives, Jerusalem). The decision was supported by vote of six for and two against, with one abstain and three government members absent.

[42] *Knesset Record* 4 (1950): 811.   [43] *Knesset Record* 4 (1950): 814.

[44] *Knesset Record* 4 (1950): 774.

Nevertheless, the Knesset debates did not focus on substantive issues but rather on the role a constitution plays under conditions of intense disagreement on the character of the state. Three principal questions were at the center of the debate. The first was whether a constitution could be an efficient instrument for conflict resolution. The second concerned the most appropriate method (essentially, either majoritarian or consensual) of reaching a decision given the profound ideological disagreements. The third was the issue of timing and pace at which the constitution should be drafted.

Constitution-making as resolving or exacerbating conflicts

Those who supported the immediate enactment of a formal constitution, among them the secular opposition parties on both the left (Mapam and the Israeli Communist Party) and right (particularly Herut), argued that a written constitution, including a bill of rights, was needed precisely because of the deep ideological divide. They believed that a formal constitution could serve as a vehicle for conciliation, helping to bridge the two sides. For them, a shared constitution would have symbolic uniting qualities, which could "bring together and unify the various world views and diverse traditions" that existed within Israeli society.[45] The constitution, it was argued, was needed for educational purposes, as a common ethical guide for the culturally diverse immigrant newcomers.

> We live in the Land of Israel under unique circumstances of ingathering of exiles, of different ethnicities, emigrants from around the globe, with different customs, and also … different – and at times, clashing and contradictory – constitutions. And from this vast diversity, we strive to create one nation. To that end we must act in every direction: the direction of education, the direction of organization, throughout all the cells of our lives, in order that we may live cooperatively and not as we live currently: separately. And this goal must find an expression also in the law, through education for one law for all.[46]

According to this position, the transformation of the multitude of immigrants into a united collective of active and contributing citizens is the true nature of Israel's national mission, and a formal constitution could contribute to this goal.

By contrast, the opponents of immediate constitution-making (which included the religious representatives as well as most of the secular Mapai

---

[45] Yaakov Gil, (General Zionists) in: *Knesset Record* 4 (1950): 745.
[46] Israel Bar-Yehuda (Mapam, United Workers Party) in: *Knesset Record* 4 (1950): 734.

Party) contended that given the extreme polarization, the process of constitution-drafting would, at best, have no positive impact on the ideological and political tensions, or, at worst, exacerbate them.

Several Mapai members stated their view that abstract constitutional declarations would have negligible impact on controversies over form of life issues, and therefore religious–secular disagreements should be resolved at the level of ordinary law, which could address particular problems more concretely:

> The constitution contains only abstract principles. A detailed system of laws is required to implement these principles in everyday life, and this is the great challenge that the Knesset needs to meet. It is not enough to proclaim independence. We need a system of laws that will translate abstract principles into practice.[47]

Other opponents claimed that drafting a constitution under existing conditions was not only unnecessary, but also against the real interests of the state. They argued that the drawn-out philosophical deliberations which would be necessary for the drafting of the constitution would divert national attention from the country's truly urgent needs.

> We fear … that the philosophical and metaphysical part of the constitution does not facilitate the building of the state, the absorption of immigrants, and does not serve the needs of our time.[48]

The most fervent warnings against the potential polarizing effects of constitution-drafting came from the Orthodox representatives, who feared that a constitution would entrench secular principles. This, they felt, could lead to a dangerous *Kulturkampf*:

> And when Mr. Nir stated cynically: "We will establish a constitution and there will be an uproar once and not every Monday and Thursday," I want to emphasize here: You are still unfamiliar with the nature of the Jewish people! The Jewish people are willing to resign themselves to many things, but the moment the issue touches upon the foundations of their faith, they are unable to compromise. If you wish to foist upon us this type of life or a constitution that will be contrary to the laws of the Torah, we will not accept it! We endured all the stages of suffering in the path of our exile and all the forces of the inquisition were no match for us! Do you think that what our haters were unable to accomplish, what blood and fire were unable to accomplish, you will be able to accomplish through the power of the state? No and no! You have yet to delve into the depth of the

---

[47] David Bar-Rav-Hai (Mapai), *Knesset Record* 4 (1950), 726.
[48] Efraim Tavori, (Mapai), in: *Knesset Record* 4 (1950): 774.

Jewish soul. It will awaken, and ignite a very large bonfire if, of all places, here in the Holy Land we strive to turn the bowl upside down, and make the lives of religious Jews unbearable.[49]

I would like to warn: the experience of drafting a constitution would necessarily entail a severe, vigorous uncompromising war of opinions. A war of spirit, which is defined by the gruesome concept of *Kulturkampf* ... Is this a convenient time for a thorough and penetrating examination of our essence and purpose? It is clear that there is no room for any compromises, any concessions or mutual agreements, since no man can compromise and concede on issues upon which his belief and soul depend.[50]

In the early years of the state, the threat of destabilization was not taken lightly by the Israeli leadership, given the fragility of the new political order. During its first years, the government faced serious challenges to its authority, which had its roots in the pre-state social and ideological fragmentation both within the Zionist movement and outside of it. The most notable example of an attempt to contest the state's governmental institutions, and particularly the state's monopoly over the use of arms, was the *Altalena* affair. The *Altalena* was an IZL ship that brought arms and soldiers to Israel in June 1948, as part of IZL's attempt to maintain its autonomy as a right-wing nationalist paramilitary organization. When the ship reached the shores of Israel, it was fired upon and sunk by the Israeli Defense Forces. A number of members of the IZL on board were killed.[51] Two additional underground groups of young ultra-Orthodox Jews condemned the state's desecration of religion. The first, Brit HaKana'im (Alliance of the Zealots) was founded in 1949 by yeshiva students who were convinced that the socialist government of Israel was determined to destroy Israel's Orthodox Judaism. Their fear was reinforced by government support for compulsive enrollment of children in secular schools for hundreds of thousands of new immigrants in the 1950s, many of whom were religious.[52] These young zealots acted against what they considered

---

[49] Minister of Welfare, Rabi Yitzhak Meir Levi in: *Knesset Record* 4 (1950): 812.

[50] Meir David Levonstein (Agudat Israel) in: *Knesset Record* 4 (1950): 744.

[51] Some view the incident as a preliminary skirmish in what could easily have become a civil war. The complete deterioration into a civil war was prevented by the decision taken by Menachem Begin, the leader of the IZL, to accept the authority of the government. For its part, the government was willing to content itself with this limited operation and did not pursue the exclusion of the IZL from political participation. Begin was elected as MK and in 1977 became a Prime Minister. Ehud Sprinzak, "Brother against Brother: Violence and Extremism in Israeli Politics from Altalena to the Rabin Assassination," *Israel Studies* 4, no. 2 (1999). Horowitz and Lissak, *Origins of the Israeli Polity*, 189.

[52] Ehud Sprinzak, *Brother to Brother: Violence and Extremism in Israeli Politics from Altalena to the Rabin Assassination* (New York: The Free Press, 1999) 62. See also

to be a violation of Shabbat observance and set on fire coffee shops, restaurants, and movie theaters that operated on Saturday in Tel Aviv, as well as, public buses that traveled on Saturday in Jerusalem.[53] The second underground group, "Hamachane" (The Camp), was formed in Jerusalem and was involved in advancing a future Orthodox revolution. They set fire to taxis, trucks and non-kosher butcher shops. They were arrested after preparing to explode a scare bomb in the Knesset to protest the drafting of women into the military. The leaders of the group were sentenced to three to twelve months in prison.[54] These two groups were not marginal in the religious camp as, later, some members became key leaders in the Orthodox political movement.[55]

The danger of direct clash over the enactment of a secular constitution was not taken lightly, even by Knesset members who supported immediate constitution-drafting. Pinchas Rosen, the Minister of Justice, for example, one of the fiercest advocates of a written constitution, admitted that "there is only one serious justification for the rejection of constitution writing now, which I don't ignore, and that is the danger of division."[56] And Yizhak Ben-Zvi from Mapai (who later became the second president of Israel, between 1952–1963) claimed that "we must remember that [the constitution] cannot only be a point of unity but also a point of division. There is more reason to assume that now, where we wish to achieve the highest point of unity among million Jews in the land of Israel and around us, million Jews in the world, we will lead, due to carelessness and indiscretion, to great schism… [the enactment] of a constitution can bring total separation."[57]

Menachem Friedman, *The Haredi (Ultra-Orthodox) Society: Sources, Trends and Processes* (Jerusalem: The Jerusalem Institute for Israel Studies, 1991) 60-66 (Hebrew).

[53] Sprinzak, *Brother to Brother* 62–64.

[54] *Ibid* 64–65. Following massive arrests of underground activists, the government ordered formation of a state investigation committee to inquire into police brutality and excessive use of force in these arrests.

[55] For example, Mordechai Eliyahu was later the Chief Mizrahi Rabbi of Israel. Yair Sheleg, *Following the Multitude: Rabbinical Attitudes Towards Democracy in Israel*, Policy Research 67 (Jerusalem: Israel Democracy Institute, 2006).

[56] *Government Meeting Minutes*, 13 December 1949. During the same meeting, Golda Meir, Minister of Labor (and later Israel's Prime Minister between 1969–1974) claimed: "There is one point which is considered to be explosive and that is the religious issue. Since we have other troubles and no lack of explosive materials in many other areas, it will be dangerous and unwise to bring up this issue now. I see this as the only reason for the postponement of the constitution and am deeply sorry that we cannot [draft] it… At this time of ingathering of the Diaspora, of people from various cultures and regimes, the constitution could have been an educational and integrating substance… But this is the reality and we are required to accept it, yet only due to necessity, and not due to ideology." *Ibid*.

[57] *Meeting of Mapai Party in the Knesset and Party Secretariat*, 14 June 1949.

Constitutional decision-making

In light of the ideological passions on both religions and secular sides, several Knesset members challenged the principle of majoritarianism as the appropriate method of reaching constitutional decisions. The pragmatic argument against majority voting rested on the assumption that imposing a decision on the minority would exacerbate the conflict and destabilize the democratic order. Those who advocated adopting a consensus-driven constitution argued that a constitution should be based on wide popular support for the ideals and norms entrenched in this significant document.

More importantly, the argument against majority voting was also made with reference to the unique conditions of the state. Israel at independence had a population of some 600,000 Jews, which constituted less than 10 percent of Jews worldwide. Given the general ideological (as well as economic and strategic) commitment to encouraging Jewish immigration to Israel, and the immediate goal of the government to double the Jewish population of the country within four years, there was an obvious argument to be made in favor of delaying the drafting of a constitution to minimize the impact of what was essentially a variation of the classic constitutional problem of precommitment.[58] The opponents of a written constitution argued that its drafting should await the anticipated mass immigration. "We are not referring to future generations," David Bar-Rav-Hai from Mapai claimed, "we are concerned with the present generation … we are concerned with those who are expected to arrive in our country in the very near future."[59] Meir David Levonstein from the Orthodox Agudat Israel Party also used the democratic argument, when he declared:

> We all see Israel as a gathering place for all parts of the Diaspora; we all look at world Jewry as our future citizens, if not actually, then at least potentially. What is the normative authority of the inhabitants of our country, which consists of seven percent of our people, and what is the authority the members of Knesset, who were elected by five percent of the people, to adopt a constitution for the homeland and the entire people?[60]

[58] The Jeffersonian argument against an entrenched constitution, through which the founding generation limits the majoritarian decision-making of future generations and thus infringes upon the most fundamental principle of democracy, was raised by several members of the Knesset. See, for example, *Knesset Record* 4 (1950): 727, 777.

[59] *Knesset Record* 4 (1950): 727.

[60] *Knesset Record* 4 (1950): 744.

Evolution or revolution

Finally, proponents and opponents of a formal constitution argued over the appropriate pace of constitution-making – whether revolutionary or evolutionary – under conditions of deep internal divisions. The supporters of a written constitution argued that this "revolutionary" period of national transformation would be the optimal moment to construct constitutional principles likely to obtain general consent. The formative years of the state, they argued, were the proper moment to determine the direction in which the state would develop in the future, "precisely because we are standing at the center of an immense process of ingathering of the Diaspora, which streams into the country as a 'mob' so diverse and multicolored in terms of its past, its habits, its development."[61]

The foundation of the state was viewed by the supporters of a constitution as a revolutionary moment, providing an extraordinary opportunity for the rebuilding of the nation: "It is only at this time of fermentation that the powers of the nation are reaching their peak … I doubt we will be able to achieve later what we could probably achieve today."[62] Mapam member Israel Bar-Yehuda declared:

> At this point we must force the issue … why can't we determine the direction of nation-building from the beginning of our work? … We forced the issue in many other areas and we must force the issue on this question as well. It is necessary, from the first moment of the state, to establish the healthy foundations, which would assist its emergence.[63]

Opponents to the immediate drafting of a constitution argued that it was precisely because of the substantial areas of disagreement and the fragility of the newly established political order that the most controversial decisions should be deferred to the future. During the internal Mapai meetings, several Knesset Members raised the issue of timing of constitution writing: Izhar Smilanski, for example, argued "If there is a true and good thing about a constitution is that it expresses a large vision which does not take into account momentarily deviations and has a great educative power… The question is whether we can now create a constitution that would educate generations…or whether we will rely on opportunistic considerations when drafting it….[if the latter] it is better to enact separate laws."[64]

[61] Moshe Aram, from the United Workers Front, in: *Knesset Record* 5 (1950): 1267.
[62] Ben-Zion Dinburg, Mapai, in: *Knesset Record* 4 (1950): 742.
[63] Israel Bar-Yehuda, Mapam, in: *Knesset Record* 4 (1950): 736.
[64] *Meeting of Mapai Party in the Knesset and Party Secretariat*, 14 June 1949.

During the Knesset debates, the postponement of the constitutional drafting was suggested by several Mapai members as the more realistic approach: "I must believe in evolution," Avraham Hartzfeld from Mapai argued, "and you prefer the way of revolution and force. My conviction is that the state could not be built in a revolutionary way, but only in an evolutionary way."[65] Moreover, constitutions, it was argued by others, should be written at the end of revolutions not at their beginning. "Any constitution is an attempt to 'freeze' certain principles, to perpetuate them, if anything can be perpetuated in the life of a nation."[66] Instead of trying to craft a complete and perfect constitution, the pragmatists called for "the minimum amount of shocks to the system and the maximum amount of solidification [of achievements]."[67]

The dispute over the time-framework for drafting the constitution reflected a longstanding and fundamental difference of opinion within the Zionist movement over the pace at which the Zionist project should proceed. Dan Horowitz and Moshe Lissak argue that the Zionist movement was historically divided as to whether the realization of the Zionist dream demanded rapid or slow progress. In the pre-state era, the supporters of an incremental approach wanted to build a Jewish presence in Palestine step by step, whereas advocates of a radical approach wished for a rapid realization of this goal through dramatic political and/or military action.[68] The question of the speed at which progress should be made was also expressed with regard to issues such as whether the creation of a Jewish state in Palestine should be publicly proclaimed as the goal of the Zionist movement, whether European Jewry should be evacuated to Palestine en masse, or gradually so as to match the economic absorptive capacity; and whether statehood should be achieved through the gradual settlement and development of autonomous political institutions or by military force.[69]

During the Knesset constitutional debates, several Mapai members argued that the incrementalist approach, which was viewed as having led to political independence, should be applied to the task of drafting a constitution.[70] Yosef Burg, one of the central leaders of the National Religious Party, claimed that this approach was particularly important due to the degree of social and ideological fragmentation in Israel:

[65] *Knesset Record* 5 (1950): 1277.
[66] David Bar-Rav-Hai, (Mapai), *Knesset Record* 4 (1950): 726.
[67] Efraim Tavori, (Mapai), *Knesset Record* 4 (1950): 775.
[68] Horowitz and Lissak, *Trouble in Utopia* 101–2.
[69] *Ibid.*, 102.
[70] For example, David Bar-Rav-Hai, (Mapai), *Knesset Record* 4 (1950): 728.

The contradictions which have been revealed here are, in my opinion, the strongest argument against the unlimited empowerment of the
Constitutional, Law and Justice Committee. This is because we could not
find the wide common foundation necessary for the framing of a constitution. I advocate the enactment of basic laws instead of a constitution not
because I object to the notion of a constitution in principle. I prefer basic
laws for reasons of method and chronology ... What we need at this time
is to pause so as to clarify and deliberate about our problems. We need to
get used to each other and together construct our common political and
public life.[71]

The reluctance to begin drafting the constitution was driven not only
by pragmatic considerations, but also by a profound trust in the supremacy of political processes, rather than legal formalities, and in the ability
of such processes to advance change and create a new social order. This
view was most clearly expressed by David Ben-Gurion, who was a leading
voice in the campaign against drafting a constitution at independence.[72]
Ben Gurion expressed his objection to the idea of a dual legal system,
which allocates a superior status to constitutional laws on several occasions: "I think no country in the world needs a constitution, except for
America where it is necessary due to its federal structure. None of the
federal states would have given up its autonomy, and the union would not
have emerged, without a constitution to guarantee...the limited authorities of the union government. Thus, there was historical necessity."[73] Such
a historical necessity does not exist in Israel according to Ben Gurion.
Moreover, he argued, writing a constitution under the current conditions
of deep disagreement would impinge upon the urgent goals facing the
young nation: "In my opinion, our whole Torah is included in one provision that states: double the Yishuv (i.e. Jewish population, HL) within two

---

[71] *Knesset Record* 5 (1950): 1310.
[72] Historians still debate the reasons for Ben-Gurion's opposition to written constitution.
Among the various explanations are his objection to limit the government, his intention to change the electoral system, and his pragmatic tendency to focus on the young
state's most urgent needs, such as security problems, economic crisis and the need to
absorb millions of new immigrants. For the different positions see: Goldberg, "When
Trees Are Planted There Is No Need for Constitution"; Shlomo Aronson, "Constitution
for Israel: The British Model of David Ben-Gurion," *Politica: An Israeli Journal for
Political Science and International Relations* 2 (1998); Nir Kedar, *Mamlakhtiyut: David
Ben-Gurion's Civic Thought* (Jerusalem: Yad Ben-Zvi and Ben-Gurion Research Institute,
Ben-Gurion University of the Negev, 2009): 154–64; Horowitz, "The Haredim (Ultra-
Orthodox) and the Supreme Court" (all in Hebrew).
[73] *Government Meeting Minutes*, 13 December 1949. See also his statement at the *Meeting of
Mapai Party in the Knesset and Party Secretariat*, 14 June 1949.

years. If this will be done than we guaranteed the existence of the state…
The disputes and debates about the constitution will weaken the energy
required to double the Yishuv… this is the most urgent task. Let's leave
the constitution for another time."[74]

In his speech during the Knesset discussions on the constitution he
grounded his opposition in his objection to empowering judges to determine state policy. He criticized the American model of judicial review
which paralyzed, in his view, the political system. He referred to the difficulties faced by President Roosevelt to realize his political goals during
the New Deal and World War II, which were due, in Ben-Gurion's eyes,
to the existence of a rigid federal system which increased the power of
appointed judges at the expense of that of elected representatives.[75] The
British model of majoritarian democracy was admired by Ben-Gurion as
the superior manifestation of the democratic ideal:

> Rule of law is impossible without the rule of democracy. The people
> respect the laws and accept their authority if the laws are made according
> to the people's opinion, derive from their needs and are subject to their
> will. A state which lacks the people's liberty to legislate through its freely
> elected representatives does not enjoy rule of law but rather it is despotic
> and tyrannical.[76]

Thus, in his view, a rigid constitution that limits the autonomy of the
legislature does not contribute to the strengthening of democracy and the
rule of law. With the example of the Weimar constitution in his mind,
Ben-Gurion seemed to be concerned that a written constitution would
entrench polarization and thereby weaken the government and the rule
of law: "The existence of an entrenched constitution would not increase
respect for the law. Rather, it would increase disrespect. Such a document
would supply plenty of excuses to disregard the law, which could be seen
as incompatible with the constitution."[77]

Informal consociationalism in the religious sphere

The Harari Resolution, which established the incremental approach to
constitution-drafting, left the future of Israel's constitution in doubt. It
did not clarify what should be covered by the Basic Laws or what their

---

[74] Ibid.
[75] *Knesset Record* 4 (1950): 817. See also Aronson, "Constitution for Israel."
[76] *Knesset Record* 4 (1950): 817.
[77] *Knesset Record* 4 (1950): 818.

status relative to ordinary legislation would be. Other issues that were left open included the legal status of the Basic Laws and the manner in which they could be amended, as well how the separate laws were to be consolidated into one constitutional document. Even the constituent authority of the Knesset and its duty to adopt a constitution were subject to legal and political dispute.

The first Basic Law – Basic Law: the Knesset – was passed in 1958, eight years after the Harari Resolution. In the meantime, Israeli constitutional law had evolved, mostly in accordance with the structure of the Jewish governmental institutions during the British Mandate.[78] The first nine Basic Laws that were passed before 1992 dealt mainly with institutional considerations, and were in essence the legal formalization of the existing structure of government.[79]

The Knesset was able to pass a number of Basic Laws dealing with institutional issues due to the fact that there was little disagreement on their content, at least in the first decades of the state.[80] But the foundational issues regarding the content of the constitution remained unresolved. The Harari Resolution enabled the Knesset to avoid any explicit formulation of the relationship between religious law and state institutions and to refrain from controversial ideological decisions concerning the religious nature of the state. But in the absence of a written constitution, the competing religious and secular claims have been dealt with through a series of informal consociational arrangements, which over time became entrenched in the political landscape.

The most notable of these consociational arrangements was the concept of the religious status quo, never clearly or formally defined, which was first introduced in the coalition agreement of 1950. Since then, it has been included in the coalition agreements of most Israeli governments as a manifestation of the delicate balance between religious and secular

---

[78] Ron Harris, "The Israeli Judiciary," in Zvi Zameret and Hannah Yavlonka, eds., *The First Decade: 1948–1958* (Jerusalem: Yad Ben-Zvi, 1997), 245 (Hebrew).

[79] These included Basic Law: The Knesset (1958), Basic Law: Israel Lands (1960), Basic Law: The President of the State (1964), Basic Law: The Government (1968), Basic Law: The State Economy (1975), Basic Law: The Military (1976), Basic Law: Jerusalem Capital of Israel (1980), Basic Law: The Judiciary (1984), Basic Law: The State Comptroller (1988).

[80] The broad consensus on issues such as the electoral system and the parliamentary regime was gradually eroded during the 1980s, as a result of the increasing political power of minority parties, and in particular of the religious parties. This ultimately led in 1992 to the changing of the electoral system as provided for in Basic Law: Government, and to its revision once again in 2001, in reaction to the problematic political consequences of direct election of the prime minister.

demands, based on what is known in the consociational literature as a mutual veto principle.[81]

The status quo arrangements, which effectively determine the non-separation between religion and state in certain areas, were shaped during the formative years of the state. Their origin is commonly attributed to a letter, dated June 1947, which was sent by David Ben Gurion and other leaders of the Jewish Agency to the non-Zionist Orthodox Agudat Israel group. The letter, designed to gain the support of the religious leadership for the Jewish state, reassured them that the establishment of a decidedly secular state would not harm the status of the Jewish religion or threaten the values and way of life of religious Jews.[82] The letter stipulated key principles that would guide governmental policy and action in four main areas: observance of the Sabbath, observance of *kashruth* (dietary laws) in governmental institutions, jurisdiction of rabbinical courts over Jews in matters of personal status (in particular marriage and divorce) and the autonomy of religious educational institutions.[83] The language of the letter is broad, and consequently its operative implications soon became highly contentious themselves.

During the first years of the state, the status quo arrangements were formulated, partly in Knesset regulations and partly through informal practice. Upon independence, the Provisional Council had decided to incorporate the existing legal framework of the British Mandate, which in turn incorporated numerous Ottoman laws, into the Israeli legal system. One result of this decision was that the authority of institutions of the various religious denominations in areas pertaining to personal law was preserved.[84] These authorities were based on the Ottoman *Millet* system, which allowed legal autonomy for religious traditions formally recognized by the state in the area of personal law.[85] Separately, various aspects of the status quo were formally defined through legislation.

---

[81] Eliezer Don-Yehiya, *Religion and Political Accommodation in Israel* (Jerusalem: Floersheimer Institute for Policy Studies, 1999), 44–5.

[82] Shulamit Aloni, *The Arrangement: From Rule of Law to Rule of Religion* (Tel Aviv: Otpaz, 1970), 90–1 (Hebrew).

[83] *Ibid.*, 82–3. Some aspects of the status quo are not included in the letter, such as the exemption of Orthodox students and religious women from military service.

[84] Based on the Palestine Order in Council 1922, Paragraph 83 in: Drayton, *Laws of Palestine*, vol. III, 2587.

[85] Fourteen religious communities are formally recognized in Israel: Jews, Muslims, Eastern Orthodox, Roman Catholics, Georgian Armenians, Armenian Catholics, Syrian Catholics, Chaldeans (Uniates), Greek Catholics, Maronites, Syrian Orthodox, Druze, Episcopal-Evangelicals and the Baha'is.

These included, for example, the recognition of the Sabbath as the day of rest,[86] observance of *kashruth* laws in military installations,[87] restrictions on production of pork,[88] exclusive Orthodox jurisdiction over Jewish marriage and divorce[89] and an independent Orthodox educational system.[90]

Other aspects of the status quo, particularly the exemption of Orthodox Yeshiva students and religious women from military service, resulted from the harsh political and military reality faced by the government during the War of Independence. "The declaration of the establishment of the State of Israel in the midst of a bloody war created a political reality which required maximal consensus," writes Menachem Friedman, "that is, the complete participation of the religious parties, including the Orthodox Agudat-Israel, in the government. This reality determined almost by itself … the application of the *status quo* principle in religious issues."[91]

In addition to the mutual veto principle, the religious–secular tension was dealt with through three other types of arrangements that are considered essential to the theory of consociational democracy, as defined by Arend Lijphart.[92] The first such arrangement was through coalition partnership. Since the first days of the state, the religious parties were almost always included in the ruling coalition. Representatives of the National Religious Party (NRP) were included in a coalition with Mapai (and later Labor), even when the latter's majority in the Knesset enabled it to form a coalition government without the religious party's support. The second standard consociational principle used was the rule of proportionality, which is reflected in coalition agreements concerning the allocation of resources to religious institutions and services, and particularly to the religious educational system. The third arrangement ensured

---

[86] *P'kudat Sidrei Ha'shilton ve'hamishpat* (Law and Administration Ordinance) (1948) and Working Hours and Rest Law (1951).

[87] Kosher Food for Soldiers Ordinance (1948).

[88] Pig Raising Prohibition (1962).

[89] Rabbinical Courts Jurisdiction (Marriage and Divorce) Law (1953).

[90] Compulsory Education Law (1949) and National Education Law (1953). For a comprehensive overview of religious legislation see Amnon Rubinstein and Baruch Medina, *The State of Israel's Constitutional Law*, vol. I (Jerusalem: Shocken, 2005), ch. 6.

[91] Friedman, "These are the Chronicles of the Status-Quo," 80.

[92] Lijphart, "Majority Rule Versus Democracy in Deeply Divided Societies," 118–19; Arend Lijphart, *Democracy in Plural Societies: A Comparative Exploration* (New Haven: Yale University Press, 1977). Don-Yehiya, *Religion and Political Accommodation in Israel*, 29–35.

that disagreements regarding the school curriculum would be resolved according to the consociational principle of autonomy. Jewish religious educational institutions in Israel, just like those in the Netherlands, enjoy autonomy and per capita governmental funding.

Israel, nevertheless, is not a consociational democracy in the full sense of the term. According to Arend Lijphart, "consociational democracy means government by elite cartel designed to turn a democracy with a fragmented political culture into a stable democracy."[93] But in Israel, as Eliezer Don-Yehiya rightly argues, not all segments of society are included in the consociational arrangements. For example, political parties that represent the Arab population in Israel are consistently excluded from any participation in governmental coalitions. Also, within the Jewish community not all groups were able to participate fully in the consociational arrangements. The non-Orthodox religious groups, such as Reform and the Conservatives, by and large do not have representatives in the official religious institutions of the state.[94]

The non-adoption of a formal constitution is another deviation of the Israeli case from Lijphart's model of consociationalism. Lijphart finds a strong link between the politics of accommodation and constitutionalism: constitutions prevent strong communities from executing their majoritarian preferences. He built his theory on the Dutch model, in which consociational arrangements were adopted in 1917 through a constitutional amendment, and are still an essential part of the constitutional infrastructure.[95] Therefore, some might argue that not adopting a constitution is anti-consociational. However, when the struggle is between rival perceptions of the foundational elements of the constitution, adopting a constitution by majority vote would itself violate the consociational principle. As noted above, the religious–secular clash in Israel differs from social conflicts in other Western democracies in that it does not concern distributive justice or issues which could be solved within a procedural constitutional framework. Rather, the conflict is over the fundamental commitments and ultimate goals that the constitution is expected to reflect, and therefore a constitution cannot serve as an instrument for entrenching consociationalism. In fact, within these constraining circumstances, a constitution might pose a rather formidable obstacle to the realization of the consociational principle. Hence, the absence of a

---

[93] Arend Lijphart, *The Politics of Accommodation: Pluralism and Democracy in the Netherlands* (Berkeley: University of California Press, 1968), 216.
[94] Don-Yehiya, *Religion and Political Accommodation in Israel*, 23–5.
[95] Lijphart, "The Politics of Accomodation," 20–2.

constitution in Israel does not undermine but actually serves the politics of accommodation.[96]

In sum, the decision not to adopt a constitution reflected the Israeli consensus regarding the need to avoid giving definitive solutions to controversial questions concerning the identity of the state. By adhering to an incremental strategy of constitution-drafting, the members of the first Knesset transferred the decisions regarding the nature of the state from the constitutional sphere to the political realm of ordinary legislation. By avoiding clear-cut choices in the religious arena in 1950, they left it to the political system to gradually construct accommodational arrangements.

A common criticism against consociational democracy is that it eventually entrenches the identity divisions within the institutional framework of the state, and ultimately perpetuates polarization instead of moderating it.[97] In the Israeli case, the consociational arrangements in the religious sphere were informal in character, but in retrospect they have proven to be extremely rigid. Without a written constitution containing accepted methods to amend existing constitutional provisions a material constitution of the informal consociational "status quo" arrangements have become more rigid than their secular framers anticipated. It could be argued that by refraining from tackling the foundational elements of the constitution in the formative years of the state, the first Knesset opened the door to the entrenchment of informal (or material) constitutional arrangements with regard to state–religion relations.

The rest of the chapter will concern this problem, which surfaced when the broad consensus that underpinned the constitutional solution of 1950 began to erode starting in the 1980s.

Escalation of the religious–secular conflict

In contrast to the relative ease with which the Basic Laws relating to political institutions were passed by the Knesset during the first decades after independence, there was consistent strong opposition to enacting a comprehensive bill of rights.[98] There was also opposition to the enactment of

---

[96] Cohen and Susser, *Israel and the Politics of Jewish Identity*.

[97] Alfred Stepan, "Paths toward Redemocratization: Theoretical and Comparative Considerations," in Guillermo O'Donnell, Philippe C. Schmitter and Laurence Whitehead, eds., *Transitions from Authoritarian Rule: Comparative Perspectives* (Baltimore and London: The Johns Hopkins University Press, 1988), 80. For an extensive criticism of the consociational model see: Brian Barry, "Political Accommodation and Consociational Democracy," *British Journal of Political Science* 5, no. 4 (1975).

[98] Nevertheless, over the years ordinary legislation protecting human rights was passed, including with respect to the rights of suspects and prisoners, children's rights, patients'

a proposed Basic Law on legislation, which was intended to entrench the legislational primacy of the Basic Laws themselves.[99] These attempts to promote the writing of a formal constitution evoked once more the old controversies regarding the fundamental values of the state. The religious parties vigorously objected to the draft of the Basic Law on Human and Civil Rights, proposed by Minister of Justice Dan Meridor in 1989. Their main concern was that it would undermine the religious status quo, even though the bill explicitly stated that the new Basic Law would not infringe upon religious regulations regarding marriage and divorce.[100]

This opposition can be understood in the context of the intensification over time of the religious–secular schism in Israeli society. There were various reasons for this intensification. One of them was the transformation of the Israeli political landscape following the Likud victory in 1977 from a system dominated by a single party (Mapai) to one with two similar-size competing blocs. In the new political reality the religious parties were often able to determine who would form a coalition government. At the same time, Israeli secular society was increasingly shifting toward Western values of liberal individualism. Furthermore the secular–religious divisions became further pronounced with the growing unity of the religious bloc. Over the years, there was a steady reduction in the political differences within the religious camp, which had characterized it during the early years of the state.

The increasing gap between the secular and religious segments of society is further attributable, among other things, to the National Religious camp's increasing religious and political conservatism, which led to growing social and cultural separatism, especially among the younger generation.[101] Concurrently, the participation of ultra-Orthodox circles in state institutions also increased. These religious institutional positions had previously been held by the National Religious Party (NRP), as part of the political arrangements dating back to the first years of the state. However, whereas the NRP tended to regard these functions as part of a broader

rights, women's rights and freedom of speech. Ruth Gavison, *The Constitutional Revolution: A Reality or a Self-Fulfilling Prophecy?* (Jerusalem: Israel Democracy Institute, 1998), 67 (Hebrew); Menachem Hofnung, "The Unintended Consequences of Unplanned Constitutional Reform: Constitutional Politics in Israel," *American Journal of Comparative Law*, 44 (1996): 592.

99   Gavison, *The Constitutional Revolution*, 66; Rubinstein and Medina, *Constitutional Law in the State of Israel*, 910–14.

100   Benjamin Neuberger, *The Constitution Debate in Israel* (Tel Aviv: Open University of Israel, 1997), 69.

101   Horowitz and Lissak, *Trouble in Utopia*, 63.

service to the state, the ultra-Orthodox Agudat Israel has tended to regard its control over these institutions in instrumental terms, using it to maximize their share of governmental resources.[102] Finally, the convergence of religiosity and hawkish political views on the one hand, and secularism and dovish views on the other, resulted in the decline of cross-cutting divisions and to the rise of the overlapping rifts in Israeli public life.[103]

Polls measuring the religiosity of Israelis and their own assessment of the situation[104] attested to the intensification of the rift between the secular and religious camps.[105] In the public sphere, the escalating rift was expressed in numerous political and judicial battles over the boundaries of the status quo.

The growing religious–secular division had an increasingly adverse effect on the relationship between the legislature and the judiciary. The tension between the two branches of government is inherent to any modern democratic regime, but in Israel it overlapped with an ideological rift between conflicting visions of the state. From the 1980s on, in the face of the growing political and legislative power of the religious camp, the liberal-secular population found support in an increasingly activist Supreme Court.[106] Many considered the Court as the central arena for the promotion of the liberal-secular Jewish agenda.[107] Although the religious status

---

[102] Emanuel Gutman, "The Religious Cleavage," in Moshe Lissak and Brian Kney-Paz, eds., *Israel toward 2000: Society, Politics, Culture* (Jerusalem: Magnes, Hebrew University, 1996).

[103] Cohen and Susser, *Israel and the Politics of Jewish Identity*, ch. 3.

[104] According to these surveys, in 1992, 71 percent of the Jews in Israel believed that the relations between religious and secular were "not so good" or "not good." See Neri Horowitz, "State and Religious 1993: Agenda Setting," in Neri Horowitz, ed., *State and Religion Yearbook 1993* (Tel Aviv: Center of Jewish Pluralism, 1994), 100 (Hebrew).

[105] Survey data between 1979 and 1992 shows a growth of the extreme groups – Haredim on the one hand and seculars on the other hand – and a decrease in the share of the middle groups, defined as "traditionalists." See Gutman, "The Religious Cleavage," 62–4.

[106] Whether Israeli Supreme Court is truly activist is a question intensely debated by legal academics. For prominent scholars writing on this issue see: Menachem Mautner, "The Decline of Formalism and the Rise of Values in Israeli Law," *Iyunei Mishpat* 13, no. 3 (1993); Gad Barzilai, "Judicial Hegemony, Party Polarization and Social Change," *Politica: An Israeli Journal for Political Science and International Relations* 2 (1998): 31–51; Ruth Gavison, Mordechai Kremnitzer and Yoav Dotan, *Judicial Activism: For and Against, the Role of the High Court of Justice in Israeli Society* (Jerusalem: Magnes, 2000) (Hebrew); Aharon Barak, *The Judge in a Democracy* (Princeton University Press, 2006); Yitzhak Zamir, "Judicial Activism: A Decision to Decide," *Iyunei Mishpat* 17, no. 3 (1993): 647–58 (Hebrew).

[107] Gad Barzilai, Efraim Yuchtman-Yaar and Zeev Segal, *The Israeli Supreme Court and the Israeli Public* (Tel Aviv: Papirus, 1994); Menachem Mautner, "The 1980s: The Years of Anxiety," *Iyunei Mishpat* 26, no. 2 (2002).

quo was recognized as a political principle for accommodating the religious–secular divide, it was never anchored as a legal imperative in Court decisions. On the contrary, over the years, the Israeli Court has attempted to alter the status quo arrangements in its rulings, especially with respect to those arrangements that conflicted with basic human rights, as provided for in the Declaration of Independence, in Basic Law: Freedom of Occupation and in Basic Law: Human Dignity and Liberty. For example, in 1994, the Court permitted the importation of non-kosher meat,[108] and in 1989 and 1994 it ruled against local authorities' refusal to appoint women or non-Orthodox Jews to local religious councils.[109]

During the late 1990s, the overlap between the social–ideological conflict and the legislature–judiciary tensions reached a climax, which led to dramatic social, political and judicial consequences. One of the major reasons for this escalation was the integration of the constitutional question as an additional layer in both the religious–secular and court–legislature conflicts.

The "constitutional revolution"

In 1992, in the face of the growing tensions between the religious and the secular parties, it became clear that the political system could not adopt a comprehensive bill of rights. But it was precisely this widening ideological rift and the increasing political power of the religious parties that created a sense of urgency among liberal Israelis regarding the need to entrench human and civil rights and to empower the Supreme Court to protect those rights. Professor Amnon Rubinstein, a Member of Shinui party in the Knesset (and later the minister of Education) spearheaded an initiative to break down the draft of the wide-ranging Basic Law on human and civil rights into its component parts and to ratify them section by section. This would have the effect of legislating at least those provisions to which the religious parties did not object. Thus, just as in the Harari Resolution of forty years earlier, the Knesset yet again embraced an incrementalist approach, this time to the enactment of a bill of rights.

---

[108] HCJ 4676/94 *Meatrael* v. *Israeli Knesset*. See: Hanna Lerner, "Democracy, Constitutionalism and Identity: The Anomaly of the Israeli Case," *Constellations* 11, no. 2 (2004): 237–57.

[109] HCJ 699/89 *Anat Hoffman* v. *Jerusalem City Council* 48(1), HCJ 4733/94 *Yehudit Naot* v. *Haifa City Council* 59(5). For more on the developments in the status quo arrangements in court rulings and in legislation see: Michael Corinaldi, "Freedom of Religion in Israel: What Changed in the 'Status Quo'?" *Sha'arey Mishpat* 3, no. 2 (2003).

In March 1992 the Knesset passed two Basic Laws on human rights.[110] Basic Law: Human Dignity and Liberty provides for the preservation of life, body and dignity, the protection of property and privacy, personal liberty and the freedom of movement. Basic Law: Freedom of Occupation guarantees the right of every Israeli national or resident to engage in any occupation, profession or trade. The goal of reaching as broad an agreement as possible led to a reduction of the scope of the rights and the extent to which they were secured, compared to the original 1989 draft on which these two Basic Laws were based.[111] The drafts of the new Basic Laws initially included an entrenchment clause, which required an absolute majority of the Knesset for amending the Basic Laws. This provision was eventually included in Basic Law: Freedom of Occupation (section 7), but was omitted (by a single vote) on the second reading of Basic Law: Human Dignity and Liberty. Both Basic Laws include a limitation clause, stating that "there should be no violation of rights under this Basic Law except by a law befitting the values of the State of Israel."[112] But the Knesset rejected an explicit reference to judicial review of legislation that infringed the rights contained in the Basic Laws.[113]

Most of the disagreements that emerged during the legislative debates on the Basic Laws stemmed from the concerns of the religious camp that restricting the legislative power of the Knesset might alter the status quo in favor of the secular community. Consequently, a special "validity of laws" clause was added to Basic Law: Human Dignity and Liberty, which provided that the Basic Law "shall not affect the validity of any law in force prior to the commencement of the Basic Law" (section 10). A similar

---

[110] Three additional drafts of Basic Laws were presented to the Committee of Law, Constitution and Justice in the Knesset: Basic Law on Judicial Rights, Basic Law on Freedom of Speech and Association, and Basic Law on Social Rights. These bills were not enacted by the Knesset due to objections of the religious parties during the Rabin government (elected in fall 1992). Rubinstein and Medina, *Constitutional Law in the State of Israel*, 919.

[111] *Ibid.*, 915–18.

[112] Basic Law: Human Dignity and Liberty, Section 8. A similar clause is included in Basic Law: Freedom of Occupation, section 4. The limitation clause was initially formulated according to a similar clause in the Canadian Charter of Rights and Freedoms. See David Kretzmer, "The New Basic Laws on Human Rights: A Mini Revolution in Israeli Constitutional Law?" *Israel Law Review* 26, no. 2 (1992): 246.

[113] The objection to judicial review was not expressed only by the religious parties, who feared that legislation enforcing religious norms would not stand up to review, but also by the defense establishment, which realized that much of the British Mandatory emergency legislation, in use to this day, did not meet the standards of the Basic Laws. See *ibid.*, 244.

clause was included in Basic Law: Freedom of Occupation, although in that case the legal effect of the validity clause is limited to a number of years (section 10). In addition, the religious parties feared potential limitations on future religious legislation. Therefore, the term "Jewish" was added to the purpose clause, stating that the purpose of the Basic Law: Freedom of Occupation is "to establish in a Basic Law the values of the state of Israel as a Jewish and democratic state" (section 2).

The inclusion of both the words "Jewish" and "democratic" in the definition reflected an attempt to bridge the ideological divide over the character of the state. The ambiguous formulation was intentional, and the drafters believed that it would help circumvent a controversial choice between competing visions of the state. In the words of the bills' sponsor, Amnon Rubinstein:

> The legal language is broad and opaque, and therein lies its advantage. It enables the achievement of a comprehensive national agreement … Hence, it was decided to favor a way which does not force deliberation and choice-making in fundamental questions regarding the relationship between the Jewish and the democratic nature of the state.[114]

By adopting ambiguous language, the drafters of the Basic Laws were following the same strategy of compromise that was adopted by the first Knesset.

The Basic Laws were enacted with surprising ease. They were both passed by simple majorities of very few Knesset members who attended the session. Twenty-three members voted in favor of Basic Law: Freedom of Occupation, with none opposing or abstaining. The Basic Law: Human Dignity and Liberty was passed by a majority of thirty-two, with twenty-one members voting against and one abstaining. In retrospect, the supporters of the Basic Laws described it as "a constitutional miracle,"[115] while its detractors named it "a parliamentary snatch,"[116] criticizing the absence of public deliberation during this crucial legislative process, that reframed the state's fundamental values.[117]

---

[114] Rubinstein and Medina, *Constitutional Law in the State of Israel*, 915.

[115] Barzilai *et al.*, *The Israeli Supreme Court and the Israeli Public*, 249–65.

[116] Yoav Dotan, "Constitution for the State of Israel? The Constitutional Dialog after the Constitutional Revolution," *Mishpatim* 28, no. 1–2 (1997): 200; Gavison, *The Constitutional Revolution*, 100.

[117] Dan Avnon, "'The Enlightened Public': Jewish and Democratic or Liberal and Democratic?" *Mishpat Umimshal: Law and Government in Israel* 3, no. 2 (1995): 423 (Hebrew). The ratification of the Basic Laws occurred in the last days of the twelfth Knesset, when the focus of public attention was on the impending elections.

The increased intervention by the Supreme Court in constitutional controversies revived the debate over incrementalist versus revolutionary approaches to writing a constitution. In several Supreme Court decisions and various publications and public statements, Supreme Court Chief Justice Aharon Barak celebrated the enactment of the two Basic Laws on human rights as a "constitutional revolution."[118] The revolution, according to Barak, stemmed, first, from the essential change in the status of some basic human rights in Israel: "They ceased to be merely 'unwritten' rights, and became 'written' rights."[119] Moreover, their normative status had changed:

> The normative anchor which determined the validity of the entire legislation … the basic rights now impose restrictions on the legislature itself. It should not be said that Israel does not have "a written constitution" (formal and rigid) with respect to human rights. The new legislation has taken Israel out of its solitude, and has placed it in the large company of states where human rights are secured by a "written" and "rigid" constitution, namely, by a document of supremacy and normative superiority.[120]

"Israel has transformed itself from a parliamentary democracy to a constitutional democracy," he claimed,[121] and, consequently, the role of the court in Israel had essentially changed.

In truth, the Knesset had not explicitly granted the Court the power of judicial review. But this, Barak claimed,

> should not be interpreted as a negative arrangement. Like the United-States, South Africa and other countries, the Supreme Court in Israel perceives the entrenched Basic Laws as constitutionally supreme – enacted by a constituent authority … There is no doubt any more that the Israeli courts are authorized to overrule any statute which infringes upon an entrenched Basic Law.[122]

In 1995, Chief Justice Barak's views were clearly presented in a decision, *United Mizrahi Bank* v. *Migdal*, in which the Court, sitting in a rare panel of nine judges, established its authority to declare any ordinary legislation

---

[118] Aharon Barak was a Supreme Court Justice since 1978, and served as its Chief Justice between 1995 and 2006.

[119] Barak, "The Constitutional Revolution," 12.

[120] *Ibid*.

[121] Aharon Barak, "Fifty Years of Adjudication in Israel," *Aley Mishpat: The Law Review of Ramat Gan Collage of Law* 1, no. 1 (1999): 12.

[122] Barak, "The Constitutional Revolution," 16–17. See also Aharon Barak, "The Role of the Supreme Court in Democratic Society," *Tel Aviv University Law Review* 21, no. 1 (1997): 13–19 (Hebrew).

as unconstitutional if it did not meet the standards set out by the Knesset in the new Basic Laws.[123] The decision, which was over 500 pages long, most of it dicta, came to be regarded as the "constitutional manifesto" of the Supreme Court.[124] Although the decision was unanimous as far as the specific issues of the case were concerned, for the most part it did not reflect a unanimously held view of the Supreme Court of the status of constitutional norms in Israel after the enactment of the new Basic Laws. In a minority opinion, Justice Cheshin objected to the concept of a "constitutional revolution" and the recognition in the new normative status of the Basic Laws. But Justice Cheshin was the sole critic on the Bench of Chief Justice Barak's judicial activism.

The Supreme Court could have expected the formalization of its constitutional revolution to continue strengthening its status. But in fact it had the opposite effect. The constitutional revolution was perceived as a threat to the independence and legislative power of the Knesset.[125] And in the specific context of the religious–secular conflict, it was perceived by the religious parties as a threat to their bargaining power and to the future of the consociational arrangements.[126] Despite the widespread public support for the Supreme Court's activism,[127] the Court's rulings relating to the new Basic Laws created a public storm and brought about a firm political reaction.

The counterrevolution

The public, political and judicial turmoil that erupted in response to the constitutional revolution led not only to an escalation of the religious–secular struggle, but also to an increased tendency to equate this battle with the controversy over the status of the Supreme Court. The tension

---

[123] CA 6821/93, *United Mizrahi Bank Ltd.* v. *Migdal Cooperative Village*, PD 49(4) 221. The decision was in response to an appeal of several District Court decisions, which claimed that the amendment to the law on debt forgiveness for Israeli collective villages ("Moshavim") contradicted the Basic Law on Human Dignity and Freedom. The HCJ decided unanimously that the law did not actually contradict the Basic Law and thus was not to be nullified. The importance of this decision was that it outlined for the first time the Court's position regarding its new legal powers in the wake of the passing of the Basic Laws.

[124] Dotan, "Constitution for the State of Israel?" 173.

[125] Hofnung, "The Unintended Consequences of Unplanned Constitutional Reform," 585–604.

[126] Rubinstein and Medina, *Constitutional Law in the State of Israel*, 917.

[127] Barzilai *et al.*, *The Israeli Supreme Court and the Israeli Public*.

between the Knesset and the Supreme Court also increased, and this in turn further complicated the constitutional problems of Israel.

The direct conflict between the Supreme Court and the Knesset came to the fore a short time after the enactment of the Basic Laws in 1992 in *Meatrael*, a Supreme Court decision (sitting as a High Court of Justice) that has been viewed by some as a "constitutional counterrevolution,"[128] or at least a "moderation of the constitutional revolution."[129] It also resulted in an amendment to the new Basic Laws, which was added in 1994.

In spring 1992, a few months after the Basic Laws were passed, the government announced the privatization of the frozen meat industry in Israel, but forbade the import of non-kosher meat. Meatrael, a private meat company, asked the HCJ to overrule this policy, claiming that it infringed its right to engage in legal economic activity under Basic Law: Freedom of Occupation. The HCJ accepted this argument, stating in its ruling in dictum that any future legislation forbidding importation of non-kosher meat contradicted the limitation clause of the Basic Law (*Meatrael* v. *Prime Minister*, 1993). The religious parties perceived the court's decision as a direct violation of the status quo. At the government's request,[130] the Knesset added a new and highly convoluted provision to the Basic Law: Freedom of Occupation:[131]

> A law that infringes upon the freedom of occupation shall be valid even though it is not consistent with provision 4 [the restrictive clause], if included in the law passed by a majority of the Knesset members is an explicit provision stating that it is valid despite what is said in the Basic Law.[132]

This provision, which was officially titled the "Effect of Nonconforming Law," was popularly referred to as the "HCJ bypass law." A few minutes after the amendment of the Basic Law, the Knesset enacted the Importation of

---

[128] Cohen and Susser, *Israel and the Politics of Jewish Identity*, 90.

[129] Avnon, "The Enlightened Public," 420.

[130] The government initiative was driven, among other things, by the coalition's need of support from Shas (the Sephardic-Orthodox party) on the Oslo peace agreements.

[131] This provision was inspired by the "Notwithstanding Clause" in the 1982 Canadian Charter of Rights and Freedoms (Article 33), which allows Parliament or the legislature of a province to "expressly declare in an Act of Parliament or of the legislature, as the case may be, that the Act or a provision thereof shall operate notwithstanding a provision" included in several sections of the Charter. Such legislation is limited for five years but may be re-enacted.

[132] Section 8. The amendment to Basic Law: Human Dignity and Liberty included the addition of Section 1(a), namely, the adjustment of the Purpose clause to conform to the one in the Basic Law: Freedom of Occupation.

Meat Law (1994), which included a provision stating that "this law is valid in spite of what is said in Basic Law: Freedom of Occupation."[133]

Meatrael highlighted the clash between the political and judicial systems. The Court was identified as the guardian of the liberal-secular vision, and the Knesset as the realm of the religious parties.[134] Moreover, *Meatrael* reflected the exacerbating effects of foundational constitutional issues on the inter-institutional tension: the Court had intervened in controversial issues affecting the identity of the state, and the Knesset had reacted by neutralizing the Court's decisions.

As the support of secular Jews for the Supreme Court increased, the opposition of the ultra-Orthodox population became progressively more strident throughout the 1990s. Verbal attacks on Supreme Court Justices included harsh statements by leaders and journalists in the ultra-Orthodox community against what they variously referred to as "judicial dictatorship," "the fourth Reich," "the persecutors of Israel" and "Isra-Nazis." Rabbi Porush, one of the leaders of Agudat Israel, even declared at one point that he would be "willing to sacrifice his life in the struggle against Justice Barak."[135] The Chief Justice had to be given protection after receiving repeated threats on his life. And following a series of Supreme Court rulings on religious issues, including on the exemption of religious students from military service, the Orthodox monopoly on authorizing Jewish conversions and the inclusion of Reform and Conservative representatives in municipal religious councils, all of which were perceived by

---

[133] The amendment of the Basic Law raised a major debate among legal theorists on the question of whether the constitutional revolution was really "revolutionary." See, for example, Y. M. Aderi, "Constitutional Revolution?" *Mishpat Umimshal: Law and Government in Israel* 3, no. 2 (1996); Dotan, "Constitution for the State of Israel?"; Menachem Elon, "The Way of Law in Constitution: The Values of Jewish and Democratic State in the Light of Basic Law: Human Dignity and Liberty," in Aharon Barak and E. Mazuz, eds., *The Landau Book* (Tel Aviv: Borsei, 1996); Gavison, *The Constitutional Revolution*; Moshe Landau, "The Supreme Court as Constitution Maker for Israel," *Mishpat Umimshal: Law and Government in Israel* 3, no. 3 (1996).

[134] *Meatrael* was not the first time in which the Knesset, de facto, overrode a Supreme Court's decision on religious issues. In 1969 the Knesset changed the Law of Return and the Law of Registration to reflect the religious definition of who is considered as Jewish, thus overriding a court decision in the case of *Shalit* to register the children of a Jewish father and non-Jewish mother as Jews. H.C. 58/68, *Shalit v. Minister of Interior* (1969) 23 P.D. (II) 477. Mark J. Altschul, "Israel's Law of Return and the Debate of Altering, Repealing or Maintaining Its Present Language," *University of Illinois Law Review* 5 (2002): 1353–4.

[135] T. M. Tenenbaum, "No to a HCJ Which Contradicts the Halacha!" *Hamodia* 22 January 1999 (ultra-Orthodox newspaper). See also Cohen and Susser, *Israel and the Politics of Jewish Identity*, xii, 93–4.

Orthodox Jews as a violation of the status quo, the ultra-Orthodox leadership issued a statement forbidding compliance with HCJ rulings. This prohibition, published in January 1999, was directed at all Haredi political leaders and civil servants, including Knesset members and government ministers.[136]

The opposition of the ultra-Orthodox community to the Supreme Court reflected its feelings of alienation from the Court, its ideology and the value system it represents. The liberal-secular philosophy manifested in the court rulings was very prominent in Chief Justice Barak's public expressions and publications. For example, his interpretation of the formulation "Jewish and democratic state" was perceived as taking sides in the religious–secular conflict. Specifically, he attempted to bring the conflicting concepts into line according to a "universal abstraction level," and attempted to equate Jewish values with Western democratic principles. Barak stated clearly that "the meaning of the Jewish nature of the state is not in the religious-Halachic sense, and hence the values of the State of Israel as a Jewish state should not be identified with the Jewish Law."[137] This comment drew intense criticism from the religious camp, including from retired Supreme Court Justice Menachem Elon.[138] Barak's use of the concept of "the enlightened public" as a judicial criterion for decisions in deeply controversial issues[139] also provoked severe criticism. This concept, it has been argued, reflects the Supreme Court's ideological choice of liberal-universal-secular values, and contradicts the Knesset resolution concerning the simultaneously democratic and Jewish nature of the State of Israel.[140]

One of the climaxes of the struggle was a massive Orthodox demonstration against the Supreme Court in February 1999 in Jerusalem. According to estimates, between 250,000 and 400,000 Orthodox Jews participated in one of Israel's largest demonstrations ever.[141] The demonstration was extraordinary even in terms of Orthodox history, since, for the first time, the leaders of all subgroups in the religious camp – from the Zionist religious (including the Chief Rabbis of the State) to fanatic anti-Zionist ultra-Orthodox fringe factions – acted collectively.[142] A counter-demonstration

---

[136] Shahar Ilan, "The Gedoley-Torah Councils: HJC Rulings are Invalid," *Haaretz*, January 17, 1999.

[137] Barak, "The Constitutional Revolution," 30–1.

[138] Elon, "The Way of Law in Constitution."

[139] Barak, "The Enlightened Public."

[140] Avnon, "The Enlightened Public."

[141] Representing between 5 and 8 percent of the Jewish population of the country.

[142] Horowitz, "The Haredim (Ultra-Orthodox) and the Supreme Court."

was held at the same time, with about 50,000 secular Jews expressing their support for the judicial system. Thousands of police were deployed to preserve order because of the fear that the ultra-Orthodox demonstrators would march on the Supreme Court building.

In the political arena, the religious parties tried unsuccessfully to prevent the appointment of Barak as Chief Justice in 1995. On the other hand, they were successful in their attempt to amend the Basic Laws following *Meatrael*, and in preventing the enactment of additional Basic Laws. The political attacks against the Supreme Court peaked in 2001 with the introduction of a bill to establish a constitutional council whose role it would be to review constitutional issues, and which would better represent the ideological fragmentation of Israeli society than would the Supreme Court. Chief Justice Barak vigorously opposed this development, fearing the politicization of adjudication and the fatal weakening of the Supreme Court.[143] Eventually, the Knesset rejected two bills for the establishment of a constitutional court.[144] Nevertheless, the issue of a constitutional court is still on the political agenda, and the initiative may still be revived in the future.

Consociationalism versus constitutionalism

The public and political storm over the constitutional revolution of 1992 can be viewed, to a certain extent, as an extension of the controversy between the incrementalist and the revolutionary approach to constitution-making which began in the 1950s in the Knesset debates over the constitution. As in the 1950s, the 1992 argument was, at heart, over the proper way to advance the constitutional project under conditions of deep internal divisions over foundational elements. However, whereas in the 1950s the constitutional debate was conducted in the legislature, in the 1990s the dispute became an inter-institutional conflict involving the Supreme Court and the Knesset. This added a new dimension to the existing dispute on constitution-drafting issues: how should authority in constitutional matters be allocated between the legislative and the judicial branches, and how should the constitutional dialogue between them be conducted?

These questions provoked a spirited debate among legal experts. Most prominently, they were expressed in the sharp public dispute between

---

[143] Aharon Barak, "Why do I Object to the Establishment of Constitutional Court?" *Yediot Aharonot*, 2001.

[144] Gidon Alon, "Suggestions for a Constitutional Court Rejected by the Knesset," *Haaretz*, January 3, 2002.

Chief Justice Aharon Barak and Professor Ruth Gavison of the Hebrew University Law School.[145] Gavison is one of the fervent opponents of the involvement of the Supreme Court in the process of constitution-drafting. She vigorously criticized what she called "the revolutionary constitutional discourse," which is intended, she claimed, to "accelerate the constitutional development and to ensure the conversion of Israel from a state without a supreme and rigid constitution to a state with such a constitution."[146] Gavison disagreed with the Supreme Court's activist interpretation of the 1992 Basic Laws. She argued that the Court's reading of the Basic Laws presented a false reality. She also argued that the Court's activism in constitutional matters weakened the status of the Supreme Court as a professional and objective institution. The Court was providing controversial interpretations of constitutional principles and hence was seen as taking sides in the conflict.[147] The Supreme Court, Gavison stressed, is neither authorized nor qualified to decide ideological and political questions such as the issue of religion and state, because the Supreme Court Justices tend to represent a secular-liberal-intellectual elite. In a provocative journalistic interview, which led to a Knesset debate on the matter,[148] Gavison said:

> It is not clear that the Court is better than Rabbi Ovadia Yossef [the spiritual leader of Shas, the largest Orthodox party in the Knesset], and it is not clear that the supra-legislative values of the enlightened public, on behalf of which it acts, are superior to the supra-legislative values of the religious public, for example. Many people in Israel believe that Ovadia Yossef is the supreme ethical authority.[149]

Gavison emphasized the need for broad agreement as the basis for a constitution. She advocated avoiding decisions on foundational issues until

---

[145] The public dispute received a personal dimension when Aharon Barak announced his objection to Gavison's nomination to the Supreme Court. Barak said he opposed her nomination since, in his words, "she has an agenda," referring to her criticism of the Court's activism under Barak. He later revised his position stating that Gavison should only be appointed to the Supreme Court after a cooling-off period. See: Yuval Yoaz, "Barak: Gavison Could be Appointed after a 'Cooling Off Period'," *Haaretz*, December 12, 2005.

[146] Gavison, *The Constitutional Revolution*, 58.

[147] *Ibid.*, 104–6.

[148] The Knesset had two discussions on "The Judiciary, the Rule of Law and the Interview with Professor Ruth Gavison" in November–December 1999. See Gidon Alon, "The Knesset Overturned its Own Decision: Recognized the Supreme Court's Power of Judicial Review," *Haaretz*, December 15, 1999.

[149] Ari Shavit, "The Head of the Opposition," *Haaretz*, November 12, 1999.

widespread agreement was reached, arguing that deferring the adoption of a constitution was preferable to adopting a controversial one:

> The State of Israel – because of its complex social character – needs, in principle, a rigid constitution, including a bill of rights. However, because of the same social and political character, Israel does not have the extensive agreement, regarding some of its key issues, which is necessary for a constitution.[150]

The promotion of a constitution by means of "short-cuts" and creative judicial interpretation was not, in her opinion, the proper method for enacting a constitution in Israel. "The constitution accepted in this way is not good, and its damage is greater than its advantages," she contended.[151] The dangers she specified were the intensification of ideological polarization, increased alienation of the Orthodox community from the Supreme Court, and the overall undermining of the Supreme Court's public legitimacy.

Justice Barak, for his part, made it clear that he did not fear ideological decisions. He believed that since the Knesset was reluctant or unable to take such controversial decisions, this role was now up to the Court.[152] Responding directly to Gavison's arguments, Barak noted that, unlike academics, judges are obligated to make value decisions in the cases that are before them, even if the Knesset is not.[153] During a meeting with the members of the Knesset's Constitution, Law and Justice Committee, Barak bluntly declared:

> You have determined that the Basic Laws on Human Dignity and Liberty and on Freedom of Occupation should reflect the values of the State of Israel. Who will determine what are the values of the State of Israel as a Jewish state? You did not determine … so we will determine. You did not determine what happens when the values of the State of Israel as a Jewish state clash with its values as a democratic state. We will have to determine it, because someone's life or property may depend on it.[154]

This view is advocated by liberal supporters of the Supreme Court, such as law professor Mordechai Kremnitzer, who argued that the Court's

---

[150] Gavison, *The Constitutional Revolution*, 20.

[151] *Ibid.*, 94.

[152] "The Role of the Supreme Court in Democratic Society," *Tel Aviv University Law Review* 21, no. 1 (1997). See also: Barak, *The Judge in a Democracy*, 177–89.

[153] Zeev Segal, M. Landau and Aharon Barak, "United Miztahi Bank Decision – after Three Years: A Symposium," *Hamishpat* 5 (2000): 262–3 (Hebrew).

[154] Aharon Barak, "The Criticism does not Affect our Considerations," sections of the protocol of a discussion in the Supreme Court, *Halishka: The Israeli Bar Journal* 33 (1996): 12.

actions of self-empowering to overrule Knesset legislation should be seen as the "lesser evil" in the way to promote a liberal constitution for Israel. In an article criticizing Gavison's position he wrote: "there is a need for a formal constitution, however if the legislature is making only small steps in this direction – the enactment of basic laws – the Supreme Court should follow up and give these steps their full importance and effectiveness."[155]

The debate on the appropriate role for the Supreme Court to take in a deeply divided society that lacked a written constitution also had implications for the debate on the future of the informal consociational arrangements. Gavison's position implicitly supports the compromise-based, nation-unifying principles of the consociational model, whereas Barak's actions represented a move away from the politics of accommodation in the religious sphere, toward politics of decisiveness. The Supreme Court's rulings, as well as various statements made by its Justices, who are portrayed (and who sometimes portray themselves) as the champions of Western democratic liberalism, have heightened the sense that Israeli society is involved in a cultural war between theocracy and liberal-democracy. As Asher Cohen and Bernard Susser put it, these rulings encourage a decision-oriented and crisis-dominated style in Israeli politics, instead of the compromise consociational model.[156]

Perhaps in recognition of the dangers of the Court's excessive activism and in light of the severe public criticism in the late 1990s, later statements by Chief Justice Barak have been characterized by relative moderation. In a public appearance in May 2001, Barak expressed regret for some of his statements, including the concept of "the enlightened public."[157] He also held several conciliatory meetings with various rabbinical leaders. Moreover, it is important to note that despite Chief Justice Barak's revolutionary rhetoric, under his presidency the Supreme Court has used its authority to overrule Knesset legislation only sparingly.[158]

---

[155] Mordechai Kremnitzer, "Between Progress towards and Regression from Constitutional Liberalism: On the Need for Liberal Constitution and Judicial Review of Knesset Legislation," in Yoav Dotan and Ariel Bendor, eds., *Zamir Book: On Law, Government and Society* (Jerusalem: Sacher Institute for Legislative Research and Comparative Law, Hebrew University of Jerusalem, 2005), 796 (Hebrew).

[156] Cohen and Susser, *Israel and the Politics of Jewish Identity*, ch. 4.

[157] Ilan Shahar, "Barak Apologizes for 'the Enlightened People' and for 'All is Justiciable'," *Haaretz*, May 15, 2001.

[158] Between 1995 and 2006 the Supreme Court struck down Knesset legislation in five cases: HCJ 1715/97 *Israel Investment Managers Association* v. *Minister of Finance*, PD

But despite moderating its revolutionary rhetoric, it appears that the Supreme Court has not abandoned its active involvement in decisions over the religious character of the state. HCJ rulings in several controversial religious issues have continued to raise questions about the Court's attitude toward the Orthodox community. A particularly heated dispute emerged from a February 2002 decision in which the Court for the first time granted formal recognition to Reform and Conservative conversions performed in Israel.[159] This decision reignited the fierce debate over the issue of "Who is a Jew?". The ruling was viewed as a dangerous precedent by Orthodox religious authorities, who since the founding of the state have held an effective monopoly over decisions pertaining to legal definitions of membership in the Jewish people.

This ruling, which undermined Orthodoxy's superior status, reinforced the perception that the Supreme Court was acting in collaboration with members of the Reform and Conservative communities, who are among the chief critics of the religious consociational politics in Israel, and who are excluded from these arrangements. Chief Justice Barak emphasized that the ruling was made since "there is no escape from judicial decision." Indeed, the Court, which began discussing the question of Reform and Conservative conversions in 1995, tried to avoid a decision and passed this contentious issue to the Knesset, which in turn avoided taking action to define conversions to Judaism.[160] However, the Supreme Court was not unanimous in its views, and some voiced objection to the role that the

---

51(4) 367 overruled the requirement of examination for investment managers who had fewer than seven years of professional experience; HCJ 6055/95 *Tzemach* v. *Minister of Defense*, PD 53(5) 241 overruled legislation that allowed for detention of soldiers for ninety-six hours before judicial hearing; HCJ 1030/99 *Oron* v. *Knesset Speaker* PD 56(3) 640 struck down an amendment to a telecommunications law which legalized certain illegal radio stations; HCJ 8276/05 *Adalah* v. *Minister of Defense* overruled an amendment to Israeli Civil Tort Law that prevented Palestinians from claiming compensation from Israeli defense forces in conflict zones; HCJ 1661/05 *Gaza Coast Local Council* v. *Knesset* IsrSC 59(2) 481 overruled clauses in the 2005 Disengagement Law which limited the settlers' right for compensation. Between 2006 and 2010, under the presidency of Chief Justice Dorit Beinisch, the Supreme Court overruled Knesset legislation in three cases: HCJ 8823/07 *Anonymous* v. *The State of Israel* (2008) ruled that a suspect charged with security offenses must be allowed to attend judicial detention hearings; HCJ 2605/05 *Human Rights Division* v. *Ministry of Finance* (2009) overruled the privatization of prison in Isael; HCJ 4124/00 *Arnon Yekutieli* v. *Minister of Religious Affairs* (2010) annulled guaranteed-income allowances to Orthodox Yeshiva students.

[159] HCJ 5070/95 *Naamat (Movement of Working Women and Volunteers)* v. *Ministry of the Interior* PD 56(2) 721.

[160] Zeev Segal, "Registration Recognized, but Conversion is Still Undefined," *Haaretz*, February 22, 2002.

Table 3.2 *Timeline: Israeli constitutional developments*

November 29, 1948	UN resolution 193 to establish a Jewish and an Arab states on the territory of Palestine.
May 14, 1948	Declaration of Independence of the State of Israel
June 22, 1948	Military attack against the IZL's arms ship *Altalena*.
July 8, 1948	The Provisional Council appoints a Constitutional Committee, chaired by Zerach Vehrhaftig.
January 25, 1949	Elections to the Constituent Assembly.
February 16, 1949	The Constituent Assembly passes the Transition Law and transfer itself into the first Knesset.
April 1949	The Knesset elects a Constitutional, Law and Justice Committee, chaired by Nachum Nir.
December 13, 1949	The government decides that a written constitution is not required
February 1, 1950	First Knesset discussion on the constitution.
June 16, 1950	The Knesset adopts the Harari Resolution, according to which the constitution will be enacted gradually through a series of basic laws.
February 12, 1958	The Knesset enacted the first basic law – Basic Law: the Knesset.
May 17, 1977	The right-wing party Likud receives the largest number of seats in the Knesset elections, ending 30 years of Mapai dominance.
March 1992	The Knesset passed two Basic Laws on human rights. Basic Law: Human Dignity and Liberty and Basic Law: Freedom of Occupation.
November 9, 1995	The Supreme Court established its authority of judicial review in the decision of *United Mizrahi Bank v. Migdal*.
May 18, 2003	The Knesset Law, Constitution and Justice Committee initiated "The Constitution in Broad Consent Project."
February 13, 2006	The Law, Constitution and Justice Committee presented the Knesset its final report of the "Constitution in Broad Consent Project". The Knesset passed a declaratory resolution stating it would "continue this effort, which aims to present a proposal for a constitution based on broad consent".

judicial system has assumed. In a minority opinion, the Orthodox Justice Yizchak Englard stated that "a great error has come out of this Court, which has assumed a controversial role in a difficult ideological dispute for Jewish society."[161]

Perpetual incrementalism

At the beginning of the new millenium the debate over Israel's constitution has returned to the public agenda. Many in the liberal camp argued for the need to complete the enactment of a comprehensive bill of rights, particularly in light of the deep divisions in Israeli society. Moreover, legal experts argued for the need to reorganize the existing Basic Laws into a unified and formal constitutional document.[162] They pointed to the grave shortcomings in the existing set of Basic Laws, rooted in vague instructions of the 1950 Harari Resolution. These shortcomings became significant after the constitutional revolution, which recognized the superior constitutional status of the Basic Laws above ordinary legislation.[163] Most Basic Laws, for example, were passed by a regular majority of Knesset members. They defer in their level of entrenchment and in their style of writing. Many of them are too detailed and often include directives which appeared, or should appear, in ordinary laws. Some of them are based on short-term political circumstances rather than long-term constitutional vision.[164] In addition, it has been argued that many ordinary laws that were enacted over the years should have been passed as Basic Laws due to their content and importance.[165]

---

[161] Zeev Segal, "Forcing Registration but not Defining Conversion," *Haaretz*, February 21, 2002.

[162] Mordechai Kremnitzer, David Kretzmer and Avishai Benish, *The Basic Laws as a Foundation for a Constitution.* (Jerusalem: Israel Democracy Institute 2002) (Hebrew).

[163] For detailed analysis see *ibid.*, 7–8.

[164] A good recent example is the April 7, 2009 enactment of Basic Law: the State Budget for the years 2009–2010 (special instructions) (ordinance), that introduced a temporary special arrangement according to which the Knesset must approve a two-year budget no later than 107 days (instead of forty-five days) after the formation of the government. The new Basic Law was overrode the relevant sections in Basic Law: the Knesset and in Basic Law: the State Economy. The official explanation to the bill noted that it was proposed to address the special circumstances of, on the one hand, the delay in approval of the 2009 budget due to the February 2009 elections, and on the other hand the worldwide economic crisis (www.justice.gov.il/NR/rdonlyres/BCC8F251-DDC6-4CA6-B232-63E153581B55/14463/424.pdf). On June 22, 2010 this Basic Law was amended to include a two-year budget for the years 2011 and 2012 as well.

[165] Among them are the Law of Return (1950), the Law of Citizenship (1950) and the Law of Equal Rights to Women (1951).

The emerging interest in the constitution yielded a variety of constitutional drafts, covenants and "future vision" documents, produced by numerous think tanks and NGOs. It also led the Knesset Constitution, Law and Justice Committee to discuss intensively a draft constitution during more than two years. Prime Minister Ehud Olmert announced his intention to promote the enactment of a formal constitution by the end of Israel's sixtieth year.[166] But the public and political debate was itself proof, perhaps, that the main reasons for the initial decision to refrain from drafting a constitution have not yet disappeared.

Particularly revealing are the discussions in the Constitution, Law and Justice Committee of the Israeli Knesset, which in 2003 initiated the most comprehensive endeavor to draft a constitution for the State of Israel – "The Constitution in Broad Consent Project." The declared goal of the project, which was headed by the Chair of the Committee, Knesset Member Michael Eitan, (Likud) was to consolidate a single constitutional document that would enjoy "wide support among Israelis and Jews worldwide."[167] Between 2003 and 2006, the Committee held over eighty meetings. In addition to seventeen committee members, nearly 400 experts, advisors, public figures and political leaders participated in the discussions. Hundreds of documents were submitted, relating to all aspects of constitution design – institutional, procedural, foundational and symbolic. In February 2006, the Committee presented the Knesset with its final report which included a draft constitutional proposal and over 10,000 pages of minutes and background materials.[168]

The constitutional draft is not a coherent constitutional document. Rather, as Professor Gavison, who served as chief legal advisor to the Committee, argued, if the Constitutional Committee had any substantial achievement, it was in the way it "exposed the opposing positions regarding the most fundamental constitutional questions".[169] Thus, instead of resolving the disputes that arose during the constitutional debates, the draft contained several versions and suggestions for further deliberation

[166] Shahar Ilan, "Olmert: Constitution Draft to the Knesset," *Haaretz*, October 8, 2007.

[167] *Constitution in Broad Consent: Report of the Constitution, Law and Justice Committee Regarding Proposals for the Constitution of the State of Israel* (Jerusalem: Knesset, 2006) (Hebrew).

[168] *Ibid*. English translation of the proposed constitutional draft can be found at: www.cfisrael.org.

[169] Ruth Gavison, "Constitution for Israel: Lessons from the Constitutional Process in the 16th Knesset," in *Constitution in Broad Consent: Report of the Constitution, Law and Justice Committee regarding Proposals for the Constitution of the State of Israel* (Jerusalem: Knesset, 2006).

and decision, in effect incorporating within it all of the competing positions. The Committee charged the Knesset with the task of transforming this internally inconsistent document into a comprehensive constitutional formula. The Knesset, in turn, passed a vague declaratory resolution stating that after the coming elections it would "continue this effort, which aims to present a proposal for a constitution based on broad consent, for the Knesset's decision and the people's ratification."[170] It is unlikely, however, that a broad agreement will be reached, as there is still no consensus on many key constitutional issues.[171]

The protocols of the February 2006 Knesset discussion as well as the 2003–6 extensive deliberations in the Constitution, Law and Justice Committee indicate that the intense division over the religious issues is still the central axis around which the Israeli constitutional debate revolves. As deputy welfare minister and member of the Orthodox Yahadut Ha-Torah Party Abraham Ravitz stressed during the Committee discussions:

> The main reasons that for fifty years we could not make any progress towards a constitution is that ... first, the Jewish people already have a constitution, and we should implement it in our daily life ... and second, we cannot compromise on the most fundamental issues which, from our perspective, are essential to our existence as a people.[172]

Both religious and secular Knesset members acknowledged their vast disagreement and admitted that no consensus could yet be achieved on issues such as personal status law, conversions to Judaism and public observance of the Sabbath.[173]

Despite its best intentions, the Knesset in 2006 could not avoid repeating the choice made by the first Knesset, in other words to reaffirm the

---

[170] *Knesset Record* (February 13, 2006): 70. This resolution was voted by a majority of thirty against nineteen (with one abstainer).

[171] There were also seven additional proposals for declaratory resolution that were presented by the various parties during the Knesset discussion. Three, submitted by Shas, Agudat Israel and the National Religious Party, demanded an explicit reference to the principles of the Jewish religion in the constitution. Two, submitted by Meretz and the Arab party Raam, objected to the proposed constitution on the grounds that it infringed basic rights. One proposal demanded a secular constitution, and one, presented by Degel Ha-Torah, merely suggested that the constitution be based "on consent" rather than "on broad consent." *Ibid.*

[172] "Constitution, Law and Justice Committee Discussions: Protocol 658," in *Constitution in Broad Consent* (February 2, 2006).

[173] For example, see the speeches of Knesset members Yischak Levi (National Religious Party), Ofir Pines (Labor), Zehava Galon (Meretz), Nissim Zeev (Shas) in: *ibid.*

incrementalist approach to constitution-making. Recognizing the lack of consensus regarding the foundational aspects of the constitution, Knesset members from all parts of the political spectrum called for the preservation of the existing ambiguous and informal constitutional arrangements, rather than for the entrenchment of a constitution that would mirror the political and ideological outlook of one or another segment of society.

The repeated deferral of drafting a constitution was reinforced by the concerns of both the religious and the secular camps. The religious parties feared future activist interpretations of new Basic Laws by the Supreme Court. Their objection to judicial activism and further legislation of new Basic Laws was unwavering and effective. Although since 1992 the Knesset has debated over twenty-five bills for new Basic Laws, none has passed.[174] In the words of Knesset member David Tal of Shas:

> Even if the Ten Commandments are proposed as Basic Laws we will oppose the legislation … because if I accept the Ten Commandments as Basic Laws … the Supreme Court may interpret them and overturn them.[175]

At the same time, secular-liberal Members of Knesset objected to the enactment of a constitution because they feared that the fragmented political system would produce a "bad constitution," which would be worse than none at all.[176] They criticized the proposed constitutional drafts that refrain from reforming the existing religious arrangements, particularly in the area of personal law.[177]

Six decades after independence, the project of an Israeli constitution is trapped in a paradoxical situation: on the one hand, the severe disagreements in Israeli society regarding the most fundamental norms and shared values that underpin the state, as well as the clash between the judiciary and the legislature, require a clear and entrenched constitution. On the other hand, the intense conflicts over the character of the state and over authority to decide about these issues hinder the adoption of a full constitution,

---

[174] Yehoshua Segev, "Why Does Israel Not Have and Will Not Have (at Least in the near Future) a Constitution? On the Advantages of 'the Decision Not to Decide'," *Moznei Mishpat* 5 (2006): 174–5 (Hebrew).

[175] *Knesset Record* 184 (1999): 537.

[176] Baruch Kimerling, "Constitution: A Task for Future Generations," *Haaretz*, April 19, 2005; Frances Raday, "A Constitution Only for Men?" *Haaretz*, March 27, 2006; Zehava Galon, "Better without a Constitution," *Haaretz*, November 14, 2007.

[177] See more on the problem of entrenched materialism in Chapter 7. See also: Hanna Lerner, "Entrenching the Status Quo: Religion and State in Israel's Constitutional Proposals," *Constellations* 16, no. 3 (2009): 443–61.

and many on both sides of the divide prefer the existing ambiguities to any unequivocal foundational choices that might be made.

Perhaps it is not surprising, then, that the following statement, which was made during the Knesset constitutional debate in 1950, still sounds so very relevant today:

> The fundamental question is what are constitutions for? All constitutions are designed to unite the people. The people as a whole unite around particular known, supreme principles. Do we have the shared base, a uniting base which is required for enactment of this constitution, or are we still lacking this base, and hence it would be better to conceal for now the issue of constitution-drafting? The truth is that we do not yet have the minimal common basis upon which we can build a constitution. Because this building depends on a difference in the approach to one cardinal question: what is the state of Israel? Is it a novel state, a new creature that never existed, or are we facing the renewal of the Kingdom of Israel?[178]

Constitutional incrementalism and the Arab minority in Israel

The religious–secular divide, which was the focus of this chapter, is only one of the major divisions which characterize Israeli society. As we have seen, the constitutional discussions in Israel have, since the early years of the state, focused largely on the conflict between religious and secular visions of the Jewish state. Nevertheless, the debate over the foundational aspect of the constitution, namely on the definition of Israel as Jewish and democratic, cannot be separated from the dispute over the relationship between the Jewish majority and the Arab minority in Israel. Why was the Arab population excluded from the discussions on the future constitutions in the early years of the state? And what was the effect of the incrementalist constitutional approach adopted by the Israeli government on the Arab minority in Israel? Both questions touch upon many difficult and complex political, legal and ideological disputes regarding minority–majority relations in Israel. These disputes are ideologically and normatively loaded and include not only competing perspectives regarding the future of Arab minority in Israel but also contradicting views regarding the past and conflicting understandings of the present status of Israeli Arabs. A comprehensive examination of the status of Arabs in Israel is beyond the scope of this section. Moreover, this discussion raises some speculative questions – such as what would have happened if Israel had adopted a written constitution

---

[178] *Knesset Record* 5 (1950): 1315.

in the early years of the state – which are impossible to answer. Thus, this section is intended primarily to provide some background to enable a better understanding of the relations between Israeli Arabs and the incremental-ist constitutional approach adopted by the Israeli leadership.[179]

The Israeli Declaration of Independence was explicit about its inten-tion to establish "a Jewish state in Eretz-Israel" which would be "open for Jewish immigration and for the Ingathering of the Exiles." At the same time, it declared that the State of Israel

> will foster the development of the country for the benefit of all its inhabit-ants; it will be based on freedom, justice and peace as envisaged by the prophets of Israel; it will ensure complete equality of social and political rights to all its inhabitants irrespective of religion, race or sex; it will guar-antee freedom of religion, conscience, language, education and culture; it will safeguard the Holy Places of all religions; and it will be faithful to the principles of the Charter of the United Nations.[180]

The Declaration also contained an appeal "in the very midst of the onslaught launched against us now for months – to the Arab inhabitants of the State of Israel to preserve peace and participate in the upbuilding of the State on the basis of full and equal citizenship and due representation in all its provisional and permanent institutions."[181]

Despite these sincere intentions, the struggle between the Zionist movement and the local Arab population, and the circumstances under which Israel gained independence, were dominant factors in shaping the Jewish–Palestinian relationship in the new state.[182] The 1948–9 war, which is called by the Israeli Jewish population the "War of Independence," is termed by the Israeli Palestinians "El Nakba," mean-ing "the Catastrophe," referring to the demographic collapse and the political and socio-economic disaster experienced by the Palestinians due to the war and to the establishment of the Jewish state.[183] According

---

[179] Since 1967, the politics of the Arab minority within Israel is tightly linked to the conflict between Israel and the Palestinians in the West Bank in Gaza. However, this section is limited to discussing the internal Israeli debate between Jews and Arabs who are citizens of the state.

[180] The Declaration of the Establishment of the State of Israel. See official translation in: www.knesset.gov.il/docs/eng/megilat_eng.htm.

[181] *Ibid.*

[182] Yosef Gorny, *Zionism and the Arabs 1882–1948: A Study of Ideology* (Oxford: Clarendon Press, 1987).

[183] The exact number of those who left, as well as the reason for their departure – whether they were forced to leave by the Jewish army, or chose to leave hoping to return after the end of the war – are still debated by historians. Benny Morris, *The Birth of the*

to estimates, out of between 750,000–900,000 non-Jews who lived in the territory that later became the State of Israel, around 600,000–750,000 left for neighboring countries.[184] As a result, in 1949, the Arab minority in Israel comprised 14 percent of the Israeli population, which was about 1,173,900 at the time.[185] In the years that followed, the Jewish population increased dramatically through waves of immigration of Jews from around the world. Nevertheless, the Arab citizenry remained around 20 percent of the Israeli population for the next six decades, particularly due to a high birth rate.[186]

Until 1966 Israeli Arabs were under military rule which limited their freedom of movement and their freedom of occupation. They lived under military supervision and military law which also restricted their political rights.[187] Since the abolition of military rule in 1966, Israeli Palestinians have enjoyed formal civic and political rights. Nevertheless, they were consistently excluded from Israeli nationhood which had always been understood in terms of Jewish identity.[188] While the Arab population living in the territory of Israel soon became citizens of the state,[189] enjoying formal political and civil rights, they were never included in the Israeli

---

Palestinian Refugee Problem Revisited (Cambridge University Press, 2004); Ilan Pappe, *The Ethnic Cleansing of Palestine* (Oxford: Oneworld, 2006). On the "historians debate" in this context see: Tuvia Friling, ed., *An Answer to a Post-Zionist Colleague* (Tel Aviv: Yediot Achronot and Sifrei Hemed, 2003) (Hebrew); Efraim Karsh, *Fabricating Israeli History: The "New Historians"* (London and Portland: Frank Cass, 2000); Eugene L. Rogan and Avi Shlaim, eds., *The War for Palestine: Rewriting the History of 1948* (Cambridge University Press, 2001).

[184] Morris, *The Birth of the Palestinian Refugee Problem Revisited*, 601–4.

[185] Central Bureau of Statistics, *Statistical Abstract of Israel 2009*.

[186] In 2009, the non-Jewish population is Israel comprised 20.1 percent of the Israeli population. For decades, the Arab birth rate was 50 percent higher than the Jewish birth rate. However in recent years the Arab birth rate has been decreasing and it is now only 33 percent higher than the Jewish birth rate. Central Bureau of Statistics, *Statistical Abstract of Israel 2009*.

[187] Menachem Hofnung, *Israel – Security Needs Versus the Rule of Law* (Jerusalem: Nevo, 1991); Ian Lustick, *Arabs in the Jewish State: Israel's Control of a National Minority* (Austin: University of Texas Press, 1980).

[188] Yoav Peled argues that, for that reason, their citizenship was always constrained. They never enjoyed equal citizenship rights understood in Israel in republican terms. Peled, "Ethnic Democracy and the Legal Construction of Citizenship."

[189] The 1952 Nationality Law allowed non-Jews to become Israeli citizens under certain conditions, such as proven residency in the area which became Israeli territory after the establishment of the state, from the day of the state's establishment to the day the law came into effect (section 3a(3)). This condition was annulled by the 1980 Amendment of the law. Kretzmer, *The Legal Status of the Arabs in Israel*, 36–40.

discourse of ethno-republican citizenship.[190] In the words of Gershon Shafir and Yoav Peled, "Jewish ethnic background was a necessary condition for membership in the political community and for contributing to the process of the Zionist redemption."[191] The exclusion of non-Jews from Israeli nationhood is reflected in national emblems such as the flag and national anthem, in state ceremonies and in legislation.[192] Such legislation includes, for example, the Law of Return, which grants Jews the right to immigrate to Israel and settle there, and the exclusion of Arab population from military service, which is obligatory for all Jewish citizens.[193] Another example is the restriction on participation in the parliamentary process of parties that deny the particularistic definition of Israel as a state of the Jewish people.[194] As legal scholar David Kretzmer argues, this law implies that "the state is the state of the Jews, both those presently resident in the country as well as those resident abroad. Even if the Arabs have equal rights on all other levels the implication is abundantly clear: Israel is not *their* state."[195]

The non-participation of Israeli Arabs in the constitutional debates is another expression of the exclusion of the Arab minority from Israeli nationhood. As we have seen, in 1948–50 the dispute over the foundational aspect of the constitution, namely over the state's vision and ultimate goals that should underpin the state, focused on the religious–secular schism within the Jewish majority population. The first constitutional committee, chaired by Zerach Warhaftig, did not include Arab members and did not discuss proposals made by Arab representatives. In his memoir on the constitutional debates Warhaftig refrained from including any reference to the Arab minority or to potential implications of proposed constitutional provisions on the Arab population in Israel. The first

---

[190] For excellent detailed study of Israel Arabs' group rights see: Ilan Saban, "The Collective Rights of Arab-Palestinian Minority in Israel: The 'Is', the 'Isn't' and the Taboo," *Iyunei Mishpat* 26 (2002).

[191] Shafir and Peled, *Being Israeli*, 156.

[192] Kimerling, "Religion, Nationality and Democracy in Israel"; Smooha, "Minority Status in an Ethnic Democracy"; Peled, "Ethnic Democracy and the Legal Construction of Citizenship," 434–5.

[193] Except for Jewish Orthodox students and religious Jewish women. See: Shafir and Peled, *Being Israeli*, 157.

[194] Kretzmer, *The Legal Status of the Arabs in Israel*, 31. According to amended Basic Law: the Knesset (section 7A) "A list of candidates shall not participate in the elections for the Knesset if its aims of actions, expressly or by implication, point to one of the following: (1) denial of the existence of the State of Israel as the state of the Jewish people; (2) denial of the democratic nature of the state; (3) incitement of racism."

[195] *Ibid.* (italics in the original text).

Knesset Constitution, Law and Justice Committee, which was supposed to draft the constitution, included one non-Jewish member: Amin-Salim Jarjora, representative of the Nazareth Democratic Party.[196] At the opening session of the Constituent Assembly Jarjora stated (in Arabic) that "it is regrettable that Arab representation in the Constituent Assembly has not found its full expression. This fact places upon us a dual responsibility concerning the realization of the tasks developing upon us towards the Arabs of the State of Israel."[197] However, the Constitution Committee never drafted a constitution, and the Knesset soon decided to defer the enactment of the constitution to the future.

Some scholars argue that members of the then-ruling party, Mapai, saw the need to limit the civic rights of the Palestinian minority as one of the reasons that led the Knesset in 1950 to avoid enacting a constitution that included a comprehensive bill of rights.[198] Whether or not this was one of the main reasons that a constitution was not adopted is still debated. Equally contentious is the question of whether a written constitution would have better protected minority rights in Israel during the first decades of the state. Ultimately, of course, the answer to this question would depend on the content of the constitution adopted. At first glance, one could argue that a written liberal constitution would have better protected minority rights in Israel.[199] However, since from the very beginning the debate on the Israeli constitution did not focus on its content but rather on the question of whether a constitution should be written at all, it is difficult to estimate what constitution could have been adopted by the Israeli Constituent Assembly. Given the violent conflict between the Jewish and Palestinian populations at independence, and the Zionist goals of strengthening the Jewish identity of the state in the early years, it remains an open question whether a written constitution would

---

[196] Three Arab representatives were elected to the Constituent Assembly, which became the first Knesset. Taufik Tubi was member of the Israeli Communist Party (which later became Hadash) and served in the Knesset until 1990. The other two members comprised the Nazareth Democratic Party: Amin-Salim Jarjora, a Christian lawyer who served in the first Knesset and later became the mayor of Nazareth, and Seif E-Din E-Zoubialso, who was an MK until 1979.

[197] *Knesset Record* 1 (February 15, 1949). An English translation of this speech is in Jacob M. Landau, *The Arabs in Israel: A Political Study* (Oxford University Press, 1969).

[198] Shapira, *Politicians as a Hegemonic Class*, 33.

[199] This argument was made, for example, by Sammy Samooha, who claimed that "in the absence of a written constitution or a bill of rights with a superior standing over other law … Arabs lack an independent legal base to fight unfair treatment" Smooha, "Minority Status in an Ethnic Democracy," 12.

have prevented or entrenched discriminatory policies toward the Arab minority.[200] For example, a written constitution could have provided an entrenched constitutional status to the Jewish Agency and the Jewish National Fund, which were two major institutions for promoting Jewish settlements in the pre-state era, and which continued to function after the establishment of the state.[201] These institutions were responsible for the unequal allocation of national land between Jewish and Arab settlements. Thus, it is difficult to determine whether a formal constitution would have better protected the rights of Arabs in the Jewish state. I will return to this hypothetical question when I discuss below the evolution of the principle of equality in Israeli constitutional law.

In contrast to the passive role played by Israeli Arabs during the constitutional debates in the first years of the state, Arab political and intellectual leaders played a more active role during the renewed constitutional discussion half a century later. This change was reflected most significantly in the publication of three constitutional proposals in 2005 by leading Arab intellectuals and NGOs.[202] These documents, collectively termed "the vision documents," were initially written as a reaction to the

---

[200] During the internal Mapai discussions, for example, Yosef Lam argued in support of an immediate constitution-writing: "If we think that the Arabs in Israel will get stronger, than within a year or two or three we can have more Arabs than today and our position in the debate on the constitution will be difficult. Today, with the Arabs in the Knesset and in the state we can manage." *Meeting of Mapai Party in the Knesset and Party Secretariat*, 14 June 1949.

[201] *The Jewish Agency for Israel (JAFI)* was founded in 1922 and was recognized by the League of Nations as the representative of Jewish community interests to the British Mandate government. After the establishment of Israel JAFI retained responsibilities for Jewish immigration to the new state, land settlement, youth work, and relations with world Jewry. This was confirmed by the World Zionist Organization–Jewish Agency (Status) Law adopted by the Knesset in 1952. *The Jewish National Fund (JNF)* was founded in 1901 by the World Zionist Movement. Its goal was to purchase land in Palestine for Jewish settlement. In 1960, the Knesset passed Basic Law: Israel Lands, to ensure that the state lands, which constitute about 90 percent of the lands in Israel, should remain national property. The law prohibits the transfer of ownership over lands owned by the state, the Development Authority or the Jewish National Fund, either by sale or by any other means, with the exception of types of land or transactions that have been specified in the law. For critical discussion of land in Israel see: Oren Yiftachel, *Ethnocracy: Land and Identity Politics in Israel/Palestine* (Philadelphia: The University of Pennsylvania Press, 2006).

[202] These documents include: the "Future Vision" of the National Committee for the Heads of Arab Local Authorities in Israel; the "Haifa Document," published in the framework of Mada Al-Carmel, The Arab Center for Applied Social Research; and the "Democratic Constitution" published by Adalah, The Legal Center for Arab Minority Rights in Israel.

non-participation of Arab representatives in parliamentary and extra-parliamentary initiatives to draft constitutional proposals which preserve the status quo in the relationship between the Jewish majority and the Palestinian minority in Israel.[203] In order to increase their influence on the public debate on the constitution, Arab political and public leaders published three vision documents, which included proposals for constitutional provisions to be considered by the drafters of the future Israeli constitution.

Despite the differences between the three vision documents, they all reflected a change in the type of demands for equality and full citizenship voiced by Israeli Palestinians. In the first decades of the state, the Arab leadership framed its demands in terms of equal individual rights. However, since the 1980s Arab political parties and public leaders begun formulating their demands in terms of collective national rights, demanding formal state recognition as a national minority.[204] This shift was expressed in an increasing Palestinian demand to redefine the identity of the State of Israel, calling for the transformation of the state from its definition as "Jewish and democratic" into a liberal-democratic state "for all its citizens," where the Palestinians will be recognized as a national minority.[205] This view rested on a growing recognition among Arab leaders and intellectuals that equality could only be achieved if the state recognized the Arab minority as a legitimate national collective and the Jewish hegemony was abandoned.[206] The Arab political leadership therefore demanded equal participation in defining the main characteristics of the state, including its most fundamental symbols and the right to power sharing.

---

[203] The Knesset Constitution, Law and Justice Committee did include one Arab representative (out of seventeen), but the influence of the Palestinian positions of the Committee's final report was limited. Similarly, civil society initiatives to draft a "constitution by consent" (e.g. the initiative of the Israeli Democracy Institute) rarely include Arab members among their drafters.

[204] Jamal, "Strategies of Minority Struggle for Equality in Ethnic States." As'ad Ghanem, *The Palestinian-Arab Minority in Israel, 1948–2000* (New York: State University of New York Press, 2001).

[205] According to polls, 90 percent of the Israeli Arab population supports this view. Sammy Smooha, *Index of Arab-Jewish Relations in Israel* (Haifa: The Jewish-Arab Center, University of Haifa, 2004), 89.

[206] Amal Jamal, "The Contradictions of State-Minority Relations in Israel: The Search for Clarifications," *Constellations* 16, no. 3 (2009): 504. See also: Yoused T. Jabareen, "Constitution Building and Equality in Deeply Divided Societies: The Case of the Palestinian-Arab Minority in Israel," *Wisconsin International Law Journal* 26, no. 2 (2008).

As mentioned earlier, the Knesset eventually reaffirmed the incrementalist constitutional approach. Despite pledges by all political leaders to promote the adoption of a written constitution, in practice the constitutional discussions faded away and disappeared from both the parliamentary and the public agenda. The perpetuation of the incrementalist constitutional approach was supported by Knesset members from all parts of the political spectrum – religious and secular, as well as Arab representatives. They argued that given the vast disagreements regarding the ultimate values and goals of the state, it was better to avoid taking a decision than to entrench in the constitution a bad compromise. This position was also taken by MK Abed el-Malech Dahamsha, of the Arab Ra'am Party, who claimed that "If the constitution does not guarantee entrenched minority group rights, and since we lived for 57 years without a constitution, it is better to wait for better days when a constitution will be enacted."[207]

This is the rationale underlying the incrementalist constitutional approach, according to which it is better to defer decisions in controversial issues since perhaps future social and political conditions will allow for a broader consensus. Whether such a strategy will indeed allow for better protection of minority rights in Israel is a complex question which is difficult to answer. Because analysis of past developments, as well as of the current conditions of Arabs in Israel, raises intense debates and disagreements, it is problematic to attempt to rely on the historical record in order to understand the effect of the incrementalist constitutional approach on the Arab citizens of Israel. For example, one of the most heated disputes among legal and political scholars revolves around the question of whether the 1992 enactment of Basic Laws: Human Dignity and Liberty contributed in any way to the promotion of equality between Arab and Jewish citizens in Israel.

In the absence of a written constitution, the principle of equality was recognized by the court as one of the normative pillars underpinning Israel's judicial system.[208] The Knesset passed several laws regarding specific areas of equality, such as the Equal Rights for Women Law (1951). However, the principle of equality was never entrenched by the legislators as a constitutional principle, and was not included in a Basic Law. This was no accident. In fact, the dispute over the principle of equality was the

---

[207] Abed el Maleck Dahamsha, *Knesset Record* (February 13, 2006): 76.
[208] Yitzhak Zamir and Moshe Sobel, "Equality before the Law," *Mishpat Umimshal: Law and Government in Israel* 5 (2000).

greatest obstacle to the enactment in 1992 of Basic Law: Human Liberty and Dignity, and came close to preventing its passing.[209] To what extent Basic Law: Human Dignity and Liberty does in fact provide a constitutional status for the principle of equality is a question still left open.[210] Indeed, former Supreme Court Chief Justice Aharon Barak has argued that "Basic Law: Human Dignity and Liberty includes the prohibition of discrimination."[211] This view was even stated in the 1995 High Court of Justice ruling against military policy of rejecting all women from aviation courses.[212] As Supreme Court Justice Dalia Dorner explained in her concurring opinion: "Discrimination against a person because he belongs to a group, and in our case discrimination against women, violates the right to dignity."[213] Nevertheless, she also emphasized that she

> doubts whether it is possible – or at least, whether it is proper – to hold by means of construction that the purpose of the Basic Law is to provide constitutional protection to the principle of general equality. The clear intention of the legislator, as can be seen from the draft versions, was precisely not to enshrine this general principle in the Basic Law. The draft versions of a law are a factor in determining its purpose ... Admittedly, the significance of the draft versions – which reveal the intentions of the members of the Knesset who enacted the Law – decreases with the passage of time since the legislation was passed, and the occurrence of political, social or legal changes that may justify a deviation from these intentions. But only a few years have passed since the enactment of the Basic Law, and *prima facie* the Basic Law should not be construed in a way that conflicts with its purpose as can be seen from the draft versions.[214]

To date the Court has not used its powers to overrule a legislative act on the basis of the principle of equality as interpreted based on Basic

[209] Yehudit Karp, "Basic Law: Human Liberty and Dignity – a Biography of Power Struggles," *Mishpat Umimshal* 1 (1993).

[210] Hillel Sommer, Tamar Waldman and Anat Yahav, "Constitutional Right of Equality" (Presented to the Knesset Committee of Constitution, Law and Justice, 2005), 15–16.

[211] Aharon Barak, "The Constitutional Revolution – Bath Mitzvah," *Law and Business* 1 (2004): 42.

[212] HCJ 4541/94 *Alice Miller* v. *The Minister of Defense* PDI 49(4) 94. This view was restated in HCJ 6427/02 *The Movement for Quality Government in Israel* v. *The Knesset* [2006], which concerned the constitutionality of the Postponement of Military Service for Yeshiva Students whose Torah Is Their Calling Law (known as Tal Law), passed by the Knesset in 2002. In this ruling the scope of the principle of equality protected by the Basic Law: Human Dignity and Equality was somewhat extended to include any infringement of equality that can be closely associated with violation of personal autonomy.

[213] HCJ 4541/94 *Alice Miller* v. *The Minister of Defense* PDI 49(4) 94, 42.

[214] *Ibid.*, 44.

Law: Human Dignity and Equality. And in the particular context of state discrimination against Arab citizens, the Supreme Court has been criticized for applying the principles of equality and affirmative action to a lesser degree than it has in cases of discrimination against women.[215]

Thus, the effect of the incrementalist constitutional approach on the status of Israeli Arabs is difficult to estimate. Attempts to address this question rely on conflicting views regarding the legal and political developments of the status of Arab citizens, as well as on opposing views of the future of majority–minority relations in Israel. Some social scientists present a pessimistic picture of the evolution of Arab minority rights in Israel. According to this perspective, recent years have been characterized not by increasing protection of, but rather increasing threats to, Arab political and civic rights. While the Supreme Court has issued some rulings that recognize the structural discrimination of the state against its Arab citizens, the Knesset has passed several laws whose intent was to entrench the exclusive Jewish character of the state and to make it more difficult for Arab citizens to participate in the Israeli political system.[216] Thus, for example, the 2002 amendment to the election law placed new restrictions on political parties by forbidding them to support, explicitly or implicitly, the armed struggle of a state or terrorist organization against the State of Israel, and prohibited any expression or conduct by Knesset Members that negated the existence of the State of Israel as the state of the Jewish people.[217] In addition, the citizenship laws were amended to prevent family unification where the marriage of the Israeli citizen was with a person from an enemy state (including, for these purposes, the Palestinian territories). This was perceived by Arab citizens as depriving them of their basic right and as creating, "for the first time, an explicit, if only consequential, distinction between their individual citizenship rights and those of Israel's Jewish citizens."[218] According to this view, while there has been an incremental improvement in the protection of individual rights of Arab citizens, Israel is still very far from fulfilling the requirements of a liberal-democratic system, and the Israeli polity should

---

[215] Meital Pinto and Hillel Sommer, "From Particular Legislation to General Doctrine: The Role of the Judiciary in Entrenching Affirmative Action in Israel," in *Affirmative Action and Guarantees of Representation in Israel*, ed. Anat Maor (Tel Aviv: Ramot, Tel Aviv University Press, 2005).

[216] Jamal, "The Contradictions of State–Minority Relations in Israel," 499; Shafir and Peled, *Being Israeli*.

[217] Jamal, "The Contradictions of State–Minority Relations in Israel," 500.

[218] Yoav Peled, "Citizenship Betrayed: Israel's Emerging Immigration and Citizenship Regime," *Theoretical Inquiries in Law* 8, no. 2 (2007).

be understood in terms of an "ethnic democracy"[219] or even a non-democratic "ethnocracy."[220]

Some historians and legal scholars, however, claim that, overall, the protection of Arab political and civic rights in Israel has increased over the years, despite the lack of a formal bill of rights. According to this view, while socio-economic discrimination still exists against Arabs in Israel, discrimination against Arab citizens in Israel has been decreasing due to changes in policy as well as to a series of judicial decisions, particularly since the 1990s.[221] Thus, for example, in 2000 the government adopted a multi-year program of affirmative action, and Knesset legislation guaranteed equal representation of Arabs in the civil service, and canceled the special children allowance given to families of IDF soldiers.[222] The Supreme Court, in a series of decisions, ruled against structural discrimination against Arab citizens in allocation of public funding and state land, and required dual-language signs in mixed Arab–Jewish cities.[223] According to this view, the Arab demands for full collective (as opposed to purely individual) rights will never be met due to the inherent conflict between these demands and the definition of Israel as state for the Jewish people.[224] The question of the implementation of the principle of equality in Israel is complex, write legal scholars Amnon Rubinstein and Barak Medina:

> On the one hand it is clear that a respect for individual rights that is based on the status of citizenship is not enough to completely fulfill the principle of equality, since membership in a particular group, and thus group rights, are critical aspect of human existence. However, on the other

[219] Sammy Smooha, "Ethnic Democracy: Israel as an Archetype," *Israel Studies* 2, no. 2 (1997).

[220] Yiftachel, *Ethnocracy.*

[221] Rubinstein and Medina, *Constitutional Law of the State of Israel*, 459–63; Alexander Yakobson and Amnon Rubinstein, *Israel and the Family of Nations: Jewish Nation State and Human Rights* (Tel Aviv: Schocken, 2003), 179–87.

[222] For critical analysis which points to substantial gap between government statements and actual representation of Arabs in Israeli civil service see Yaser Awad and Ali Haider, "Representation of Arab Population in the Civil Service 2006–2007" (Sikkuy, The Association for the Advancement of Civic Equality in Israel, 2008).

[223] See for example: HCJ 6698/95 *Ka'adan* v. *Israel Land Administration*; HCJ 4112/99 *Adalah et al.* v. *The Municipalities of Tel Aviv-Jaffa et al.* HCJ 2773/98 and HCJ 1163/03 *The High Follow-Up Committee for the Arab Citizens in Israel et al.* v. *the Prime Minister of Israel.*

[224] Rubinstein and Medina, *Constitutional Law of the State of Israel*, 414; Yakobson and Rubinstein, *Israel and the Family of Nations*; Ruth Gavison, "Jewish and Democratic? A Rejoinder to the 'Ethnic Democracy' Debate," *Israel Studies* 4, no. 1 (1999).

hand, the character of the state as a Jewish state – and not as a bi-national, Jewish-Arab, or as a "civic" nation-state – is a given, and it implies that the scope of protection of group rights for the Jewish collective is more substantial than that of the Arab collective in Israel.[225]

In the absence of a written constitution, the task of balancing Israel's character as both Jewish and democratic is often left to the judicial system, which is required to make controversial choices under conditions of deep societal and political divisions. Whether the legal system is the appropriate venue for advancing a particular worldview under conditions of deep societal and political divisions is disputed, as we have already discussed above. Former Chief Justice Barak expressed his cautious approach in one of the landmark Arab anti-discrimination decisions of recent years. In *Ka'adan* v. *Israel Land Administration* (March 2000) the Supreme Court struck down state prohibition of selling property to an Arab family in a Jewish community town which was built on state land. The ruling was criticized, on the one hand, as representing judicial intervention in the highly sensitive political dispute regarding Jewish–Palestinian relations in Israel.[226] On the other hand, it was criticized for refraining from advancing a more significant change toward greater Jewish–Arab equality.[227] Barak, who wrote the majority opinion in this case, was aware of the difficult role played by the court:

> We must keep in mind that we are taking the first step on a difficult and sensitive path. It is therefore appropriate that we step heel to toe so that we do not stumble and fall but rather advance carefully from case to case, according to the circumstances of each case. However, even if the road before us is long, it is important that we always bear in mind, not only whence we came, but also to where we are headed.[228]

---

[225] Amnon Rubinstein and Barak Medina, *Constitutional Law of the State of Israel*, 6th edn. (Tel Aviv: Schocken, 2005) 463.

[226] Ruth Gavison, "Zionism in Israel? The Ka'adan Ruling," *Mishpat Umimshal: Law and Government in Israel* 6 (2001); Steven V. Mazie, "Importing Liberalism: *Brown* v. *Board of Education* in the Israeli Context," *Polity* 36, no. 3 (2004); Shimon Shitrit, "The Issues of Equality and Separate Inhabitation in Community Settlements and Villages: Was the *Ka'adan* Ruling Inevitable?" *Karka (Land): A Journal for Discussing Land Issues* 56, no. 27–65 (2003).

[227] Marwan Dalal, "The Guest, the House, and the Judge: A Reading in the Unread in the Qa'dan Decision," *Adalah's Review* 2 (2000); Ronen Shamir, "Zionism 2000: Past, Future, and the Qa'dan Family," *Adalah's Review* 2 (2000); Neta Ziv, "Communities, Lawyers, and Legal Strategies for Social Change – Before and After Qa'dan," *Adalah's Review* 2 (2000).

[228] HCJ *Ka'adan* v. *Israel Land Administration* CA 6698/95.

Whether the adoption of a constitution in the early years of the state would have made such steps easier, is a question left open for further discussion. The challenge of promoting liberal values in the absence of written constitutional provisions will be further discussed in Chapter 7, where I address the difference between formal and non-formal mechanisms of constitutional amendment.

4

Constructive ambiguity in India

> The real work of this Constituent Assembly ... is the high adventure of giving shape, in the printed and written word, to a Nation's dream and aspirations.
>
> Jawaharal Nehru, *Constituent Assembly Debates*, vol. I, p. 59

One of the major political goals of India's leaders at independence was to forge a common national identity in the face of unparalleled social and cultural diversity. Translating this goal into legal language of constitutional formulations was the greatest challenge for the Indian Constituent Assembly when it drafted the constitution between December 1946 and January 1950. The aim of this chapter is to examine how the Indian framers addressed this challenge and how they navigated the country's seemingly irresolvable tensions.

India, the second most populated country in the world, is one of the most diverse in religious, cultural, ethnic and linguistic terms. The Muslim community is the largest religious minority in India. Constituting roughly 20 percent of India's population prior to partition, even after partition the Muslim community still comprised 10 percent of the population, making India the third largest Muslim country in the world. Other important religious minorities are Sikhs, Christians, Buddhists, Jains and Parsis; all together their share in the population is around 5 percent. Hindus, who comprise around 83 percent of India's population, are themselves socially segmented into thousands of sects, castes and subcastes, traditionally stratified and ranked in hierarchical order. India is extremely linguistically diverse as well. At independence there were close to twenty languages spoken by communities numbering at least one million people each, and the total number of lesser represented languages and dialects exceeded 1,600. Hindi was spoken by no more than 40 percent of the population[1]. In addition to the vast religious, cultural and linguistic diversity, the

---

[1] The 1951 Census of India reported that Hindi, Urdu, Hindustani and Punjabi were all together spoken by 42 percent of the population. *Census of India, Paper No. 1: Languages*

framers faced the challenge of incorporating under the constitution the 562 princely states, which for the most part had their own monarchic traditions, together with what was then British India. In some rare cases this was achieved by military force.[2]

Unlike Israel, which was unable to resolve its own internal tensions and consequently resorted to refraining from drafting a constitution altogether, in India the possibility of not adopting a written constitution was never considered. From its inception, the demand of the Indian nationalist movement for self-government was conceived in constitutional terms. The first known "Constitution of India Bill," dated May 8, 1895, represents a non-formal attempt to draft a constitution for India.[3] In May 1928 the All Party Conference appointed a committee to consider and determine the principles of the constitution for India, chaired by Motilal Nehru, which published its report in August that year, including specific constitutional recommendations. In 1934 the first formal demand for an independent Indian Constituent Assembly was made in a resolution of the Swaraj (self-government) Party conference.[4] As independence approached, it was clear that a written constitution was needed in order to tie together the vast and diverse components of India's federal system. The main difficulty was to agree on its content, given the country's tremendous diversity and internal tensions that ran along religious, ethnic, linguistic, social and economic lines.

Thus, unlike their Israeli counterparts, the Indian drafters included the incrementalist strategy in a written constitution. They adopted ambiguous provisions in order to avoid making difficult, unequivocal choices with respect to the most contested foundational issues. Two particular disputes will be used to illustrate this strategy: the uniform civil code and the national language.

The incrementalist approach was not adopted by the Indian framers to address all conflicts and disputes that arose during the three years of constitutional deliberations. The drafting of a constitution was perceived by

1951 Census. (India Republic Census Commissioner, 1954) 6–7. The 1961 census distinguished between the results of these four languages, and reported that Hindi was spoken by 30.37% of the total population. R. C. Nigam, *Language Handbook on Mother Tongues in Census*, Census of India 1971, New Delhi, 1972.

[2] Narendra Luther, *Hyderabad: Memoirs of a City* (Hyderabad: Orient Longman, 1995).

[3] B. Shiva Rao, *The Framing of India's Constitution*, vol. V (New Delhi: The Indian Institute of Public Administration, 1966), 1. The text of the Bill appears in *ibid.*, 5. This five-volume collection chronicles the historical documents of the Constituent Assembly and includes many of the documents, letters, reports and resolutions which were related to process of the making of the Indian constitution.

[4] *Ibid.*, 76.

India's leadership as a vehicle for advancing not only political unity but also solid democratic order and a comprehensive social reform in a country marked by widespread illiteracy, endemic poverty and entrenched social hierarchies. These goals were achieved by various institutional mechanisms. For example, India's democracy was designed as a "top-down" federalism comprising a centralized administration, a federal government with extensive financial and legislative powers, a unified court system, single citizenship and universal franchise.[5] It represented a commitment to social reform by abolishing untouchability and by entrenching caste-based affirmative action programs and civil liberties and individual rights.[6]

There is considerable debate among scholars over the achievements and failures of the Indian constitution and the degree to which these can be attributed to the character of India's democracy. This chapter will not address all aspects of this debate.[7] Its main purpose is to explore a particular constitutional strategy that was adopted by the drafters in order to manage the ideological tensions between competing visions of Indian identity at a time when resolution of these tensions was seen as impossible. It will trace the two stages, before and after partition, of the making of India's constitution. It will show how in both stages the drafting of the constitution brought to the fore a struggle between competing perceptions of Indian nationalism – between an exclusivist model that regarded national identity as homogeneous and uniform, and an inclusivist model that permitted variety and diversity. Before partition, the dispute over the foundational aspects of the Indian constitution and the kind of nationalism that it should reflect was primarily between the largely Hindu Congress Party, which envisioned a centralized federal state based on a pluralistic conception of Indian national identity, and the Muslim League,

---

[5] Granville Austin, *Working a Democratic Constitution: The Indian Experience* (New Delhi and New York: Oxford University Press, 1999), 146.

[6] For a comprehensive study on caste in India see: Nicholas B. Dirks, *Castes of Mind: Colonialism and the Making of Modern India* (Princeton and Oxford: Princeton University Press, 2001).

[7] The debate over the nature of India's democracy encompasses extensive literature. To name just few excellent recent examples of the different approaches in the debate see Rajeev Bhargava, ed., *Politics and Ethics of the Indian Constitution* (New Delhi: Oxford University Press, 2008); Steven I. Wilkinson, *Votes and Violence: Electoral Competition and Ethnic Violence in India* (Cambridge University Press, 2004); Ashutosh Varshney, *Ethnic Conflict and Civic Life: Hindus and Muslims in India* (New Haven and London: Yale University Press, 2002); Ashutosh Varshney, "Why Democracy Survives," *Journal of Democracy*, 9, no. 3 (1998): 36–50; Sanjay Ruparelia, "How the Politics of Recognition Enabled India's Democratic Exceptionalism," *International Journal of Politics, Culture, and Society*, 21, no. 4 (2008): 39–56.

which perceived nationalism as implying a high degree of uniformity, and which consequently viewed Hindu dominance in a majoritarian democratic system as a threat. After partition, the dispute on whether Indian unity required cultural uniformity (which, of course, would be essentially based on the culture of the Hindu majority) or could accommodate diversity, continued in the Congress-dominated Constituent Assembly. This was primarily because even after partition India remained extremely diverse religiously, culturally and linguistically.

To a certain extent, partition was the consequence of the failure to draft a constitution – or even to form a Constituent Assembly – that was acceptable to the Muslim leadership. After partition, it was clear that a different approach would be needed. In light of the intense tensions around foundational issues, the Assembly discussed such questions as the appropriate methods of constitutional decision-making given the existing societal tensions, and whether the constitution should be essentially descriptive or prescriptive in issues relating to linguistic and religious identity. Ultimately, the framers opted for constitutional incrementalism rather than revolutionism in such matters. Instead of making unequivocal choices, the constitutional drafters formulated intentionally ambiguous provisions, choosing to defer controversial choices to the future. The consequences of this constitutional approach are still very much alive today.[8]

A proposal for regional federalism: the Cabinet Mission plan

At the beginning of March 1946 three members of the British Cabinet – the Secretary of State for India Lord Pethick-Lawrence, the President of the Board of Trade Sir Stafford Cripps and the First Lord of the Admiralty Mr. A. V. Alexander – arrived in New Delhi. Their mission was to formulate a legal structure that would resolve what the British referred to as "the Indian problem," namely the rift between the Hindu majority and the Muslim minority, and which they regarded as the major obstacle to the transition of power into Indian hands.[9] The British government assumed that the two communities could not resolve their differences on their own; the goal of the Cabinet Mission was to settle the conflict between the Congress and the

---

[8] Some of these consequences will be discussed in the last section of this chapter, however mostly they will be discussed in Chapter 7.

[9] In 1944, the British historian Reginald Coupland, who was a member of the Cripps Mission, published three volumes under the title "The Indian Problem: Report on the Constitutional Problem in India." In the report, he stated that it is "in the Hindu–Muslim schism which that conflict reflects, that the supreme obstacle to an agreement is to be found." Reginald Coupland, *The Indian Problem: Report on the Constitutional Problem in India* (New York and London: Oxford University Press, 1944), part III, p. 16.

Muslim League and to facilitate a smooth transfer of power, while maintaining legal continuity between the existing political order and its successor.

The members of the Cabinet Mission held intensive negotiations with representatives of the various religious groups in India for two-and-a-half months. On May 16, 1946 they published a plan for a general framework of the government of an independent India, which included a proposal for the structure of its Constituent Assembly. According to the plan, India was to be formed as a federal state, composed of provinces that incorporated both British India and the princely states. The authority of the Union (i.e. the federal government) was to be limited to only three areas: foreign affairs, communications and defense. The Union government was also granted the power to raise the finances required for state action in these areas.[10] The plan provided that "any question raising a major communal issue in the legislature should require for its decision a majority of the representatives present and voting from each of the two communities."[11] In all other issues the provinces would enjoy full autonomy.

The most controversial part of the plan was to organize the provinces into three geographical groupings, with each grouping having a regional parliament and government (Table 4.1). One of the groupings would be predominantly Hindu (consisting of Madras, Bombay, United Provinces, Bihar, Central Provinces and Orissa), one predominantly Muslim (including Punjab, Sind and the North-West Frontier Province), and a third in which the populations of the two communities would be nearly equal (Bengal and Assam). The constitutions of the federal union and of each region were to provide that "any province could, by a majority vote in the legislative assembly, call for a reconsideration of the terms of the constitution after an initial period of ten years and at ten yearly intervals thereafter."[12]

On the basis of this general framework, the Cabinet Mission made its recommendations for the Constituent Assembly that would draft the Union constitution. While stating its preference for a broadly elected assembly, the Mission acknowledged that universal adult suffrage would lead to a "wholly unacceptable delay in the formation of the new constitution." It therefore recommended "utiliz[ing] the recently-elected provincial legislative assemblies as the electing body,"[13] in full knowledge of the fact that these assemblies had been elected in 1946 in elections in

[10] Cabinet Mission's plan, para. 12 in Rao, *The Framing of India's Constitution*, 212.
[11] Cabinet Mission's plan, para. 15, in Rao, *The Framing of India's Constitution*, vol. I, 213.
[12] Cabinet Mission's plan, para. 15, in Rao, *The Framing of India's Constitution*, vol. I, 213.
[13] Cabinet Mission's plan, para. 18, in Rao, *The Framing of India's Constitution*, vol. I, 214.

Table 4.1 *Representation in the Constituent Assembly according to the Cabinet Mission plan*

Section A:				
Province	General	Muslim	Total	
Madras	45	4	49	
Bombay	19	2	21	
United Provinces	47	8	55	
Bihar	31	5	36	
Central Provinces	16	1	17	
Orissa	9	0	9	
Total	167	20	187	
Section B:				
Province	General	Muslim	Sikh	Total
Punjab	8	16	4	28
North-West Frontier Province	0	3	0	3
Sind	1	3	0	4
Total	9	22	4	35
Section C:				
Province	General	Muslim	Total	
Bengal	27	33	60	
Assam	7	3	10	
Total	34	36	70	

Total for British India	292
Maximum for Indian State	93
Total	385

Source: Rao, *The Framing of India's Constitution*, vol. I, 215.

which the vast majority of the population had been prevented from voting through tax, property and educational requirements.[14]

The Mission's plan called for the provinces to be represented in the Assembly in proportion to their population (in approximate ratio of one per million), with seats of delegates from each province allocated

---

[14] The 1946 provincial elections were held under the Government of India Act 1935. Estimates for the percentage of adults who were allowed to participate in the elections range from 15 to 28 percent. Shibani Kinkar Chaube, *Constituent Assembly of India: Springboard of Revolution*, 2nd edn. (New Delhi: Manohar Publishers & Distributors, 2000) 45; Austin, *The Indian Constitution*, 10 n. 38.

proportionately to representatives of only three officially recognized communities: general (i.e. Hindus and others), Muslims and Sikhs.[15] The princely states were also to be represented in the Constituent Assembly in proportion to their population.[16]

The initial work of the Constituent Assembly would be split into three, the members meeting in three group assemblies to frame their provincial constitutions and then their group constitution. Only then would the representatives reassemble to draft the national constitution.[17] In order to assure the Muslims that the Constituent Assembly would not unfairly exploit Hindu majority power, the Cabinet Mission determined that, as in the case of ordinary laws passed by the national legislature, "any major communal issue shall require a majority of the representatives present and voting of each of the two major communities." The chairman of the Assembly would decide which resolutions required the special majorities and would, if so requested, consult the Federal Court before giving his decision.[18]

Both the Congress and the Muslim League were disappointed with the Cabinet Mission's plan. For both parties, the plan did not coincide with their vision for India. The Congress aspired to an India that was united around centralized governmental institutions, which go beyond communal differences. The constitutional vision of the Congress was very much expressed in the 1928 Nehru Report, which stated that "logic or sense have little to do with communal feelings."[19] The report objected to the recognition of Muslims as a separate electorate, and recommended limited arrangements of reserved seats in the national legislature and in some provinces, for a limited time of ten years. While the report is named after the Committee's chair, Motilal Nehru, in many ways it mirrors the views of his son, Jawaharlal Nehru, who served as the general secretary of the Congress at the time, and played a central role in the drafting of the report. Jawaharlal Nehru perceived national unity and democracy as essential tools for promoting India's integration into the modern world, which was his main concern. As he wrote in 1938, in an article titled *The Unity of India*: "India's socio-economic transformation can be tackled

---

[15] Cabinet Mission's plan, para. 18, in Rao, *The Framing of India's Constitution*, vol. I, 214.
[16] Cabinet Mission's plan, para. 19, in *ibid.*, 215.
[17] Cabinet Mission's plan, para. 19, in *ibid.*, 216.
[18] Cabinet Mission's plan, para. 19, in *ibid.*
[19] Report of the Committee appointed by the All India Conference to Determine the Principles of the Constitution for India, 1928. In Ravinder Kumar and Hari Dev Sharma, eds., *Selected Works of Motilal Nehru*, Vol. 6 (New Delhi: Vikas, 1995), 27.

only on a national planned basis without vested interests to obstruct the planning."[20]

"National unity and democracy," the two doctrines upon which the Congress was founded and on which it stood most firmly,[21] were precisely the source of concern from the perspective of the Muslim League. For Jinnah, "talk of Indian unity as one central constitutional government of this vast sub-continent is simply a myth."[22] India's "so-called present geographical unity is entirely the creation of the British who hold it as one administrative unit by a system of bureaucratic government whose ultimate sanction is the sword and not the will or the sanction of the people behind the government."[23] He viewed India as comprising diverse nationalities and races, among them the two major ones being Hindus and Muslims. As a religious minority in a mostly Hindu society, the Muslims feared that majoritarian democracy in independent India would mean imposition of the norms of the majority on the Muslim minority. In his 1944 book, *The Meaning of Pakistan*, F. K. Khan-Durrani summarized the problem bluntly: "The Hindus claim the right of majority rule. Majority rule means Hindu-Raj. Muslims cannot agree to it."[24] What the Muslim League demanded was full autonomy for Muslim-majority provinces.

The concerns of the leaders of the Muslim League with regard to a Hindu majoritarian rule stemmed from a long and complex history of inter-communal relations. There were three main reasons for the growing estrangement between the sides in the years before independence. First, the Muslim mistrust of the Indian National movement emerged due to what some of them saw as the elitist nature of the Congress and its cultural and religious character which was predominantly Hindu. The Muslims rejected the argument that the Congress was an inclusive organization that represented all religious, linguistic and social groups of Indian society. Indeed Congress included members from almost all minority groups in India, some even holding senior positions. Maulana Azad (1888–1958),

[20] Jawaharlal Nehru, *The Unity of India: Collected Writings, 1937–1940* (London: L. Drummond, 1948).

[21] Jawaharlal Nehru, *The Discovery of India* (Delhi and New York: Oxford University Press, 1989), 384.

[22] Mohammad Ali Jinnah, "Forward," in M. R. T., *Nationalism in Conflict in India* (Bombay: Home Study Circle, 1942), 1.

[23] *Ibid.*

[24] F. K. Khan-Durrani, "*The Meaning of Pakistan*," *Lahore: Sh. Muhammad Ashraf* (1944): 62, in Chaube, *Constituent Assembly of India*, 18.

for example, was the Congress president in the years 1939–45. He was born in Mecca to a Muslim family, grew up in Calcutta and together with Gandhi and Nehru was one of the leaders of the struggle against British rule.[25] Nevertheless, there was never large-scale participation of the Muslim community in the Congress.[26] Moreover, even when attempting to broaden its lines, the Congress Party drew on Hindu culture and religion for its basic philosophy, especially under the leadership of Mahatma Gandhi. Given Gandhi's religiosity, which was expressed both in his private and public life, many Muslims saw Indian nationalism under Gandhi as Hindu nationalism.[27]

The second reason for the growing estrangement between the sides in the years before independence was the Muslim concern that the special protections they had received as a minority group under the British would be abolished. Beginning in the nineteenth century, the British advanced a "divide and rule" policy through a complex system of safeguards for minorities, particularly for Muslims, in education, employment and the political system.[28] Since the inauguration of autonomous governmental institutions in 1909, the British advanced a method of separate electorates for Muslims and Hindus, which was retained in 1919 despite the Montagu-Chelmsford Report which assessed the policy as undemocratic.[29] As a result of the Report, the Government of India Act of 1919 reserved seats in the legislature for Muslims, Sikhs, Indian Christians, Anglo-Indians and Europeans. In Madras and Bombay seats were reserved for lower-caste Hindus in the provincial legislatures in order to assure them adequate

---

[25] Azad was one of the chief objectors of India's partition. After independence he became India's minister of education. Maulana Abul Kalam Azad, *India Wins Freedom: An Autobiographical Narrative* (New York: Longmans Green, 1960).

[26] For the history of the Indian National Congress see D.C. Gupta, *Indian National Congress* (Delhi: Vikas Publications, 1970); Christophe Jaffrelot, *The Hindu Nationalist Movement in India* (New York: Columbia University Press, 1996); S. R. Mehrotra, *A History of the Indian National Congress* (New Delhi: Vikas Pub. House, 1995).

[27] Ronald E. Miller, "Indian Muslim Critiques of Gandhi," in Harold Coward, ed., *Indian Critiques of Gandhi* (Albany: State University of New York Press, 2003), 193–216. The growing estrangement between the two sides was also caused by the power struggle between Jinnah and Gandhi. For Jinnah's view see Ayesha Jalal, *The Sole Spokesman: Jinnah, the Muslim League and the Demand for Pakistan* (Cambridge University Press, 1994). For Gandhi's view see B. R. Nanda, *Mahatma Gandhi: A Biography* (New Delhi: Oxford University Press, 1989).

[28] Penderel Moon, *Divide and Quit* (Berkeley: University of California Press, 1962), 285; Mehrotra, *A History of the Indian National Congress*, vol. I, 42.

[29] Report on Indian Constitutional Reform, p. 150. Cited in Chaube, *Constituent Assembly of India*, 19.

representation. In 1935 the Government of India Act extended this system of separate voting to a total of eighteen communities and minority groups.[30]

The Muslims' fears of oppression under Hindu majority rule had been reinforced after the provincial elections of 1937, which were the first exercise of limited self-rule under the Raj. These elections, held under the new Government of India Act of 1935, resulted in a sweeping victory of the Congress Party. The growing political power of the Congress, especially in the United Provinces, generated a heated political struggle with the Muslim League, which protested against what it saw as administrative and educational discrimination against its voters.[31]

These political developments created a paradoxical situation: the more successful the Indian national movement was and the closer the end of British rule, the greater the fears of the Muslims of an independent government in India. The Muslim League, which initially collaborated with the Congress Party,[32] increasingly came to see autonomy in majority Muslim provinces as a necessary element of any political arrangement.

However, the League–Congress split should not be perceived only in terms of competition over the allocation of power. The controversy which eventually led to the partition of the country rested on a fundamental ideational division between two different conceptions of national identity.

Rival paradigms of Indian nationalism

The struggle over the constitutional definition of Indian identity can be described in terms of a struggle between competing understandings of Indian nationalism: between an exclusivist paradigm that defined

---

[30] The communities and interest groups were: Men – general; backward areas and tribes; Sikhs; Muslims; Anglo-Indians; Europeans; Indian Christians; commerce, industry, mining and plantation; landholders; universities; labor; in Bombay, reservation for Marhattas; women – general; Sikhs; Muslims, Anglo-Indians; Indian Christians. See *ibid.*, 20 n. 11.

[31] See, for example, "Presidential address delivered at the Lucknow session of the All India Muslim League, October 1937," in *Speeches and Writings of Mr. Jinnah*, collected and edited by Jamil-un-Din Ahmad, Vol. 1 (Lahore: Shaike Muhammad Ashraf, 1960), 24–36. See also Mushirul Hasan, *India's Partition: Process, Strategy and Mobilization* (Delhi and Oxford: Oxford University Press, 2001), 17–18.

[32] The greatest achievement of collaboration between the Congress and the Muslim League was the Lucknow Pact of 1916, which set out a joint plan for postwar reform of the Indian political system.

national identity in "communal" terms of cultural-religious homogeneity, and an inclusivist paradigm that defined national identity in secular-political terms, attempting to overcome communal differences. Gyanendra Pandey terms the two competing understandings as "communalism" and "new nationalism," and argues that in many ways these two conceptions were defined in opposition to each other during the colonial period and the struggle for independence.[33] While a "communalist" conception of nationalism recognized the grievances of the religious communities and perceived Indian politics in terms of tension and strife between the Hindu and Muslim communities, a new concept of Indian nationhood challenged this view and envisioned the Indian nation in "purely national" terms and its foundation as going beyond religious communities and caste.[34]

The "communalist" paradigm of nationalism was at the root of the "two-nation theory" advocated by the Mohammad Ali Jinnah, the leader of the Muslim League. In his words:

> It is a dream that the Hindus and Muslims can ever evolve a common nationality … The Hindus and Muslims belong to two different religious philosophies, social customs and literature. They neither intermarry not interdine together, and indeed they belong to two different civilizations which are based mostly on conflicting ideas and conceptions … It is quite clear that Hindus and Mussalmans derive their inspiration from different sources of history … To yoke together two such nations under a single state, one as a numerical minority and the other as a majority, must lead to growing discontent, and final destruction of any fabric that may be so build up for the government of such a state.[35]

Jinnah feared that the Muslims in India would be a permanently subordinated minority in a Hindu-dominated India, despite constituting almost a quarter of the population. In his view, Muslims were a single community or "nation," and he was determined to secure their protection in Muslim-majority autonomous areas. Although until the 1940s the notion of Muslim autonomy was not synonymous with separation, ultimately, this exclusivist definition of national identity led to the demand for political self-determination.[36]

---

[33] Gyanendra Pandey, *The Construction of Communalism in Colonial North India* (Delhi: Oxford University Press, 1990).

[34] *Ibid.*, 241.

[35] "Presidential Address by Muhammad Ali Jinnah to Muslim League, Lahore session, March 1940," in *Speeches and Writings of Mr. Jinnah*, 160–1.

[36] It was not until the famous Lahore resolution of 1940 that the League called for an independent Muslim state in the north-western and eastern zones of India, and signaled

Leaders in the Congress Party, by contrast, and Jawaharlal Nehru above all, offered an alternative paradigm of nationalism, one that was inclusivist, secular and democratic.[37] In their view, the politics of communalism was part of the "pre-modern" world that served the interests of the colonial regime. It represented a backward-looking and reactionary perspective of politics. By contrast, the new idea of Indian nationalism they envisioned was "forward-looking, progressive, 'modern' in Indian politics ... [and] reflected the spontaneous urge of the Indian people for economic advancement and freedom from exploitation."[38] "Real or Indian nationalism," Nehru wrote, "was something quite apart from these two religious and communal varieties of nationalism [Hindu and Muslim] and strictly speaking, is the only form which can be called nationalism in the modern sense of the word."[39]

Nehru believed that India's diversity should not be regarded (as it typically was in colonial thinking) as a disadvantage. According to Nehru, "a diverse economy was less prone to scarcities, breakdowns and foreign pressures; a diverse culture offered greater imaginative and intellectual resources."[40] Instead of concealing it, Nehru wished to embrace India's "infinite diversity" as a definitive element of its national identity.[41] For

the rise of the separatist camp within the Muslim League. "The problem of India is not of an inter-communal character but of an international one," Jinnah affirmed in his speech. Yet even the Lahore Resolution was obscure with regard to the constitutional scheme which would satisfy Muslim national aspirations, and it did not even include the word "Pakistan." R. J. Moore, "Jinnah and the Pakistan Demand," in Mushirul Hasan, ed., *India's Partition: Process, Strategy and Mobilization* (Oxford University Press, 2001), 185.

[37] Pandey, *The Construction of Communalism in Colonial North India*, 240–2. Not all Congress Party leaders shared Nehru's vision. Many of them advocated for Hindu nationalism or sought to the preserve Hindu traditions and culture in the emerging independent state. Often in the Constituent Assembly debate they supported unity on the basis of Hindu identity, rather than the universalistic pluralistic approach promoted by Nehru. See: Christophe Jaffrelot, "Composite Culture is not Multiculturalism: A Study of the Indian Constituent Assembly Debates," in: Ashutosh Varshney, *India and the Politics of Developing Countries*, (New Delhi: Sage Publications, 2004), 126–149. See also: Jaffrelot, *The Hindu Nationalism Movement in India*.

[38] Nehru, *Glimpses of World History* (1934, 2nd edition Bombay, 1964), 1129, cited in *ibid.*, 240.

[39] *Ibid* 241.

[40] *Ibid.*

[41] Another leading proponent of this approach was Abul Kalam Azad, the president of the Congress Party, who stated during his presidential address in 1940: "As a Muslaman I have a special interest in Islamic religion and culture, and I cannot tolerate any interference with them. But in addition to these sentiments I have others also which the realities and conditions of my life have forced upon me. The spirit of Islam does not come in the way

Nehru, India's national identity was not linked to a particular religious, national or cultural identity. Rather, it represented an ethical, philosophical identity, which rested on the acceptance and respect of its cultural, religious and linguistic diversity. Nehru, who opposed religious sentimentality,[42] wished to distance India's identity from any aspect of Hindu religiosity:

> The correct word for "Indian," as applied to country or culture or the historical continuity of our varying traditions, is "Hindi", from "Hind", shortened from Hindustan … "Hindi" has nothing to do with religion, and a Moslem or Christian Indian is as much a Hindi as a person who follows Hinduism as a religion.
>
> Whatever the word we may use, Indian or Hindi or Hindustani, for our cultural tradition, we see in the past that some inner urge towards synthesis, derived essentially from the Indian philosophic outlook, was the dominant feature of Indian cultural, and even racial, development. Each incursion of foreign elements was a challenge to this culture, but it was met successfully by a new synthesis and a process of absorption. This was also a process of rejuvenation and new blooms of culture arose out of it, the background and essential basis, however, remaining much the same.[43]

Sunil Khilnani defines Nehru's distinctive pluralist concept of national identity as "layered nationalism": an intricate conception of Indianness which "was defined not as a singular or exhaustive identity, but as one which explicitly recognized at least two other aspects. Indian citizens were also members of linguistic and cultural communities."[44] As opposed to the model of European nationalism with its emphasis on uniformity, Nehru preferred the "idea that identity and patriotism were necessarily complex and multilayered affair and that there was no way of being an Indian without first being a Tamil or Maratha or Bengali."[45]

---

of these sentiments … I am proud of being an Indian. I am a part of the indivisible unity that is Indian nationality. I am indispensable to this noble edifice, and without me this splendid structure of India is incomplete." Presidential Address to the Fifty-Third Session of the Indian National Congress, Ramgarh, 1940, in A. M. Zaidi, ed., *Congress Presidential Addresses*, Vol. 5 (New Delhi: Indian Institute of Applied Political Research, 1985), 17–38.

[42] Sunil Khilnani, "Nehru's Faith," in Anuradha Dingwaney Needham and Rajeswari Sunder Rajan, eds., *The Crisis of Secularism in India* (Durham and London: Duke University Press, 2007).

[43] Nehru, *The Discovery of India*, 76.

[44] Sunil Khilnani, *The Idea of India* (New York: Farrar Straus Giroux, 1999), 175.

[45] Sudipta Kaviraj, "Modernity and Politics in India," *Daedalus* 129, no. 1 (2000), 154.

The failure of the May 16 plan

Congress and the Muslim League's conflicting visions of what independent India should look like were reflected in their reactions to the Cabinet Mission plan. The May 16 plan was underpinned by the singular or exclusivist paradigm of Indian nationalism. It guaranteed for Muslim autonomy, short of total independence, under a decentralized government dominated by the Hindu majority. The main objection of the Congress Party to the plan was to the division of the country into three political geographically based groupings.[46] In its Working Committee Resolutions, as well as in letters to British officials, the Congress leadership claimed that the compulsory grouping created a weak center, while failing to provide real provincial autonomy as the individual provinces were linked to arbitrarily created regional groups.[47] Moreover, Muslim provinces were over-represented in two of the three geographical groups.[48] To guarantee provincial autonomy, Congress wished to permit any province to leave its originally designated group at any time. Provided that its suggested revision of the grouping provision was accepted, Congress was willing to join the proposed Constituent Assembly.[49] The decision to support the British plan may be understood in light of the primary role that the Congress had historically attached to the Constituent Assembly in the struggle for Indian independence. More importantly perhaps, the Congress' willingness to accept the plan had to do with the Cabinet Mission recommendation to elect the Constituent Assembly members through the provincial legislatures. This would assure the predominance of the Congress in the Assembly since the party's control over the provincial legislatures (based on the December 1945 elections) was overwhelming.[50]

---

[46] Paragraph 15 of the Cabinet Mission plan.

[47] Congress Working Committee Resolution, May 24, 1946, in Rao, *The Framing of India's Constitution*, vol. I, 257.

[48] "As section B and C have been formed it is obvious that one province will play a dominating role in the section, the Punjab in section B and Bengal in section C. It is conceivable that this dominating province may frame a provincial constitution entirely against the wishes of Sind or the North-West Frontier Province or Assam. It may even conceivably lay down rules, for elections and otherwise, thereby nullifying the provision for a province to opt out of a group. Such could never be the intention as it would be repugnant to the basic principles and policy of the scheme itself." Letter from Azad to the Secretary of State, May 20, 1946, in *ibid.*, 251.

[49] Congress Resolution Accepting the Cabinet Mission's plan, June 25, 1946, in *ibid.*, 278.

[50] In the elections for provincial legislatures held in December 1945, the Congress won 58 percent of the total number of seats (925 out of 1,585), but it captured about 85 percent of the non-Muslim seats. Granville Austin, *The Indian Constitution*, 9.

The Muslim League, for its part, initially supported the plan, despite Jinnah's criticism of the grouping idea which divided the Muslim provinces between two groups.[51] The Muslim League resolution included several reservations relating to the proposed electoral system for the Constituent Assembly and the fact that communal safeguards in the union legislature were not well defined.[52]

Based on the initial expression of support from both parties, the preparations for the establishment of a joint Constituent Assembly continued as planned. During the month of July 1946, the representatives of the Constituent Assembly were elected, according to the Cabinet Mission's plan.[53] However, the differences between the sides soon became irreconcilable.

The dispute over the grouping provision, combined with Congress's enthusiastic embrace of the system by which the Assembly's representatives were to be elected, reinforced the League's suspicions about the true intentions of Congress.[54] The League was concerned that Congress would use its dominance in the Assembly to adopt a constitution which would suppress the rights of the Muslim minority.[55] These concerns were reinforced by the fact that Congress conditioned its agreement to the

[51] In its initial reaction to the Cabinet Mission plan, Jinnah objected to the grouping idea because it divided the Muslim provinces between two groups. "Muslim League Resolution on the Cabinet Mission's plan," June 6, 1946, in Rao, *The Framing of India's Constitution*, 264.

[52] For example, it was not clear "who will decide and how as to what is a major communal issue and what is a minor communal issue and what is a purely non-communal issue?" See: "Muslim League Resolution on the Cabinet Mission's plan," June 6, 1946. For Jinnah's objections to the Cabinet Mission's statement see: Jinnah's Statement, May 22, 1946 in *ibid.*, 252–4.

[53] The elections were held by the recently elected Legislative Assemblies of the provinces included in British India. Due to its overwhelming majority in most provincial legislatures (see note 36 above), the Congress candidates filled 208 seats out of the total of 296 seats allotted to the provinces under the Cabinet Mission plan. The Muslim League won all but seven seats reserved for Muslims. Besides the Congress and the Muslim League, other groups that won seats in the Constituent Assembly included Akali Sikhs from Punjab (three seats), Unionists from Punjab (three seats), the Communists (one seat), the Scheduled Castes Federations (one seat) and independents (eight seats). In addition, ninety-three members of the assembly were nominated by the princely states Austin, *The Indian Constitution*, 9.

[54] See the exchange of letters between Pethick-Lawrence, the British Secretary of State and A. K. Azad, the president of the Congress, in Rao, *The Framing of India's Constitution*, vol. I, 191–203.

[55] Muslim League Resolution Withdrawing Acceptance of the Cabinet Mission's Plan, July 27–9, 1946, in *ibid.*, 284–5.

Mission's plan on acceptance of its own interpretation of the grouping provisions.[56]

From Jinnah's perspective, this conditional approval was effectively a rejection of the entire plan. Consequently, at the end of July, the Muslim League resolved to withdraw its acceptance of the Cabinet Mission's proposals.[57] On August 16, 1946 the League held a Direct Action Day to press its demands for an independent Pakistan. There was a spate of communal rioting involving both communities throughout the country. The most severe violence occurred in Calcutta, where, within seventy-two hours, by some estimates 6,000 people were killed and a further 20,000 were injured.[58] The Calcutta Killings as they soon became known were a turning point in the emergence of Pakistani national consciousness. The possibility of India's division, which had first surfaced as a theoretical notion only a decade before, became after the riots a realistic, and perhaps inevitable, option.[59]

The British wished to push the transfer of power forward. On November 20, 1946, with negotiations between the parties proving futile, Viceroy Archibald Wavell invited the participants of the Constituent Assembly to convene in less than three weeks. The next day Jinnah wrote to him that he was "entirely playing into the hands of the Congress" and that "no representative of the Muslim League [w]ould attend the Constituent Assembly."[60]

In a last-minute attempt to resolve the deadlock, Prime Minister Clement Attlee invited the leaders of the Congress, the Muslim League

[56] In a press conference held in Bombay on July 10, 1946, Nehru stated that Congress would enter the Constituent Assembly "completely unfettered by agreements and free to meet all situations as they arise." In his autobiography, Azad, the Muslim Congress president, described this statement as "one of those unfortunate events which changed the course of history." Azad, *India Wins Freedom*, 181.

[57] "The Congress have made it clear that they do not accept any of the terms or the fundamentals of the scheme but that they have agreed only to go into the Constituent Assembly and to nothing else; and that the Constituent Assembly is a sovereign body and can take such decisions as it may think proper in total disregard of the terms and the basis on which it was proposed to be set up." Muslim League Resolution Withdrawing Acceptance of the Cabinet Mission's Plan, July 27–9, 1946, in Rao, *The Framing of India's Constitution*, vol. I, 284.

[58] Leonard Mosley, *The Last Days of the British Raj*, 1st American edn. (New York: Harcourt Brace & World, 1962), 11, see also pp. 33–40.

[59] Leonard A. Gordon, "Divided Bengal: Problems of Nationalism and Identity in the 1947 Partition," in Mushirul Hasan, ed., *India's Partition: Process, Strategy and Mobilization* (Delhi and Oxford: Oxford University Press, 2001), 309.

[60] Jinnah's Statement Finally Dissociating the League from the Constituent Assembly, November 21, 1946, in Rao, *The Framing of India's Constitution*, vol. I, 325.

and the Sikhs to a summit in London. On December 2, one week before the convocation of the Assembly, Nehru, Jinnah and the Sikh representative, Baldev Singh, flew to London. The effort proved fruitless. On December 9, 1946 207 members of the Indian Constituent Assembly convened in New Delhi to open its first session. None of the seventy-three Muslim League representatives attended.

All attempts to reconcile the parties failed. On June 3, 1947, seven months after the establishment of the Constituent Assembly of united India, Attlee, the British prime minister, announced his decision to divide the country and to transfer all government powers to two separate dominions: India and Pakistan. Within six weeks, the British left the subcontinent, leaving behind them a country torn apart along hastily sketched borders, with about a million dead and seventeen million displaced. Trains packed with dead passengers crossed over from both sides of the border. The period is remembered in the history of the subcontinent as a holocaust.[61]

Formalization of the conflict

Whether the partition of India was inevitable is a question long debated by historians.[62] From a constitutional perspective, the collapse of the Cabinet Mission plan demonstrates the fragility and limited potential of constitutional procedures in the context of a deeply divided society. One may ask whether the May 16 plan could be seen as a form of "interim constitution," since it had set strict limitations on the process of permanent constitution-making. On the one hand, like the well-known cases of the Hungarian and the South African interim constitutions in the late 1980s and early 1990s, the Cabinet Mission's plan was designed to facilitate the peaceful dismantling of the old regime while maintaining legal continuity, and establish a more or less viable enforceable form of political competition.[63] The Cabinet Mission also attempted to provide a legitimate beginning to the constitution-making process by involving all the major political forces in a series of negotiations on the

---

[61] Mosley, *The Last Days of the British Raj*, 243; Khushwant Singh, *Train to Pakistan* (New York: Grove Press, 1956).

[62] The literature on the origins of partition is vast. For few examples see: Hasan, *India's Partition*; C. H. Philips and Mary Doreen Wainwright, *The Partition of India: Policies and Perspectives, 1935–1947* (Cambridge, MA: The MIT Press, 1970); Anita Inder Singh, *The Origins of the Partition of India, 1936–1947* (Delhi and New York: Oxford University Press, 1990).

[63] Andrew Arato, "Interim Imposition," *Ethics and International Affairs* 18, no. 3 (2004).

plan itself. However, unlike the "interim constitution" model, the procedural constraints to be imposed on the constitution-making body were not adopted by mutual agreement, but rather were imposed by a colonial ruler. Eventually, the Constituent Assembly began to function while only part of its members accepted the plan. Furthermore, the British plan did not merely put constraints on the procedures of the constitution-making body, but also determined the end result of these procedures by imposing the three-tiered federal structure. Thus, while the Cabinet Mission's plan was presented as ostensibly allowing Indian society to resolve its political problems, it did not provide a genuine "learning process" to use Andrew Arato's terminology.[64] Thus, likening the May 16 plan to an interim constitution is misleading.

The lesson that can be learned from the failure of the first round of constitution-making in India concerns the limitations of constitutional procedures to address deep divisions over the vision of an emerging state. While the preliminary constitutional negotiations and deliberations may not have exacerbated the conflict, they certainly failed to mitigate it. The two main parties to the conflict used the disagreement over constitutional procedures for political advantage. Instead of bringing the sides together, the constitutional debate turned into a focus for political tension which emphasized the differences between the two sides.

The study of the letters and protocols in the tripartite negotiations between the Congress, the League and the British government regarding the Cabinet Mission plan shows how the leaders of the Congress Party and of the Muslim League used the Mission plan and its legal formulations as a battering ram, rather than as a vehicle for compromise. They imported their political disputes into the constitutional debate and used the legal dispute to emphasize the ideological differences between their positions. The dispute over the proposal of provincial grouping heightened the tensions and exposed fundamental disagreements between the Congress and the League.

Another example of a legal debate which was exploited by the two parties for political gain is the debate which arose in December 1947 over the validity of the Constituent Assembly in light of the absence of the League's representatives. In this dispute, the Cabinet Mission plan itself had served as political ammunition in the hands of the two parties. Presuming that the main purpose of the Cabinet Mission scheme was to sustain legal continuity in India during the transformation of power, the legal issue

---

[64] *Ibid*, 30

was whether the absence of representatives of the largest minority group, for whose protection special provisions had been devised, violated the Cabinet Mission plan and undermined the validity of the Assembly itself. The Muslim League naturally argued that the plan could only be given effect if the two major parties agreed to accept it, and that, consequently, in the absence of the support of the major communities (the Congress not having accepted the plan without reservations), both the elections for the Constituent Assembly and its convening lacked legitimacy.[65]

By contrast, the perspective of Congress was that the fundamental purpose of the plan was to guarantee the representation of Indian pluralism. And this condition was realized, as K. M. Munshi claimed, even without the participation of the League. Munshi pointed to the method of election as indicated in Clause 18 of the plan, which did not allocate seats in the Assembly to any specific party. The Constituent Assembly, he claimed, "is clearly representative of the population of India as a whole and not of a conference of representatives of certain groups," while the allocation of seats to provinces and communities was, in his opinion, merely "a matter of convenience."[66]

Despite its intention to create a constitutional blueprint that could lay the groundwork for reconciliation between the sides, the British plan succeeded only in proposing a formal legal framework which colored the conflict with legal argumentations. The constitutional debates mirrored the competing visions of the Congress and the Muslim League with regard to the Indian polity. As one of the British architects of the partition plan suggested, the nine months of negotiations over the composition of the Constituent Assembly were not wholly in vain: "they had at any rate brought home to everyone, except perhaps Gandhi, the necessity of partition."[67]

Whether the framing of the Hindu–Muslim tensions in constitutional terms exacerbated the conflict and promoted partition is one of those historically hypothetical questions that is very difficult to answer, particularly in retrospect. Nevertheless, already the political leaders of the time recognized the complicated role the process of constitution-making plays under circumstances of deep divisions regarding the identity of the state. As the disagreements became increasingly more apparent, it was Jinnah

---

[65] Muslim League Resolution on H. G. M. Statement, January 31, 1947, in Rao, *The Framing of India's Constitution*, vol. I, 353–9.

[66] K. M. Munshi's Views, in *ibid.*, 390–1.

[67] Moon, *Divide and Quit*, 64.

who supported a gradual process of consensus building prior to drafting a formal constitution. During the negotiations over the structure of the Constituent Assembly he contended that the long-term plan of constitutional design should be postponed until a more conducive atmosphere was created and agreement was reached on points of difference.[68] Viceroy Wavell also acknowledged in his own way the correlation between writing a constitution and the process of long-term political integration. He hoped to use the framework of the interim government as an opportunity for building trust and cooperation between the sides.[69]

Even within the Assembly voices were raised in support of a more gradual approach. Bhim Rao Ambedkar, who represented the untouchable caste and was the Chair of the Drafting Committee,[70] argued in his speech during the first session of the Assembly that the goal of political unity should trump constitutional procedures and that advancing unity is more important at this early stage than insisting on the legal right.

> Let us leave aside slogans, let us leave aside words which frighten people. Let us even make a concession to the prejudices of our opponents, bring them in, so that they may willingly join us on marching upon that road which as I said if we talk long enough must necessarily lead us to unity.[71]

Finally, Nehru himself understood the direct link between national unity and constitutional legitimacy. In his first speech in the Assembly, referring to the absent representatives of the Muslim League, he stated, "we do hope that those who have abstained will soon join us in our deliberations, since this constitution can only go as far as the strength behind it can push it."[72] At the same time, however, independence was more important and more urgent for him than reconciliation: "it is, at the same time, manifested that when a great country starts to advance, no party or group can stop it. This house, although it has met in the absence of some of its

---

[68] Less than one month before the Constituent Assembly had convened Jinnah wrote to the Viceroy: "In my opinion ... you should announce immediately the postponement of the Constituent Assembly *sine die* and let us all forthwith concentrate every ounce of our energy upon restoring peace and order first". "Jinnah's Letter to the Viceroy," November 17, 1946, in Rao, *The Framing of India's Constitution*, vol. I, 325.

[69] Chaube, *Constituent Assembly of India*, 54.

[70] Ambedkar was the first member of the untouchables (Dalit castes) who was educated in the UK and United States and became a prominent leader in Indian politics. He was the first law minister in independent India. Christophe Jaffrelot, *Dr. Ambedkar and Untouchability: Fighting the Indian Caste System* (New York: Columbia University Press, 2005).

[71] *CAD* I, 101.   [72] *CAD* I, 57.

Table 4.2 *Timeline: the making of the Indian constitution*

December 28, 1885	Foundation of the Indian National Congress
1906	Foundation of the Muslim League
1909	Indian Councils Act (based on Morley-Minto Reforms)
1916	The Lucknow Pact
1919	Government of India Act (based on Montagu-Chelmsford Reforms)
September 1920	Congress adopts the goal of Swaraj and launches the Satyagraha
March 10, 1922	Gandhi calls for *swaraj* (self-government)
August 1928	Nehru Report published
October 1929	The Indian Statutory (Simon) Commission Report submitted
November 12, 1930	Round Table Conference in London
August 1935	Government of India Act
March 22–4, 1940	The Lahore resolution of the Muslim League
December 1945	Elections for provisional legislatures in British India
May 16, 1946	The Cabinet Mission plan is published
August 16, 1946	Muslim League held Direct Action Day, which became the Calcutta Killings
July 11–12, 1946	Provincial legislatures elect the members of Constituent Assembly
December 9, 1946	First meeting of the Constituent Assembly in Delhi. Muslim League representatives do not attend
June 3, 1947	Mountbatten's declaration on the partition of India and Pakistan
August 14, 1947	The establishment of the Dominion of Pakistan (since 1956 the Islamic Republic of Pakistan)
August 15, 1947	India gains independence. The British transfer all powers to Indian interim government
December 1949	End of Constituent Assembly debates
January 26, 1950	The constitution of India was formally adopted

members, will continue functioning and try to carry out its work at all costs."[73]

Although probably all sides acknowledged that the advancing of unity is necessarily a gradual, incremental process, suspending the Assembly discussions, or the transfer of power, was not an option which the Congress

[73] *CAD* I, 57–8. Not everyone agreed with Nehru in the Constituent Assembly, though.

and the British were willing to consider. As W. H. Auden wrote in his poem *Partition* on Lord Mountbatten, who was the last Viceroy in India:

> "Time", they had briefed him in London, "is short. It's too late
> For mutual reconciliation or rational debate:
> The only solution now lies in separation …"[74]

The Constituent Assembly after partition

In November 1947, three months after partition, the Congress Working Committee adopted a resolution stating that "the Committee believes that the destiny of India will yet be realized and that, when passions have cooled, a new and stronger unity based on good-will and co-operation will emerge."[75]

Whether the belief in the provisionality of partition was genuine or not among the leadership of the Congress Party, the separation of Pakistan did not have a dramatic impact on the image of independent India held by the leadership of the Constituent Assembly, including Nehru. The framers of the constitution realized that partition would not resolve the problem of India's cultural, religious and linguistic diversity. As Nehru wrote three years before partition:

> Any division of India on a religious basis as between Hindus and Moslems, as envisaged by the Moslem League today, cannot separate the followers of these two principle religions of India, for they are spread out all over the country. Even if the areas in which each group is in a majority are separated, huge minorities belonging to the other group remain in each area. Thus instead of solving the problem, we create several in place of one.[76]

The percentage of Muslims in the Indian population dropped from 20 percent before partition to less than 10 percent in post-independence India. Still, it remained the third largest Muslim community in the world (after Indonesia and Pakistan). Other religious minorities in India included Christians (2.3 percent of the population), Sikhs (almost 2 percent), and Buddhists, Jains and Parsis (together comprising about 2.5 percent).[77] In

---

[74] W. H. Auden, *Collected Poems*, ed. by Edward Mendelson (Modern Library Edition, 2007), 803.

[75] Cited in: Michael Brecher, *Nehru: A Political Biography* (London and New York: Oxford University Press, 1959), 378.

[76] Nehru, *The Discovery of India*, 530.

[77] *Census of India, Paper No. 2: Religion–1951 Census* (India Republic Census Commissioner, 1953) 1.

addition, India was (and remains) one of the richest countries in the world in terms of its linguistic and ethnic diversity.

The creation of Pakistan, in short, did not change the vision of India which the leaders of Congress, and Nehru in particular, wished to promote through the drafting of the constitution. At the same time, the partition of India and the transfer of power from British to Indian hands resulted in increased dominance of the Congress in the Constituent Assembly, which in turn made it possible for its leadership to incorporate in the constitution elements of its vision of Indian unity. In this respect, three main changes should be noted.

First, partition increased the influence and power of the Congress Party in the Assembly. Since Congress also controlled the government, both at the provisional and national levels, the Constituent Assembly became a "one-party body in an essentially one-party country. The Assembly was the Congress and the Congress was India."[78]

Congress leaders tended to stress the inclusive nature of the party, which attempted to encompass all major sections and interests in Indian society.[79] The Congress Party indeed invited representatives of various minority groups to participate in the Assembly on a Congress ticket, even though they were not members of the party.[80] Moreover, the atmosphere during the assembly deliberations was inclusive, and resolutions were adopted after long intensive debates including representatives of various ethnic religious and caste groups.[81] Nevertheless, in fact the decision-making process in the Constituent Assembly was highly centralized. The Committee system of the Assembly was dominated by a group of eleven members.[82] Eight of them were members of the Congress Party. Of them,

---

[78] Austin, *The Indian Constitution*, 8–9.

[79] Rajni Kothari, *Politics and the People: In Search of a Humane India* (Delhi: Ajanta Publications, 1989), 23, 27, 51. See also Arend Lijphart, "The Puzzle of Indian Democracy: A Consociational Interpretation," *American Political Science Review* 90, no. 2 (1996): 259–60.

[80] As reported by the president of the Assembly on January 20, 1947, out of total of 296 members of the Constituent Assembly, 160 were Hindus, thirty-three representatives of Schedule Castes, five Sikhs, seven Indian Christians, five representatives of Backward Tribes, three Anglo-Indian, three Parsis, and eight Muslim (only four of whom attended the first session) (*CAD* II, 267). These ratios of religious representation remained more or less the same after partition, since the elections in the divided provinces were held through a system of separate electorates.

[81] "Nearly 250 members [out of 305] spoke in the Assembly, over 200 of them frequently." Austin, *The Indian Constitution*, 316.

[82] Prasad, Azad, Patel, Nehru, Pant, Sitaramayya, Ayyar, N. G. Ayyangar, Munshi, Ambedkar, Satyanarayan Sinha. Austin refers to this group as the "inner circle." Together

four key figures in the Congress, namely Jawaharlal Nehru, the prime Minister, Sardar Patel, the deputy prime minister, Rajendra Prasad, the president of the Assembly, and Abul Kalam Azad, a minister in the Union government, constituted what has been referred to as the "oligarchy" of the Assembly.[83] Between them, Nehru, Patel and Prasad chaired seven of the eight most important committees of the Constituent Assembly. Ambedkar, who chaired the Drafting Committee, was also elected with the support of the Congress Party.[84] The Assembly leadership exercised its power informally on the House floor or behind the scenes, but also formally through the means of the Party Whip.[85]

Second, under the 1947 Indian Independence Act, the Constituent Assembly assumed full powers for the government of India. It was also mandated to exercise the powers of a federal legislature under the 1935 Government of India Act, which meant that the Constituent Assembly simultaneously acted as India's provisional parliament.[86] On August 29, 1947 the Assembly decided to distinguish between its two functions, and subsequently held morning sessions as a legislature, while sitting as a Constituent Assembly in the afternoons.[87]

Third, partition resolved lingering doubts on the Assembly's sovereignty. When the Assembly initially convened in December 1946, the pervasive view was that the Assembly could not automatically be regarded as sovereign, due to the fact that it was not born of a revolutionary movement, but rather was a negotiated compromise that was reached between the rulers and the ruled. To the extent that it was revolutionary in spirit, it was a "revolution by consent."[88] As Gandhi noted, "it is no use declaring somebody

---

with the members of the Drafting Committee and several other Congress personalities, there were roughly twenty key members of the Assembly. *Ibid.*

[83] *Ibid.*, 21.

[84] In 1946 Ambedkar entered the Constituent Assembly on an independent ticket from Bengal, with the support from the Muslim League. After partition he lost his seat but was re-elected to the Assembly on a ticket from Bombay, with the support of the Congress Party. Jaffrelot, *Dr. Ambedkar and Untouchability*, 100.

[85] Austin, the Indian Constitution., 316.

[86] Section 8, Indian Independence Act, 1947, see Rao, *The Framing of India's Constitution*, vol. I, 543.

[87] *CAD* VI, 330. India differs in this from Israel, which, at its establishment, elected a Constituent Assembly. Yet, while the Indian Assembly continued to function as the Constituent Assembly and eventually adopted a constitution, the Israeli Constituent Assembly declared itself as the first Knesset (legislature) in its first session after the elections, and a year and a half later formally decided to postpone the drafting of the constitution.

[88] Dhirendranath Sen, *Revolution by Consent?* (Calcutta: Saraswaty Library, 1947).

else's creation a sovereign body."[89] The effect of partition was to remove the procedural constraints that had been imposed on the Assembly under the Cabinet Mission plan. The report to the Assembly given by K. M. Munshi, on the proceedings of the Order of Business Committee on July 14, 1947, expressed a sense of relief that was shared by many of his colleagues:

> We have no sections and groups to go into, no elaborate procedure as was envisaged by [the Cabinet Mission plan], no double majority clause, no more provinces with residuary powers, no opting out, no revision after ten years and no longer only four categories of powers for the centre. We, therefore, feel free to form a federation of our choice, a federation with a centre as strong as we can make it.[90]

In short, after partition the Constituent Assembly was stronger, more confident in its status and more united around the leadership provided by the Congress Party. It was thus ready to tackle the question, which was to be debated over the next three years, of how best to make use of a national constitution to promote common norms and values that could be widely accepted and shared by the multitude of cultural, religious and linguistic segments that made up Indian society.

"Unity amidst diversity"

Throughout the Constituent Assembly deliberations Nehru gave a clear expression to his conception of Indian national identity:

> The ultimate objective is not separatism but building up an organic nation, not necessarily a uniform nation because we have a varied culture and in this country ways of living differ in various parts of the country, habits differ and cultural traditions differ[. The] glory of India has been the way in which it has managed to keep two things going at the same time: that is, its infinite variety and at the same time its unity in that variety. Both have to be kept.[91]

Nehru understood that the promotion of a homogenizing and unifying perception of national identity would undermine the fragile balance between the various communities in India. Thus, he strove for an inclusivist multi-layered definition of Indianness, which recognizes the traditions and values of the country's religious and cultural communities. This,

---

[89] To Louis Fischer in an interview held on July 22, 1946. Cited in Austin, *The Indian Constitution*, 7.
[90] *CAD* IV, 546.
[91] *CAD* VII, 323. Nehru had articulated his view on "the variety and unity of India" in Nehru, *The Discovery of India*, 59–63.

claims Sunil Khilnani, is the most remarkable achievement of Nehru and the Congress Party after independence: that in spite of the colonial legacy, partition and Congress's aspirations for centralized political authority and economic planning, "no attempt was made to impose a single or uniform 'Indian' identity."[92]

From the very start of the assembly deliberations, Nehru wished to frame the debate in terms of his inclusivist multi-layered conception of Indian nationalism. On December 13, 1946, the fourth day of the Assembly's discussions (and seven months before partition), he proposed his Objective Resolution, which offered to present to Indians and to the world at large the outline of the constitutional plan and "to indicate the direction in which the Constituent Assembly would go."[93] The Resolution reflected Nehru's complex vision of India. It included a variety of social and political principles, embracing a mixture of Western democratic values and Indian traditional tenets, individual rights and special group rights:

> This Constituent Assembly [shall guarantee and secure] to all the people of India justice, social, economic and political; equality of status, of opportunity, and before the law; freedom of thought, expression, belief, faith, worship, vocation, association and action, subject to law and public morality; and wherein adequate safeguards shall be provided for minorities, backward and tribal areas, and depressed and other backward classes, and … this ancient land attains its rightful and honored place in the world and make its full and willing contribution to the promotion of world peace and the welfare of mankind.[94]

Nevertheless, despite Nehru's dominant influence in the Congress Party and in the Constituent Assembly, his intricate formulation of India's shared norms and values was challenged throughout the three years of constitutional discussions. In the sessions before partition, his request to translate this complex pluralistic set of ethical and nationalist principles into a legal system of constitutional provisions raised many objections, the most serious of which was that it did not refer to the issue of grouping which stood at the heart of the tension with the Muslim League. After long and intense discussions, the resolution was adopted, but only at the end of January 1947, when it was already obvious to all that the chances for reconciliation with the League were exhausted and that partition was a foregone conclusion.

Yet, nor did partition itself end the struggle over the fundamental principles and ultimate goals of independent India. The competing exclusivist

---

[92] Khilnani, *The Idea of India*, 173.
[93] *CAD* VII, 57.   [94] *CAD* VII, 59.

paradigm of Indian nationalism did not disappear from the constitutional debate after the division of India's territory. Hindu nationalists openly and forcefully expressed their vision of a culturally unified India. Ultimately, as Sudipta Kaviraj argues, "the influence of European examples was so deep that it determined the manner in which the constitution-makers framed their question."[95] This was especially clear in the debates over uniform civil code and over the question of India's national language.

These two issues touched upon the most fundamental aspects of Indian identity and raised difficult questions regarding the foundational elements of the Indian constitution.[96] Not surprisingly they also stirred heated debates in the Assembly: how should the constitution facilitate political unity, based on shared commitments and values, in a society characterized by immense cultural, religious and linguistic diversity? The study of these debates reveals the enormous difficulties of the task of drafting the state's constitutive document under conditions of considerable social segmentation. As we will see, the Assembly addressed these difficulties by making a particularly creative use of the constitutional language. By deliberately leaving certain constitutional formulations ambiguous, the Assembly acknowledged that the gaps between rival perspectives were unbridgeable. By refusing to adopt unequivocal language, the Assembly effectively shifted the burden of resolving – or at least continue discussing – the controversies to the new political institutions that it created.

Uniform civil code

Under British rule, personal law (in issues such as marriage, divorce, maintenance, succession to property, inheritance, custody and adoption) as it related to Hindus and Muslims was administered by separate Hindu and Muslim courts, in accordance with the different traditional laws and practices.[97] As independence approached, it became urgent to provide a

---

[95] Sudipta Kaviraj, "Writing, Speaking, Being: Language and the Historical Formation of Identities in India," in Dagmar Hellmann-Rajanayagam and Dietmar Rothernund, eds., *Nationalstaat Und Sprachkonflikte in Sud- Und Sudostadien* (Stuttgart: Franz Steiner Verlag, 1992), 54.

[96] The question of national identity was raised in the context of additional issues; such as, use of national symbols and definitions of citizenship. See, for example, Jaffrelot, "Composite Culture is not Multiculturalism." I focus on the debates on national language and the uniform civil code because the discussion in the Assembly in these cases revolved not only on the substantial issue but also on the broader question of what role the constitution should play under conditions of deep societal division.

[97] See: Marc Galanter, *Law and Society in Modern India* (Delhi and New York: Oxford University Press, 1989) ch. 6.

response to a pressing question: should the constitution secularize and unify personal law by providing for a uniform civil code, or should it perpetuate the existing system of separate personal law regimes based on affiliation to the various religious communities in the country? This issue went to the heart of the definition of Indian national identity – was it exclusivist, in which case a uniform civil code was imperative in order to advance the goal of national unity, or was it inclusivist, in which case supporting religious and cultural pluralism by maintaining the various legal traditions could do no harm to national unity?

From the outset, the debate over a uniform civil code revolved around the question not of whether such a principle should be included in the constitution, but rather of whether it should be included in the justiciable or non-justiciable section of the constitution. The Indian framers identified a particular section of the constitution ("The Directive Principles of State Policy") whose provisions were non-justiciable.[98] Namely, the articles in this part, in contrast to all other constitutional provisions, are not enforceable by any court. These provisions represent principles that are "fundamental in the governance of the country," and that it is "the duty of the state to apply these principles in making law."[99] That is, these principles are intended only as guidance for the legislature in reconstruction of Indian society.[100]

As far as the issue of unifying personal law was concerned, the question was whether the provision that stated the principle of a uniform civil code should be justiciable or not, i.e. whether this provision should be enforceable by a court of law or merely represent a recommendation for future action by the national government. As we shall see below, this debate was accompanied by a wider debate on whether the framers should in general use the constitution's power to promote radical social and cultural reform.

---

[98] The source of inspiration for the non-justiciable section in the Indian constitution was a similar provision which appears in the 1937 Irish constitution, Article 45 of which identified a set of social policy principles which are "intended for the general guidance of the Oireachtas," and stipulated that "the application of those principles in the making of laws shall be the care of the Oireachtas exclusively, and shall not be cognisable by any Court under any of the provisions of this Constitution." The decision in the Indian Constituent Assembly to adopt non-justiciable provisions was reached only after intense debate in committee, as well as on the Assembly floor.

[99] Article 37 of the Indian constitution.

[100] India, in turn, inspired various other countries that adopted similar non-justiciable sections in their constitutions, such as Namibia, Ghana, Brazil, Germany, Portugal and Spain. See Jeffrey Usman, "Non-Justiciable Directive Principles: A Constitutional Design Defect," *Michigan State Journal of International Law* 15 (2007): 696, n. 5.

The debate over the uniform civil code began already before partition, during the discussions of the Sub-Committee on Fundamental Rights, which met between February and April 1947. The demand for legal uniformity in the sphere of personal law did not come only from extreme Hindu nationalists. M. R. Masani, a Parsi member of Congress from Bombay, and Amrit Kaur, a Christian member of Congress who represented CP and Behar, were two of three Congress Party members who jointly demanded that the provision be included in the justiciable part of the constitution so that it could be enforceable by court.[101] They argued that "One of the factors that has kept India back from advancing to nationhood has been the existence of personal laws based on religion which keep the nation divided into watertight compartments in many aspects of life."[102] However, the majority of subcommittee members opposed this demand, and the provision was left in the Directive Principles section of the constitution. The decision of the subcommittee was made in April 1947, two months before the British announcement on partition. As Austin points out, "the reason behind this action was not, as it might at first appear, the wish to avoid a clash with Hindu orthodoxy, but a sensitivity, particularly on Nehru's part, to the fears of the Muslims and the Sikhs."[103]

After partition, the issue of the justiciability of the uniform civil code clause was raised again by the same three members of the Advisory Committee. In July 1947 the three wrote a letter to Patel, the chairman of the committee, asking the committee to reconsider its decision "in view of the changes that have taken place since [i.e. partition] and the keen desire that is now felt for a more homogenous and closely knit India nation."[104] Despite their efforts, the clause remained in the Directive Principles.

The next round of debates regarding the uniform civil code arose during the deliberations over the draft constitution. The most interesting exchange of opinions occurred on November 23, 1948, around several amendments to the draft uniform civil code, which concerned the demand to limit the state interference and to protect the personal laws of religious minorities. Although all amendments restricting the uniform civil code were proposed by Muslim representatives, they mostly claimed to speak for all religious communities in India. By stressing the cultural and religious diversity which characterized Indian society, many

---

[101] Mehta and Kaur were among the few women members of the Assembly.
[102] "Minutes of Dissent to the Draft Report, April 14, 1947," Rao, *The Framing of India's Constitution*, II, 162.
[103] Austin, *The Indian Constitution*, 80.
[104] Letter dated July 25, 1947. Law Ministry Archives, File CA/24/Com/47-III (cited in *ibid.*, 81).

of the objectors to the uniform civil code implied that it undermined the pluralism of the Indian state. In the words of B. Pocker Sahib Bahadur, a Muslim League representative from Madras: "there are ever so many multitudes of communities following various customs for centuries or thousands of years. By one stroke of the pen you want to annul all that and make them uniform."[105] Pocker Bahadur also attacked the uniform civil code as representing the tyranny of the majority. The standards of which community, he asked, would be taken as the basis for the uniformity of the code?[106] The answer was obvious.

A further argument against the enactment of the uniform civil code was raised by another representative of the Muslim League from Madras, Mohamad Ismail, who claimed that the code conflicted with the principle of freedom of religion, as provided in Article 19 of the draft constitution. Ismail maintained that obedience to particular personal laws should be seen as the exercise of religious beliefs: "If anything is done affecting personal laws, it will be tantamount to interference with the way of life of those people who have been observing these laws for generations and ages."[107] Hence, the right of a group or a community of people to follow and adhere to its own personal law "is among the fundamental rights and this provision should really be made amongst the statutory and justiciable fundamental rights," he said.[108]

Like other opponents of the uniform code, Ismail accepted the basic definition of India as a secular state, but he emphasized the limits of this definition and the particular interpretation of secularism that he believed should be applied in the Indian context: "this secular state which we are trying to create should not do anything to interfere with the way of life and religion of the people."[109]

The main champion of the provision was K. M. Munshi, a Hindu member of Congress, who later became the minister of food and agriculture.[110] He argued that the state should not be prevented from legislating for social reform. In his speech he presented the ultimate goals he believed should guide the Constituent Assembly, namely the restriction of religion to the private sphere and the promotion of unity and societal integration on the basis of civic national identity:

> There is one important consideration which we have to bear in mind –
> and I want my Muslim friends to realize this – that the sooner we forget

---

[105] *CAD* VII, 545. [106] *Ibid.* [107] *Ibid.*, 540. [108] *Ibid.* [109] *Ibid.*, 540–1.
[110] Munshi was later among the founders of the right-wing Swatantra Party, which challenged the socialist principles of Congress.

this isolationist outlook on life, it will be better for the country. Religion must be restricted to spheres which legitimately appertain to religion, and the rest of life must be regulated, unified and modified in such a manner that we may evolve, as early as possible a strong and consolidated nation. Our first problem and most important problem is to produce national unity in this country … There is no use clinging always to the past. We are departing from the past … we want the whole India to be welded and united together as a single nation. Are we helping those factors which help the welding together into a single nation, or is this country to be kept up always as a series of competing communities?[111]

The dispute over the fundamental question of the relationship between unity and uniformity explains only one aspect of the debate concerning the uniform civil code. The second aspect was related to an essentially constitutional issue: the role of the constitution in promoting social, religious and cultural reforms. On the one side, as we have seen, stood Assembly members such as Masani, Kaur and Mehta, who wished to use the legal power and status of the constitution to modify religious customs and advance secularization and legal uniformity among all religious groups. On the other side were those who believed that a constitution should reflect the spirit of the nation as it currently was and should not impose deep social and cultural changes. Naziruddin Ahmad, a Muslim representative from West Bengal, expressed this view when he warned against overly radical constitutional provisions:

> I have no doubt that a stage would come when the civil law would be uniform. But then that time has not yet come. We believe that the power that has been given to the state to make the Civil Code uniform is in advance of the time … What the British in 175 years failed to do or were afraid to do, what the Muslims in the course of 500 years refrained from doing, we should not give power to the state to do all at once. I submit, sir, that we should proceed not in haste but with caution, with experience, with statesmanship and with sympathy.[112]

Ahmad supported the fundamental notion of uniformity, but argued against pervasive state interference in internal affairs of religious communities. "This is not a matter of mere idealism," he stated. "It is a question of stern reality which we must not refuse to face and I believe it will lead to a considerable amount of misunderstanding and resentment amongst the various sections of the county."[113] Emphasizing pragmatism, Ahmad indicated the difficulty the state would face "at this stage of our society"

---

[111] *CAD* VII, 548–9. [112] *Ibid.*, 542–3. [113] *Ibid.*, 543.

in asking people to give up their conception of marriage, for example, which is associated with religious institutions in many communities. The solution he proposed was to act patiently: "I submit that the interference with these matters should be gradual and must progress with the advance of time."[114] Ahmad stressed the importance of obtaining consent of the communities whose religious laws would be affected by the new code: "The goal should be towards a Uniform Civil Code but it should be gradual and with the consent of the people concerned."[115] He therefore recommended that the decision regarding the application of a uniform civil code should not be entrenched in the constitution but should rather be left to Parliament, which could obtain the consent of the communities through their representatives.

Eventually, the framers decided to include the reference to a uniform civil code as Article 44, which provides that "the State shall endeavour to secure for the citizens a Uniform Civil Code throughout the territory of India." The Article is included in the "Directive Principle of State Policy" part of the constitution.

By including the uniform civil code in the non-justiciable section of the constitution, the Indian framers created a constitutional mechanism which in fact evaded the hard choice between the inclusivist and the exclusivist perceptions of India's religious identity. The Constituent Assembly decided not to give up the uniform civil code provision, and announced it as one of the ideals the state should aim at. Yet this decision could not have been seen as a victory of the approach that espoused national homogenization. Following the pragmatic and principal considerations similar to those presented by Naziruddin Ahmad, the members of the Assembly formulated the code as merely a policy recommendation. Ambedkar, the chair of the Drafting Committee, explained that the provision merely required the state to "endeavor to secure a civil code for the citizens of the country. It does not say that after the Code is framed the state shall enforce it upon all citizens."[116] Ambedkar stressed that Parliament would retain the authority to implement this policy recommendation, and that it was "perfectly possible" that it would decide that "in the initial stage the application of the Code may be purely voluntary."[117] A similar view was expressed by Nehru in 1954, when he stated that he thought a uniform civil code was an eventual goal, but that the time was not ripe to push it through.[118]

---

[114] *Ibid.*, 542.   [115] *Ibid.*   [116] *Ibid.*, 551.   [117] *Ibid.*
[118] *The Times of India*, September 16, 1954, p. 11. Cited in: Donald Eugene Smith, *Nehru and Democracy* (Bombay: Orient Longmans, 1958), 165.

The exportation of the civil code debate from the Constituent Assembly to the legislature did not mitigate the conflict. Already in 1948, an attempt to draft a comprehensive Hindu Code Bill to be passed by the legislature encountered intense opposition from conservative hardliners and Hindu fundamentalists within the Congress Party.[119] The Bill, which was initiated by Nehru, proposed to reform Hindu personal law and introduced principles of gender equality in issues of marriage and divorce, property and adoption, and abolished barriers of inter-caste marriage. While Nehru viewed the Bill as the cornerstone of modernization in India, given the intense opposition he agreed to break it into four different parts to enable their separate enactment.[120] Eventually, the legislation of the four parts of the Hindu Code was completed in 1961.[121] Nevertheless, while the legislation advanced secular reforms affecting the Hindu community, traditional Muslim personal law continued to apply to the Muslim community.[122]

The Assembly's decision to include the reference to a uniform civil code in the non-justiciable section of the constitution and its resulting distinction in legal status between members of different religious communities is still a hotly debated political and legal issue.[123] As will be discussed further in Chapter 7, the decision is often criticized for having allowed traditional patriarchal practices that restrict basic rights of women to persist.[124] The decision was also criticized as indecisive and an exercise in

---

[119] Jaffrelot, *The Hindu Nationalist Movement in India*, 102–4. The debate over codification of reformed Hindu law goes back to the Hindu Women's Rights to Property Act (1937) and the 1941 Hindu Law Committee appointed under the British rule.

[120] Reba Som, "Jawaharlal Nehru and the Hindu Code: A Victory of Symbol over Substance?" *Modern Asia Studies* 28, no. 1 (1994): 171.

[121] The Hindu Code includes the Hindu Marriage Act (1955), which outlawed polygamy and dealt with inter-caste marriage and divorce; the Hindu Adoption and Maintenance Act (1956) concerned the adoption of daughters and the rights of wives; the Hindu Succession Act (1956), which dealt with inheritance rights of daughters, and the Dowry Prohibition Act (1961).

[122] The validity of the different systems of personal laws for different religious groups and the power of the state to create new rules applicable to particular communities was upheld by the Indian Supreme Court in 1952 in *State of Bombay* v. *Narasu Appa Mali*. See Galanter, *Law and Society in Modern India*, 155.

[123] Gary Jacobsohn, *The Wheel of Law: India's Secularism in Comparative Constitutional Context* (Princeton University Press, 1993); Shylashri Shankar, "The War of the Worlds: Political Equality and Religious Freedom in India and Israel" (PhD dissertation, Columbia University, 2002).

[124] Flavia Agnes, "Law and Gender Inequality: The Politics of Women's Rights in India," in *Women and Law in India* (Oxford and New York: Oxford University Press, 2004). This point will be further discussed in Chapter 7.

evasion, a missed opportunity to provide a clear and unambiguous definition of India's identity as a Hindu or a secular nation.[125]

However, the Assembly's decision regarding uniform civil code
may also be seen as an intended decision to defer controversial choices
between rival sets of beliefs and commitments, so as to assuage the fears
of minority groups under conditions of deep mistrust between religious communities. Moreover, the Assembly's decision also represents
the drafters' acknowledgment in the moderate pace by which Indian
national unity would emerge. The Assembly recognized the limitations of constitutional provisions in the face of the complicated societal
reality which the constitution is expected to reflect. For this reason, it
preferred to follow an incrementalist rather than revolutionary constitutional approach. The Assembly transferred the decision regarding the
secular identity of the state from the legal back to the political arena,
leaving the decision on whether and how to implement its recommendation to future parliamentarians.

National language

Another area where the incrementalist principle was applied by the
Assembly was the issue of a national language.[126] The question whether
India should adopt a single national language was one of the most
drawn-out and hotly debated issues addressed by the Constituent
Assembly.

The complexity of the language problem in India stems from the
fact that India's linguistic diversity is among the richest in the world.
Moreover, the exact number of languages, mother tongues, dialects,
and speech varieties spoken throughout the country is a subject of con-
tinuous debate, and varies between different censuses and linguistic

---

[125] This line of criticism is voiced by both proponents and opponents of the uni-
form civil code. For example this was part of the Hindi-nationalist BJP's cam-
paign for national elections in 1996 and 1998. Khilnani, *The Idea of India*, 189–90;
see also: Seval Yildirim, "Expanding Secularism's Scope: An Indian Case Study,"
American Journal of Comparative Law 52 (2004); Rajkumari Agrawala, "Uniform
Civil Code: A Formula Not Solution," in Tahir Mahmood, ed., *Family Law and and
Social Change* (Bombay: MN Tripathy, 1975); Tahir Mahmood, *Personal Law in Crisis*
(New Delhi: Manohar, 1986).

[126] For an illuminating analysis of the unique relationship between language and Indian
culture and identity, before and after independence, see Kaviraj, "Writing, Speaking,
Being."

studies.[127] Hindi, which is a family name of various dialects, was spoken by less than 40 percent of the population. In fact, the only language commonly used throughout India for administrative and educational purposes was English. However, opposition to the language of the ruler had been at the heart of Gandhi's struggle for national independence as far back as 1918, and it was unthinkable that the Constituent Assembly would agree to its adoption as India's first language. As Nehru stated during the Assembly debates, "no nation can become great on the basis of a foreign language."[128] The two basic questions before the Assembly were, first, which language would replace English as the language of government, and, second, to what extent would English continue to be used for administrative purposes before being replaced by a native language.[129]

The two main factions in the Assembly debate over the national language were the representatives of the Hindi-speaking areas, mostly from north-central India and the representatives of non-Hindi-speaking regions particularly from the south, as well as the moderate leaders of the Congress Party. The Hindi-speaking representatives demanded that Hindi be declared as the national language and that it should replace English immediately.[130] They claimed that a multilingual society was incompatible with Indian unity. Seth Govind Das, a Congress representative of the Central Provinces and Berar, stated that "we want one language and one script for the whole country. We do not want it to be said that there are two cultures here."[131]

Representatives of non-Hindi-speaking regions contested the necessity of national linguistic homogeneity. "Not uniformity but unity in

---

[127] For example, the 1961 census counted 1,652 mother tongues, while the 1991 census recorded the total number of languages to be 114, and the total number of mother tongues to be 10,400. On the complexity of ethno-linguistic classification in India see: Asha Sarangi, ed. *Language and Politics in India* (New Delhi: Oxford University Press, 2009), 13–18.

[128] *CAD* IX, 421.

[129] A related debate was centered around the issue of the status of the regional languages and the reorganization of the provinces along linguistic borderlines. It was settled by Article 3, which provided that Parliament would be able to redraw state boundaries by a simple majority vote. In 1955 Parliament established a States Reorganization Commission, and the boundaries of India's states were eventually redrawn in conformity with linguistic lines. See Paul R. Brass, *Language, Religion and Politics in North India* (Lincoln, NE: An Authors Guild Backinprint.com, 2005).

[130] Seth Govind Das, *CAD* IX, 1331. [131] *Ibid.*

diversity," asserted Shri Shankarrao Deo from Bombay, who was the general secretary of the Congress.[132]

> When people use the term "national language" my heart does not respond to it. I admit India is a nation and I am an Indian, but if you will ask me "what is your language?", Sir, you will excuse me if I say "my language is Marathi" ... If you mean by national language one language for the whole country then I am against it. I must make it quite clear. India is a nation and I am an Indian but my language is Marathi.[133]

The moderate Congress leaders, headed by Nehru himself, recognized the practical difficulties in adopting Hindi as the national language.[134] The vast majority of the population did not speak the language, and imposing Hindi on a non-Hindi-speaking, largely illiterate population was virtually impossible. It was even argued that Hindi lacked the appropriate modern vocabulary required to govern a modern state.[135] Maulana Abul Kalam Azad, the Muslim president of the Congress Party, and a minister of education in Nehru's government, stressed, during the Assembly debate, the central role of English as the de facto language of law and government:

> This change [from English] should be ushered in only when a national language can be read and written in every part of the country and becomes mature enough for the expression of highly technical subjects ... Languages are never made; they evolve. They are never given a shape; they shape themselves. You cannot shut the mouths of people by artificial locks. If you do that, you will fail. Your locks would drop down. The law of language is beyond your reach; you can legislate for every other thing but not for ordering its natural evolution. That takes its own course, and only through that course it would reach its culmination.[136]

The dispute between extremists and moderates also touched upon the procedural question of how the decision on a national language should be reached. The proponents of Hindi demanded a simple majority decision, while its opponents emphasized the importance of a consensual, preferably unanimous, decision. Seth Govind Das represented the Hindi-speaking position:

---

[132] *Ibid.*, 1433.   [133] *Ibid.*, 1443.
[134] For a study of Nehru's approach to India's linguistic conflicts see Robert D. King, *Nehru and the Language Politics of India* (Delhi: Oxford University Press, 1997).
[135] *CAO*, IX, 1443.   [136] *CAD* IX, 1457.

> We have accepted democracy and democracy can only function when majority opinion is honoured. If we differ on any issue, that can only be decided by votes. Whatever decision is arrived at the majority must be accepted by the minority respectfully and without any bitterness.[137]

By contrast, S. P. Mookerjee (Christian Congress representative from Bengal, who later became the governor of Bengal), pointed to the difficulty of imposing a majoritarian decision on the minority: "If it is claimed by anyone that by passing an article in the Constitution of India one language is going to be accepted by all by a process of coercion, I say, Sir, that that will not be possible to achieve." Similarly, Prasad, the president of the Constituent Assembly, alerted the members to the tight link between consensus and the legitimacy of the constitution:

> whatever decision is taken with regard to the question of language, it will have to be carried out by the country as a whole … The decision of the House should be acceptable to the country as a whole. Even if we succeed in getting a particular proposition passed by majority, if it does not meet with the approval of any considerable section of people in the country … the implementation of the Constitution will become a most difficult problem.[138]

Eventually, it was the pragmatic consensus-seeking approach that triumphed. It was largely achieved by the insistence of Nehru himself, "who was the voice of moderation, the defender of English and regional Indian languages against the Hindi fanatics."[139] On September 14, 1949, after three years of debate, the Assembly overwhelmingly approved a compromise resolution, known as the Munshi-Ayyangar formula, which later became Articles 434–51 of the Indian constitution. Instead of declaring a "national language," Hindi was labeled the "official language of the Union" (Article 343), while English was to continue to be used "for all official purposes" (Article 351). It was decided that this arrangement would apply for a period of fifteen years, during which time Hindi was to be progressively introduced into official use. What would happen at the end of this interim period was left undetermined, with the constitution providing for the establishment of a parliamentary committee to examine the issue in the future (Article 344). In addition, the constitution recognized fourteen other languages for official use (listed in the Eighth Schedule of the constitution). The provincial governments were permitted to choose one of the regional languages, or English, for the conduct of their internal

---

[137] *Ibid.*, 1327. [138] *Ibid.*, 1315.
[139] Brecher, *Nehru: A Political Biography*, 424.

affairs, while English (unless Parliament would replace it with Hindi) would remained the language of inter-provincial communication.

As with the issue of a uniform civil code, the inability of the Assembly to reach broad agreement on the language issue led the framers to endorse a strategy of ambiguity, allowing the postponement of contentious decisions. In this way, the Constituent Assembly sustained the balance between its nationalist aspirations and their pragmatic realization.[140] On the one hand, the Indian constitution gave formal expression to the ideal of an Indian national language. On the other hand, the final decision on how to realize this ideal was deferred. The Assembly recognized that such a fundamental choice regarding the identity of the state could not be made simply by drafting a constitutional provision. But as the issue could not be ignored, the Assembly opted instead for an ambiguous formulation which avoided making a clear pronouncement, and preserved the conflicting opinions of the members within the constitution itself. In other words, their solution was to adopt an incrementalist strategy in the hope that the issue could be resolved in the future.

Ultimately, fifteen years after the enactment of the constitutional provisions on an Indian national language, Hindi was not widely used by the Union government. On the provincial level, only the Hindi-speaking states adopted Hindi for official use, and even then, not always widely. In other states regional languages replaced English as the language of subordinate courts and of legislative proceedings, but otherwise English remained the principal language of the government.[141] Paradoxically, in the years after independence, English became more entrenched in the Indian administrative and business world because, as Sudipta Kaviraj put it, "the earlier political compulsion of using vernaculars to underline self-respect had less relevance."[142]

But it was only after a series of violent riots in non-Hindi-speaking states in the 1960s that Parliament renounced the ideal of an Indian national language. In 1965, when the fifteen-year interim period prescribed by the constitution elapsed, northern Hindi-speaking states demanded that Hindi be declared as the national language. Growing concern among the non-Hindi-speaking population in the south, and in particular the Tamil elites, that the exclusive use of Hindi in the examination for the Indian Administrative Service and in Indian courts would limit their career

---

[140] See also Khilnani, *The Idea of India*, 175.
[141] Austin, *Working a Democratic Constitution* ch. 6.
[142] Kaviraj, "Writing, Speaking, Being," 54.

prospects, resulted in riots breaking out in Madras and in other towns in February 1965. Troops opened fire on protesters, causing an estimated 100 dead and leading to the arrest of some 10,000 people.[143] To bring an end to the crisis, the government announced that English would remained the de facto formal language of India.[144]

Today, twenty-two languages are recognized in the Eighth Schedule of the Indian Constitution and may be used officially at the level of state administration.[145] India's functional multilingualism is expressed in many other ways. For example, newspapers and periodicals are published in about ninety-seven languages; sixty-seven languages are used for primary education; and, All India Radio broadcasts in 104 languages.[146] While linguistic identity in India is a constant cause of political debate and struggle, language is no longer a source of endemic group conflict and violence in India.[147] Indeed, the resolution of language issues succeeded due to the compromise regarding the question of national language, as well as, the continuing process of territorial reorganization of the Indian states along linguistic lines. Since 1956, the government of India occasionally reconfigurated state boundaries in response to demands for the formation of culturally unified states, while, at the same time, attempting to safeguard the rights of linguistic minorities.[148]

Constructive ambiguity

In the conclusion of his comprehensive study of the making of the Indian constitution, Granville Austin notes the ability of the Constituent

---

[143] Brass, *Language, Religion and Politics in North India*, 123.

[144] It is interesting to compare the Indian decision to maintain English as a de facto formal language of the state with an opposite decision, which led to destructive consequences, in Sri Lanka, where Sinhalese politicians eliminated English as the language of administration. It is commonly claimed that this decision was one of choices "that contributed to turning the non-issue of Tamil separatism in the 1940s into one of the world's most intractable and bloody conflicts." Linz *et al.*, *Crafting State Nations*, 94.

[145] For comparative perspective, in other multi-linguistic democracies such as Belgium, Canada and Switzerland the number of official languages is between two to four. South Africa recognizes eleven formal languages. Indonesia, where the number of dialects is over 560, has only one official language – bahasa-indonesia.

[146] Sarangi, *Language and Politics in India*, 17.

[147] Paul Brass, "Elite Interest, Popular Passion, and Social Power in the Language Politics of India," in: *Ibid*, 213.

[148] On the various political considerations in the government's decisions regarding state organization see: Joseph E. Schwartzberg, "Factors in the Linguistic Reorganization of Indian States", in: *ibid*, 139–182.

Assembly to encompass conflicting principles as one of its most original contributions to the theory of constitution-making. The Assembly, he comments, was able "to reconcile, to harmonize, and to make work without changing their context, apparently incompatible concepts – at least concepts that appear conflicting to the non-Indian, and especially to the European or American observer."[149] Others, however, have criticized the Indian constitution precisely on this issue. Stressing its lack of theoretical consistency and its failure to present a coherent system of values and beliefs, they point to internal contradictions between various provisions which represent competing principles and perspectives, such as modernity and traditionalism, social reform and social conservatism,[150] church–state separation versus state intervention in religious affairs,[151] liberalism and individual rights versus communitarianism and special group rights.[152]

However, the adoption of ambiguous constitutional formulations in the area of personal law and national language represented a conscious strategy of the Indian Constituent Assembly. B. N. Rau, the key legal advisor of the Constituent Assembly, expressed this view when he stated: "we have to bear in mind that conditions in India are rapidly changing; the country is in a state of flux politically and economically; and

---

[149] Austin, *The Indian Constitution*, 317.

[150] Alongside reformist provisions such as the abolition of the status of untouchability (Article 17) and the prohibition of child labor in factories (Article 26), the constitution also includes recommendations for the prohibition of alcohol (Article 47) and of cow slaughter (Article 48), which are "indigenous" Hindu laws. However, these two Articles are found in the non-justiciable part of the constitution, a decision which was criticized in the Assembly as a failure to adequately represent and protect the traditional institutions and principles of Hindu thought *CAD* VII, 832.

[151] For example, Article 25 which permits extensive state intervention in religious matters in the interest of social reform, conflicts with the principle of autonomy for religious institutions, which is one of the tenets of of secularism. This criticism was most clearly presented by Anthony Smith, *The Ethnic Origins of Nations* (Oxford and New York, B. Blackwell, 1986), 101, 26. Nevertheless, it is worth noting that the lack of constitutional uniformity in questions of religion and culture is highly valued by legal and political scholars who claim that it should be seen as a successful attempt to craft a multi-dimensional system of values and principles corresponding to the intricate needs of Indian society. For analysis of the complex, multi-valued ethos of the Indian "contextual secularism" see Rajeev Bhargava, *Secularism and Its Critics, Themes in Politics Series* (Delhi and New York: Oxford University Press, 1998); Rajeev Bhargava, "What Is Indian Secularism and What Is It For?" *India Review* 1, no. 1 (2002).

[152] Thus, for example, Article 15 is included under the title "equality before the law," yet it also provides for the making of special provisions for women and children (section 15.3) as well as for "backward" classes and scheduled castes and tribes (section 15.4).

the constitution should not be too rigid in its initial years."[153] As such, it reflects a coherent constitutional approach that rejects a cohesive value-system (such as the one proposed by the advocates of a uniform Indian identity) and refrains from imposing, through the means of majority voting, Hindu tradition and values on non-Hindu religious and cultural communities. B. R. Ambedkar used similar terms when he explained the underlying objective of the Directive Principles of State Policy: "It is no use giving a fixed, rigid form to something which is not rigid, which is fundamentally changing and must have regard to circumstances and keep on changing."[154] Nevertheless, according to Ambedkar, the Directive Principles had an important role in guiding future legislatures to promote the principles of economic democracy: "Because we did not want merely a parliamentary form of government to be instituted through the various mechanisms provided in the Constitution, without any direction as to what our economic ideal or as to what our social order ought to be, we deliberately included the Directive Principles in our Constitution."[155]

The debates in the Indian Constituent Assembly demonstrate the unsuitability of the liberal-procedural constitutional model for deeply divided societies. The issues of national language and religious identity stood at the heart of India's self-definition and could not be ignored. The Assembly could not simply remove these contentious issues entirely from its agenda and draft a purely proceduralist constitution based on a lib-eral-institutional mechanism of conflict resolution. The framers there-fore embraced the conflicts and imported them into the constitution by crafting ambiguous constitutional formulation.

In the religious domain, the constitution is clear about the aim of uni-fying the nation's personal law on the basis of secular principles, but it leaves Parliament to decide in what way and at what pace this goal should be pursued in practice. Similarly, while the framers included in the consti-tution clear statements regarding the primacy of liberal values and prin-ciples, they also acknowledged the constraints under which they labored. The uncertainty faced by Muslims who decided to remain in India after the partition riots and the need to reassure them that the constitution would protect their cultural identity compelled the authors of the consti-tution to compromise and adopt an ambiguous constitutional arrange-ment which opened the door for legal pluralism.

---

[153] B. N. Rau, "The Indian Constitution" an article contributed to Independence Day spe-cial issue of *The Hindu*, August 15, 1948, reprinted in B. N. Rau, *India's Constitution in the Making* (Bombay: Orient Longmans, 1960), 360–6.
[154] *CAD* III, 494.   [155] *CAD* III, 494–5.

In the linguistic domain, the tension between the nationalistic aspirations of the framers, based on the model of the monolingual European nation-state, clashed with the Indian reality of many vernacular languages. The ambiguity of the framers in addressing this problem is reflected in their decision to defer the decision on national language, without even providing clear instructions or criteria for how governments of the future should act. While the drafters accorded legitimacy to regional identities, they also wished to promote "a second order self-identification of the people as Indians."[156] This ambiguity resulted in a growing divergence between the declared policy of Nehru's government – which gently advocated Hindi as the official language for the Union government and communication between states – and the actual use of language in government.[157]

To conclude, the constitution reflected its authors' understanding of the need for an incrementalist approach when it came to key issues relating to national identity and the state's underlying commitments. The debates in the Assembly demonstrated the framers' realization that in the context of a deeply fragmented society, the expectation that the constitution could provide a sense of unity or common identity was unrealistic. The Indian constitution preserved within it the competing beliefs and values of the various factions which aspired to leave an imprint on the formal document. By that, the Indian framers were committed to what Isaiah Berlin referred to as moral pluralism, his conviction that

> [t]he old perennial belief in the possibility of realizing ultimate harmony is a fallacy … that Great Goods can collide[.] But the collisions, even if they cannot be avoided, can be softened. Claims can be balanced, compromises can be reached … Priorities, never final and absolute, must be established.[158]

The Indian constitution, in sum, demonstrates how complex segmented societies may adopt complex segmented constitutions. In other words, the constitution of a deeply divided society may end up reflecting the conflicted identity of "the people" in whose name it is written. The Indian framers recognized the limits of the process of constitution-making in resolving internal conflicts, and used ambiguous legal language to facilitate further deliberation over contentious issues. These constitutional ambiguities in the issues of religion and language resulted in the prolongation of the

---

[156] Kaviraj, "Writing, Speaking, Being," 48.   [157] *Ibid.*, 54.
[158] Isaiah Berlin, "The Pursuit of the Ideal," in Henry Hardy, ed., *The Crooked Timber of Humanity: Chapters in the History of Ideas* (Princeton University Press, 1990), 17.

debates in the political and judicial spheres. The incrementalist strategies lend strength to Rajeev Bhargava's observation that the Indian constitution reflects a faith in political deliberation. The Constituent Assembly's endorsement of inclusive and open-ended principles "indicate the willingness of people to modify their existing preferences – in short, to justify outcomes by reference not to self-interest but to reason."[159]

Thus, the achievement of the Indian constitution is that by refraining from resolving certain contentious issues in a clear and decisive manner it succeeded in creating strong institutional structures which helped preserve democratic order despite the continuing tensions around the foundational aspects of the constitution. As Linz *et al.* show, despite the fact that India is more culturally and linguistically diverse than any other stable democracy, the democratic form of government is supported by the overwhelming majority of Indians across these diverse communities.[160] According to an Indian National Election Study conducted in 1998, there is no difference in levels of support of democracy among the members of the major religious groups in India.[161] Indians to this day have among the highest degree of trust in state institutions of any democratic country. Finally, although less than 30 percent of the Indian population speak Hindi, are Hindu, or live in a territory which experienced the homogenizing influences of the British colonial rule or the independence movement, 87.7 percent of the population expressed their pride in being Indian.[162]

The embodiment of the incrementalist approach to constitution-making in the constitution's foundational aspect thus provides a key to explaining the persistence of Indian representative democracy despite unprecedented historical odds. In the words of Rajeev Bhargava, "the refusal of the framers to give us well-deliniated criteria to settle all moral conflicts is the strength, not the weakness, of the constitution."[163]

---

[159] Bhargava, *Politics and Ethics of the Indian Constitution*, 25.

[160] Linz *et al.*, *Crafting State Nations*.

[161] 60.1 percent of Hindus, 59.2 percent of Muslims, 61.8 percent of Christians and 66.4 percent of Sikhs preferred democracy over any other form of government. *Ibid.*, 60.

[162] In answer to the World View survey question "How proud are you to be Indian?" 69.9 percent said they had a "great deal" of pride and 18.1 percent answered they were "quite" proud. *Ibid.*, 84.

[163] Bhargava, *Politics and Ethics of the Indian Constitution*, 28.

5

Symbolic ambivalence in Ireland

The constitution of Ireland (Bunreacht na hÉireann) was adopted in 1937. However, in the words of J. M. Kelly, author of one of the most important studies on the Irish constitution, "while all branches of our law depend for their formal validity on the 1937 Constitution, this enactment was very largely a re-bottling of wine most of which was by then quite old and of familiar vintages."[1] The old wine that Kelly is referring to is the constitution of the Irish Free State (Saorstát Éireann), which was adopted in 1922.

Just as in the Israeli and Indian cases, the 1922 Irish constitution was drafted under conditions of a deep ideological rift over the fundamental norms and ultimate goals of the state. The polarization over the definition of Irish nationalism and Irish sovereignty was so intense that it split the Irish nationalist movement, Sinn Féin, and caused a nearly year-long civil war which claimed more lives than the two-and-a-half years of war against the British. It was in the midst of that war, between the proponents of two competing visions of independent Ireland, that the Irish Free State constitution was drafted.[2]

The constitutional debates on the 1922 constitution were inter-linked with the debates on the Anglo-Irish Treaty (henceforth "the Treaty"), which defined the relationship between Ireland and the British Commonwealth. Indeed, the drafting of the 1922 Irish Free State constitution differs from the constitutional debates in Israel and India in that it was shaped to a considerable extent by the demands of a foreign

---

[1] Gerard Hogan and Gerry Whyte, *J. M. Kelly: The Irish Constitution*, 4th edn. (Dublin: Lexis Nexis Butterworths, 2003), ix.

[2] The split in Sinn Féin which occurred in 1922 as a result of ideological disagreements over the Anglo-Irish Treaty and the constitution led to the creation of what are still the two largest parties in Irish politics, Fianna Fáil and Fine Gael. In over eight decades of Irish democracy the two parties have never been able to come together to form a coalition government. As Bill Kissane noted, "the key issue of the civil war – how Irish republicanism could be reconciled to a democratic but 26 (rather than 32) county state – remains a source of contention in Ireland even in the early twenty-first century." Bill Kissane, *The Politics of the Irish Civil War* (Oxford University Press, 2005), 213.

power – the British government – which imposed some of its provisions through a military ultimatum. The question at the center of the constitutional debates – whether and to what extent Irish nationalist goals should be expressed in the document – was the direct result of British pressure on the drafting process.

Nevertheless, as in the cases of Israel and India, the Irish Free State constitution was debated and ratified by a democratically elected Irish Parliament (Dáil Éireann). Moreover, as in the cases of Israel and India, the internal Irish debates on the constitution reflected a fundamental disagreement over the role of the constitution in deeply divided societies, and revolved around the question of whether a revolutionary or incrementalist approach was more appropriate. This chapter will seek to show how the unique conditions under which the Irish Free State constitution was drafted not only dictated the question that stood at the center of the constitutional debate, but also affected the type of incrementalist strategy used by the framers: the adoption of an ambivalent constitutional document that includes conflicting and contrasting statements regarding the meaning of Irish nationalism and Irish sovereignty.

The drafting of the 1922 constitution will be the focus of this chapter. It will first discuss the dispute over the Anglo-Irish Treaty, which triggered the split within Sinn Féin and led to civil war. It will then trace the various stages of constitutional debates and negotiations in Ireland and in London, which resulted in the ambivalence in the constitution regarding the definition of Irish sovereignty and nationalism. Finally, it will briefly discuss the enactment of the new constitution in 1937 and the constitutional developments of 1998 (the amendments to Articles 2 and 3 as part of the Good Friday Agreement), which can be seen as a continuation of the debate between the revolutionist and pragmatist approaches of constitution-drafting in a deeply divided society. This debate began in Ireland with the split between Michael Collins and Eamon de Valera in 1922 – between the perception of the constitution as a moment of realization of all national aspirations, and an incrementalist view of the constitution as an evolutionary process based on the gradual emergence of societal consensus.

The treaty debates

The Articles of Agreement for a Treaty between Great Britain and Ireland, commonly known as the Anglo-Irish Treaty, were signed on December 6, 1921, bringing to an end two-and-a-half years of violent war and 750 years of various systems of British rule in Ireland.[3] The Treaty established the Irish Free State, which was assigned a constitutional status of dominion. Under the Treaty, the relationship between the United Kingdom and the Free State would be similar to that between the United Kingdom and Canada, including the appointment of a Governor-General to formally oversee politics in the dominion. Ireland assumed a portion of the United Kingdom's national debt, and agreed not to raise a defense force greater, in proportion to its population, than that of Britain. Further, the British were guaranteed the use of several Irish ports in peacetime for at least five years, and they were allowed to use additional facilities in wartime. One of the most controversial Articles of the Treaty required the members of the Free State Parliament to swear allegiance to King George V.[4]

The Treaty provided that the constitution of the Irish Free State would be drafted by the Irish themselves, under the guidelines set in the Treaty, and according to a strict timetable: the constitution had to be adopted within one year.[5] The Anglo-Irish Treaty had to be ratified by both British and Irish parliaments. After the enactment of the constitution, the six

---

[3] The Treaty was signed after three months of negotiations in London between the Irish and the British delegations. The Irish delegation included Arthur Griffith, Michael Collins, Robert Barton, Eamon Duggan and George Gavan Duffy. The British signatories were Lloyd George, Austern Chamberlain, Lord Birkenhead, Winston Churchill, Worthington Evans, Hamar Greenwood and Gordon Hewart. For the full text of the Treaty, as well as for a detailed description of the negotiations between the delegations, see Frank Pakenham Longford, *Peace by Ordeal: The Negotiation of the Anglo-Irish Treaty, 1921* (London: Pimlico, 1992).

[4] Nevertheless, while in other dominions the oath was to the king personally, the Irish were only asked to swear to the king "in virtue of the common citizenship of Ireland with Great Britain and her adherence to and membership of the group of nations forming the British Commonwealth of Nations" (Article 4). See Alan J. Ward, *The Irish Constitutional Tradition: Responsible Government and Modern Ireland, 1782–1992* (Washington, DC: Catholic University of America Press, 1994), 163–4.

[5] The Treaty did not recognize the authority of the existing Dáil Éireann and required that the constitution be ratified by representatives elected in May 1921 in accordance with the provisions of the Government of Ireland Act. The first Dáil Éireann was convened in January 1919 by twenty-nine members of Sinn Féin who held seats in the British Parliament. It was proscribed by the British soon after its establishment and had to hold its meetings in secret. Most of its members were arrested and overall it held only twelve meetings between 1919 and 1921. The first Dáil adopted a very short constitution, which included five articles concerning the procedures of the Dáil. The Dáil sent representatives to the Paris peace talks demanding recognition of the Irish right of self-determination, but it never received the international recognition to which it aspired. The second Dáil, comprising 124 representatives from the south and one from the north, was elected in May 1921. See *ibid.*, 153–9. See also: Brian Farrell, *The Founding of Dáil Éireann: Parliament and Nation-Building* (Dublin: Gill and Macmillan, 1971).

northern counties of Ireland (part of the province of Ulster) would be allowed to opt out of the Irish Free State and maintain their status as part of the United Kingdom. Should they decide to do so, a boundary commission would be appointed for the demarcation of the border between the north and the south.

The Dáil Éireann agonizingly debated whether to ratify or reject the Treaty during twelve public sessions and one secret one, spread over nearly a month. At stake was the future of Ireland and the realization of Irish national aspirations. The question of Ulster and the potential territorial division between north and south received little attention during the Dáil debates on the Treaty, and relations between Catholics and Protestants in Ireland were hardly mentioned. The debate centered on the definitions of Irish nationalism and sovereignty.[6]

The supporters of the Treaty emphasized its implicit recognition of Irish sovereignty and independence from Britain. The Treaty was made between two separate nations, equally recognizing each other, argued Arthur Griffith, the founder of Sinn Féin and one of the signatories of the Treaty, during the Dáil debates:

> We have come back from London with that Treaty – Saorstát na hÉireann recognized – the Free State of Ireland. We have brought back the flag; we have brought back the evacuation of Ireland after 700 years by British troops and the formation of an Irish army. We have brought back to Ireland her full rights and powers of fiscal control. We have brought back to Ireland equality with England.[7]

The proponents of the Treaty viewed it as a "stepping stone" toward complete independence, one that gave the Irish "the freedom to achieve freedom," in the words of Michael Collins.[8] Collins, who was the military leader of the armed struggle against Britain, was among the signatories of the Treaty, and later became the first Chairman of the provisional government of the Irish Free State. The Treaty, he argued, provided the Irish with

---

[6] Private session of second Dáil, *Dáil Debates* (December 15, 1921). All protocols of the Dáil Debates from January 21, 1921 are available online at the website of Ireland's Parliamentary Debates: http://historical-debates.oireachtas.ie.

[7] *Dáil Debates* (December 19, 1921). Griffith, who became the first president of the Irish Free State, was one of the strongest supporters of a compromise with the British. Already in 1904 he proposed that Ireland adopt the Austro-Hungarian model of a dual monarchy, symbolically representing the common interest of the people of the two islands, with an independent Irish parliament in which popularly elected representatives would control the government. Arthur Griffith, *The Resurrection of Hungary: A Parallel for Ireland*, 3rd edn. (Dublin: Whelan and Son, 1918).

[8] *Dáil Debates* (December 19, 1921).

de facto sovereignty. England had "renounced all right to govern Ireland and the withdrawal of her forces [was] the proof of this."[9] He believed that even if the Treaty did not itself provide for full Irish independence, the limited sovereignty which it granted could be leveraged by the Irish to further their nationalist aspirations: "obtaining by the Treaty the constitutional status of Canada, and that status being one of freedom and equality, we are free to take advantage of that status and we shall set up our constitution on independent Irish lines."[10] During a public meeting of the Dáil Éireann on December 19, 1921, Collins argued that possibly even more important than the military withdrawal was the fact that the Treaty provided for economic separation between Ireland and Britain, thus stopping the economic penetration that "has destroyed our Gaelic civilization."[11] Collins also argued that the Treaty should be accepted for pragmatic reasons, since its rejection by the Irish would inevitably lead to war against the British.[12]

By contrast, hard-line Republicans refused to accept any agreement with the British short of complete independence. Dominion status and the fact that the British Parliament had to approve the Irish constitution were perceived by them as a British victory. Eamon De Valera, the president of the Dáil and the leader of Sinn Féin, led the campaign against the Treaty in the Dáil debates. Dominion status, he argued, was not a guarantee against British interference in Ireland. What guaranteed the freedom of Canada, Australia and South Africa was their size and distance from the British Isles, as well as the historical nature of the relationship between Britain and these former settler colonies.[13] De Valera saw the Treaty as a solemn, binding and unbreakable contract. Consequently, it was not a stepping stone but a barrier to independence. If the Irish people entered into it voluntarily, the British government would hold them to the terms of the agreement should any future leader try to alter the nature of the relationship.[14] "This Treaty means that the Ministers of the Irish Free State will be His Majesty's Ministers and the Irish Forces will be His Majesty's Forces," he stated.[15]

The central fear of the Republicans was that, while the limitations that the Treaty imposed were mostly symbolic, they nevertheless compromised

[9] Michael Collins, *The Path to Freedom* (Dublin: The Talbot Press, 1922), 38.
[10] *Ibid.*, 37–8.   [11] *Dáil Debates* (December 19, 1921).   [12] *Ibid.*
[13] Maurice Moynihan, ed., *Speeches and Statements by Eamon De Valera 1917–1973* (New York: St. Martin's Press, 1980), 95–6.
[14] *Ibid.*, 94.   [15] *Ibid.*, 91.

Irish national sovereignty. The most controversial clause was Article 4, which required the members of the Irish Parliament to pledge allegiance to the king. De Valera's position was that symbols, including the crown, should not be taken lightly:

> You may sneer at words, but I say words mean, and I say in a Treaty words do mean something – else why should they be put down? They have meanings and they have facts, great realities that you cannot close your eyes to.[16]

Against the argument that the Free State should be seen as a starting point which would lead to greater freedom and autonomy in the future, Erskine Childers, one of the vocal objectors to the Treaty, noted that the only other two Free States in the world were the colony of the "Congo Free State" and the Boer "Orange Free State" which was a minor province inside the Dominion of South Africa.[17] Childers also argued against the analogy with Canada. Ireland's geographical proximity to Britain, he claimed, would always prevent equal status.[18]

On January 9, 1922 the Dáil Éireann approved the Treaty, sixty-seven members voting in favor and fifty-seven voting against. In protest at the decision, de Valera resigned and withdrew from the Dáil along with all the other members who opposed the Treaty. Arthur Griffith was elected as the new president. One week later the British transferred all executive powers to the provisional government of the Irish Free State, headed by Michael Collins. The new provisional government began preparing for the drafting of the constitution immediately after the formal transfer of power by appointing a committee to undertake the task. However, the successful passage of the Treaty in the Dáil and the launching of the constitution-making process in no way represented the end of the debate over the Treaty which had divided the Irish public. The debates around the constitution essentially continued the dispute over the Treaty, and revolved around the symbolic and foundational aspects of the constitution, that is around the question of whether the constitution would reinforce Ireland's continued subjugation to Britain and block its aspirations for full independence or whether it would facilitate Ireland's emergence as an independent political entity

---

[16] *Ibid.*

[17] Erskine Childers, *What the Treaty Means* (Printed from 'The Republic of Ireland', 1922), 4.

[18] Erskine Childers, *Dáil Debates* (December 19, 1921). On the Treaty debates see also: Nicholas Mansergh, *The Unresolved Question: The Anglo-Irish Settlement and Its Undoing, 1912–72* (New Haven: Yale University Press, 1991).

The drafting of the constitution began against the background of the split within Sinn Féin, which, within half a year after the Treaty was approved by the Dáil, led to civil war. The war lasted eleven months, and estimates of casualties are around 1,000.[19]

The acrimonious nature of the debate around the Treaty and the constitution and its grave consequences regarding the unity of the Irish Free State attest to the fact that these debates reflected a deep division within the Irish nationalist movement. The division touched upon the basis of Irish political identity, upon the meaning of Irish nationalism, and of Irish national aspirations and upon its relations with the British Empire.

Conflicting visions of independent Ireland

Historians of the Irish civil war attribute the violent escalation of the Treaty divide into a civil war and its enduring impact on Irish political culture to the ideological schism which divided the leadership of the nationalist movement from its very first days. The split was rooted in the two rival traditions of Irish nationalism that developed gradually in the second half of the nineteenth century between what John Hutchinson calls "cultural nationalism" and "political nationalism."[20] Cultural nationalism originated with the Gaelic revival and celebrated the distinctiveness of Irish identity, rejecting any cultural, economic or political synthesis with the British.[21] Political nationalism, by contrast, was embodied in an Anglo-Irish tradition which followed an assimilationist logic. It worked the channels of representation at Westminster to achieve the kind of economic and educational progress that was not prized by the cultural nationalists.[22] The middle-class leaders of the political nationalists were "men long immersed in British political and cultural life, secularists in their outlook and who admired its liberal democratic ideals."[23]

Political nationalists conceived of the nation largely in legal-historical and constitutional terms. They argued against the dissolution of Ireland's native Parliament by the Act of Union, and called for Home Rule in order

---

[19] Kissane, *The Politics of the Irish Civil War*. Hopkinson claims that the number of dead was much higher, and even reached 4,000. Michael Hopkinson, *Green against Green: The Irish Civil War* (Dublin: Gill and Macmillan, 1988).

[20] John Hutchinson, *The Dynamics of Cultural Nationalism: The Gaelic Revival and the Creation of the Irish Nation State* (London: Allen & Unwin, 1987).

[21] Kissane, *The Politics of the Irish Civil War*, 23–7.   [22] *Ibid.*, 27–8.

[23] Hutchinson, *The Dynamics of Cultural Nationalism*, 152.

to guarantee the Irish people an equal status within the British Empire.[24] Cultural nationalists, by contrast, understood the Irish nation in organic terms, portraying Ireland as a living personality whose individuality had to be cherished in all its manifestations.[25]

While in practice there was considerable cooperation between the two strands of Irish nationalism, they differed substantially in their ideals and goals. Cultural nationalists aimed at reviving a distinctive Irish community, whereas the goal of political nationalists was the normalization of Ireland's place among the nations of the world by regaining its independence.[26] The practical implication of the cultural tradition was isolation if not autarky, whereas for the political tradition the aim was that an autonomous Ireland modeled on English liberal lines be given its proper status as a partner in the British imperial mission.[27]

Bill Kissane argues that the rival traditions within the nationalist movement should be seen as the root causes of the 1922 split over the Treaty settlement.[28] To some, the Treaty offered a chance to show that the Irish were as worthy of self-government as anybody else, while to others it amounted to an abandonment of their national birthright.[29] The Treaty was thus perceived as either the cradle or the grave of Irish national aspirations. For this reason, both sides claimed to speak in the name of "the people" in its struggle for national realization and to represent its authentic will. Public opinion largely agreed with the provisional government,[30] which fact was generally disregarded by the anti-Treatyites, who considered themselves as "above the political process."[31] In 1926 de Valera

---

[24] Kissane, *The Politics of the Irish Civil War*, 28.

[25] Hutchinson, *The Dynamics of Cultural Nationalism*, 153.   [26] *Ibid.*, 152.

[27] *Ibid.* Tom Garvin makes a somewhat similar distinction between what he views as two subcultures or collective political styles within the nationalist movement. On the one side were the "republican moralists," who saw the Republic as a moral and transcendental entity analogous to the church, an entity whose citizens were duty bound to defend with their lives. On the other side stood the "nationalist pragmatists," who saw the establishment of the Republic as a strategic step toward achieving rational-legal self-government for as much of Ireland as possible, regardless of formal political labels. While the republican nationalists envisioned the Irish state in terms of a national moral community, the nationalist pragmatists viewed it as a state of its citizens, whose individual identity was a private rather than a public matter. Tom Garvin, *1922: The Birth of Irish Democracy* (Dublin: Gill & Macmillan, 1996), 143–5.

[28] Kissane, *The Politics of the Irish Civil War*, 36–7.   [29] *Ibid.*, 29.

[30] The Treaty was supported by the general public, by the church and by local governments. *Ibid.*, 67.

[31] Peter Hart, *The IRA at War 1916–1923* (Oxford and New York: Oxford University Press, 2003) 97. As Liam Deasy, one of the leaders of the IRA, wrote in his memoirs, "the results

summarized the Treaty dispute in one sentence: "[It was] the conflict between the two principles, majority rule on the one hand and the inalienability of national sovereignty on the other, that was the dilemma of the Treaty."[32]

Both sides used democratic arguments to support their position. After the Treaty vote in the Dáil, anti-Treatyites wished to disregard the majority's approval, arguing that it defied the true and essential voice of the Irish people, referring to the sovereign nation of the island which expressed their will in 1918 and 1921. Instead, they argued that the threat of war with Britain meant that approval had been granted only "under duress." Given these conditions, they stressed, the public acceptance of the Treaty was not an expression of the will of the people but of "the fear of the people."[33]

In his speeches in the Dáil during the Treaty debates, de Valera also claimed to "truly represent" the "will of the nation." He drew a parallel between his opposition to the Treaty and the Easter Rising of 1916, which was initiated by a small minority of individuals with little public support, who nevertheless "truly represented the heart and feeling of the nation."

> Those who said we had no right to "rebel", as it was called, because we didn't represent the views of the people, were proved to have told untruths. Whatever may have been said about the chances of success and other matters, there is one thing that stands proved historically – that these men did represent the hearts and souls and aspirations of the Irish people. I say that no election taken under duress or anything else will disprove that today … there would never be peace which neglects the fundamental fact … that the Irish people want to live their own lives in their own way without any outside authority whatever being imposed upon them, whether it is the authority of the British Crown or any other authority whatever.[34]

show a swing … in favor of the Treaty, yet, this had little effect on the morale of the Republican Army[.] From the first by-election in 1917 we were never unduly influenced by election results." Liam Deasy, *Brother against Brother* (Dublin and Cork: The Mercier Press, 1982), 43.

[32] Cited in the Earl of Longford and Thomas P. O'Neill, *Eamon De Valera* (London: Hutchinson, 1970), 186.

[33] Kissane, *The Politics of the Irish Civil War*, 183, n. 25.

[34] Moynihan, *Speeches and Statements by Eamon De Valera 1917–1973*, 92. Later in the speech De Valera took a personal approach: "the first fifteen years of my life that formed my character were lived amongst the Irish people down in Limerick; therefore I know what I am talking about; and whenever I wanted to know what the Irish people wanted I had only to examine my own heart. And it told me straight off what the Irish people wanted." *Ibid.*, 93.

Arthur Griffith, by contrast, emphasized the broad public and electoral support for the Treaty. For this reason, in his public statements he repeatedly linked Irish sovereignty with the need for democratic mechanisms of majority rule. "There [is] but one sovereign and supreme power in Ireland, and that [is] the people, and it [is] for the people to say whether they would have the Treaty or not."[35] Griffith insisted that the Irish had to adhere to the basic principles of democracy, since they "could have no workable system of government unless they had majority rule in the country. It might have its defects. The majority might sometimes be wrong, but they had chaos unless as a democracy they submitted to majority rule."[36]

Despite the intense division between the pro- and anti-Treatyites and the split within Sinn Féin, the provisional government began drafting the constitution in the hope, which was soon dashed, that the drafting process would bridge the divisions and heal the rifts within Irish society.[37]

Collins' goal of consensus

Michael Collins, as the chairman of the provisional government, chaired the drafting committee, but was not involved in most of its day-to-day deliberations.[38] The journalist and poet Darrell Figgis was selected as deputy chairman and secretary of the committee, and was its only paid member. The composition of the rest of the committee reflected an attempt to avoid any type of partisan representation: James Douglas was a Dublin businessman, deeply involved in humanitarian activities and a close friend of Michael Collins. Five members of the committee were legal experts: there were three barristers – Kevin O'Shiel, John O'Byrne (subsequently a high court justice) and Hugh Kennedy (who became the first Chief Justice of the Irish Supreme Court), as well as two other legal experts: C. J. France, an American lawyer, and James Murnaghan, law professor

---

[35] Speaking at a meeting in support of the Treaty at Dundalk, on March 12, 1922. Arthur Griffith, *Arguments for the Treaty* (Dublin: Martin Lester, 1922), 30.

[36] Speaking at the annual convention (Ard Fheis) of Sinn Féin, held in Dublin on February 21, 1922. *Ibid.*, 23.

[37] Brian P. Murphy, "Nationalism: The Framing of the Constitution of the Irish Free State, 1922 – the Drafting Battle for the Irish Republic," in Joost Augusteijn, ed., *The Irish Revolution, 1913–1923* (New York: Palgrave, 2002), 136.

[38] The most detailed historical account of the constitution-making process, based largely on contemporary British documents, is D. H. Akenson and J. F. Fallin, "The Irish Civil War and the Drafting of the Free State Constitution, Part I, II, III," *Éire-Ireland* 5, no. 1, 2, 4 (1970).

at University College, Dublin. Four members were civil servants: James MacNeill, R. J. P. Mortished, P. A. O'Toole and E. M. Stephens. Perhaps the most atypical member of the committee was Alfred O'Rahilly, a professor of mathematical physics at University College, Cork, and a fierce defender of the interests of the Roman Catholic Church in the new state.

The non-partisan character of the committee was also reflected in the fact that three of the committee members (Douglas, MacNeill and France) were former leaders of the Irish White Cross, a non-sectarian relief agency founded in January 1921 to assist Irish civilians who suffered during the war with Britain, funded by the American Committee for Relief in Ireland, which succeeded in remaining above politics throughout the war.[39]

In the first meeting of the drafting committee, on January 24, 1922, Collins presented guidelines for drafting the constitution. He instructed the committee to omit from the constitution everything that was already covered in the Treaty concerning the relations between Great Britain and Ireland, and to focus exclusively on establishing the mechanisms of Irish government. He insisted that the constitution should rest solely upon authority derived from the Irish people. Referring to the Treaty as a mere "legal formality," Collins argued that,

> You are not to be bound by legal formalities but to put up a constitution of a Free State and then bring it to the Provisional Government who will fight for the carrying of it through. It is a question of status and we want definitely to define and produce a true democratic constitution. You are to bear in mind not the legalities of the past but the practicalities of the future.[40]

Hoping to frame an independent constitution which would be acceptable at least to the more moderate anti-Treaty forces, Collins wished to leave out all mention of the oath of allegiance to the Crown, all treaty clauses dealing with the Governor-General, all reference to the powers vested in the king.[41]

In addition to bridging the ideological rift within the Catholic majority, Collins believed that the constitution-making process could also prevent the territorial division of the island. Hence, Collins led the drafting of the Irish Free State constitution on the assumption that it was being written for a unified state on the entire territory of the island. The Anglo-Irish Treaty

[39] On the White Irish Cross see *ibid.*: 20.
[40] Hugh Kennedy, "Character and Sources of Constitution of the Irish Free State," *American Bar Association Journal* 14, no. 8 (1928): 443.
[41] Douglas, "Memoirs" book I, sec. 2, pp. 47–9, in Akenson and Fallin, "The Irish Civil War and the Drafting of the Free State Constitution, Part I," 24.

indeed gave Northern Ireland the right to opt out of the new arrangements if its parliament so desired. However, the boundaries between Ulster and the rest of the island were to be determined only after the enactment of the constitution. The boundary would be revised by a commission comprising representatives from the Irish Free State, Northern Ireland and Great Britain. Before signing the Treaty, Collins was led by the British to believe that the boundary commission would render Northern Ireland a non-viable entity and that a merger with the south would follow. Furthermore, Collins was persuaded by Birkenhead and Churchill, during their talks in London, that the north-east would be left with only four counties and that the British would make a four-county government impossible.[42]

Thus, Collins assumed that the new constitution, if carefully formulated, could convince the Ulster Unionists to remain part of the Irish Free State.[43] For this reason, during the first weeks of the constitutional drafting, he repeatedly emphasized to Douglas the importance of a decentralized government. The constitution, Collins asserted, should allow some level of autonomy to the local political institutions, and he even considered the creation of subordinate Irish legislatures.[44]

Deeply divided committee

Guided by Collins' directives to find common ground between Republicans and pragmatists, between the north and the south and between Ireland and Britain, the constitutional drafting committee began its deliberations in late January 1922.[45] However, despite the efforts made to ensure

---

[42] F. S. L. Lyons, *Ireland since the Famine* (Glasgow: Fontana/Collins, 1975), 45. See also Michael Laffan, *The Partition of Ireland 1911–25* (Dundalk: Dundalgan Press, 1983), ch. 5. In the event, the findings of the commission proved so unsatisfactory from the Saorstát point of view that they were set aside and the boundary remained as it had been settled by the Government of Ireland Act 1920.

[43] Collins was not the only one who expected that the island would remain united under the Irish Free State. After the adoption of the constitution in December 1922, the first governor-general of the Irish Free State, Timothy Healy, expressed the hope that "in a few years the spirit of mutual concession will bring about a reunification and make the storied little island one governmental entity." *Washington Post*, December 7, 1922.

[44] Douglas, "Memoirs," book I, sec. 2, p. 38, in Akenson and Fallin, "The Irish Civil War and the Drafting of the Free State Constitution, Part I," 34.

[45] They even produced an initial draft, known as Document no. 39, which included all the provisions upon which they agreed, while the undecided clauses were presented in their alternative forms. The members of the drafting committee never reached a consensus regarding the disputed clauses. Akenson and Fallin, "The Irish Civil War and the Drafting of the Free State Constitution, Part II," 43–7.

that the drafting committee was non-political and non-partisan, the pervasive political frictions of Irish society entered into the constitutional deliberations and created a split within the committee. Consequently, the committee members could not agree on a unified draft, and on March 8, 1922 they submitted to the provisional government two separate draft versions of the new constitution.[46]

Collins hoped that severing the link between the constitution and the Treaty would avoid confrontation, but this hope turned out to be futile. As has been pointed out, what Collins failed to appreciate when he instructed the committee not to include the Treaty provisions in the constitution was "that the divisions in Ireland ran deeper than merely support for or opposition to the Anglo-Irish Treaty."[47] The split within the drafting committee was a microcosm of the larger split in Irish society. It demonstrated the depth of the disagreement over foundational aspects of the Irish constitution. While both drafts contained similar provisions relating to procedural and institutional issues, including the structure of the lower house, the judiciary, the electoral system, amendment mechanisms and civil rights, they differed considerably in their fundamental conception of the nature of the Irish state and of Irish nationhood.[48]

Draft A, which was signed by Figgis, MacNeill and O'Brien, was the result of a realistic and pragmatic appraisal of the political and legal constraints facing the Irish nation. This draft represented the pragmatic approach of the "political nationalists", to use Hutchinson's terminology. By contrast, Draft B, which was signed by Douglas, Kennedy and France, contained language expressing a stronger sense of national unity, based on a romantic view of Irish identity, and it reflected the tendencies of the "cultural nationalists."

The fundamental differences between the two visions of the nature of Irish nationalism is clearest in the preambles to the two drafts.

---

[46] In fact, there were actually three drafts that were submitted. The third, Draft C, was prepared by the two university professors on the committee, Alfred O'Rahilly and James Murnaghan, and was modeled after the Swiss constitution and based on principles of religious conservatism. This draft was deemed impractical from the start, and was never seriously considered by the provisional government. The full text of Draft C has been lost. For segments of Draft C and commentary on it see: *ibid.*, 51–7.

[47] Jeffrey Prager, *Building Democracy in Ireland: Political Order and Cultural Integration in a Newly Independent Nation* (Cambridge University Press, 1986), 75.

[48] For the full text of the two draft constitutions see Akenson and Fallin, "The Irish Civil War and the Drafting of the Free State Constitution, Part II," 57–93.

Here are the two preambles with the salient differences between them emphasized:

> Draft A
>
> We, the people of Ireland, in our resolve to renew and re-establish our State and found it upon *principles of freedom and justice*, take control of our destiny in order that Ireland may take her place among the Nations of the world as a *free democratic State*. In the exercise of our sovereign right as a free people and to provide the welfare and to preserve and develop the heritage and the spiritual aspirations of our people we hereby declare Saorstát Éireann established and give it this Constitution.

> Draft B
>
> We, the people of Ireland, acknowledging that *all authority comes from God*, and in the exercise of our right as a free people, do hereby create Saorstát Éireann and give it this constitution. *Through it we shall endeavor to re-establish our national life and unity* that Ireland may take her rightful place among the Nations of the earth.

The values, expectations and aspirations expressed in the two versions are significantly different.[49] First, the secular conception of political authority underpinning Draft A stands in a sharp contrast to the philosophical stance of Draft B, which views God as the ultimate source of authority. While Draft A defines the Irish nation as an evolving political collectivity, Draft B perceives the Irish nation in essentialist terms of a holy nation whose actions were theologically justified. Second, the two drafts proffered different conceptions of the role of the state. Draft A makes an explicit normative commitment to the civic and democratic principles, and refers to the ideals of freedom and justice. Draft B mentions none of these. And whereas Draft A recognizes the importance of establishing viable representative governmental institutions, Draft B reflects a romantic belief in the possibility of a harmonious non-hierarchical interaction based on the collective will of the Irish people. Third, the preambles give expression to two fundamentally different conceptions of the role of the constitution. For the framers of Draft A, a constitution creates a civic definition of nationalism, providing for integration of a heterogeneous society and protection of basic rights. The framers of Draft B, in contrast, envision a constitution as a means to recreate a moral community, based on a republican image of a unified Irish people.

---

[49] This analysis is largely based on Jeffrey Prager, *Building Democracy in Ireland: Political Order and Cultural Integration in a Newly Independent Nation* (Cambridge and New York: Cambridge University Press, 1986), 78–80.

The different perspectives of the committee members were also reflected in some of the provisions of the constitution itself. The most important difference was between the two proposed structures for the cabinet. While Draft A followed the British model, Draft B recommended that the cabinet would include two types of member: the first group would comprise four members of the Dáil, who would hold the positions of president, vice president and ministers of finance and external affairs, and who alone would be responsible for foreign affairs, while the second group would comprise other ministers who would not need to be members of parliament. As anti-Treatyites had made clear that they would not enter the Dáil as long as the Treaty provisions necessitated Dáil representatives to swear allegiance to the Crown, this innovative scheme may have been intended to allow anti-Treatyites to join a coalition government.[50]

The politicization of the constitution

The provisional Irish government was determined to find a constitutional formulation that would be acceptable to moderate Republicans, without incurring the opposition of the British or the Ulster Unionists. To this end, it entered into talks with Treaty opponents immediately after the ratification of the Treaty in the Dáil in January 1922.

At Sinn Féin's annual convention (Ard Fheis) held on February 22, 1922, Griffith, the acting (pro-Treaty) president of the Dáil, and de Valera, who still served as the (anti-Treaty) president of the party, reached an agreement intended at averting a formal rift within Sinn Féin and avoiding immediate elections, which would be postponed until after the constitution had been drafted.[51] Politically this made sense, as postponing the

---

[50] Akenson and Fallin, "The Irish Civil War and the Drafting of the Free State Constitution, Part II," 45–6, 50; Akenson and Fallin, "The Irish Civil War and the Drafting of the Free State Constitution, Part III," 38. Another distinction between the two drafts, concerning the role of the Senate, reflected two different institutional approaches: strong political institutions on the one hand and a distrust of political elites on the other. Draft A proposed that the members of the Senate would be elected by the members of the lower house (Article 31), while Draft B suggested popular elections. The powers of the Senate were also intended to be different under the two drafts. As opposed to Draft A, Draft B restricted the legislative powers of the Senate, which was perceived as distant from the popular voice, and excluded it from the appropriation process or taxation (Article 34) and denied it from any function in regard to money bills (Article 37). Akenson and Fallin, "The Irish Civil War and the Drafting of the Free State Constitution, Part II," 49.

[51] The full text of the agreement can be found in Dorothy Macardle, *The Irish Republic: A Documented Chronicle of the Anglo-Irish Conflict and the Partitioning of Ireland, with a*

elections would permit the Irish people to express support for or opposition to the constitution at the polls. However, the intention to view the constitution as the central issue of the elections reinforced public perception of it as a political document and put paid to any attempt by the provisional government to portray it as a vehicle for national reconciliation.

Collins, who understood the risks associated with the internal Sinn Féin agreement, tried to mitigate them by signing on May 20, 1922 what came to be known as the Collins–de Valera Pact, which fixed in advance the post-election balance of power between parliamentary supporters and opponents of the Treaty. In accordance with its terms, Sinn Féin would propose for the June 1922 elections a slate of sixty-six pro-Treaty and fifty-eight anti-Treaty candidates, which ratio reflected the composition of the existing Dáil. It was also agreed that the Cabinet would consist of four anti-Treaty and five pro-Treaty members. The pact enabled the provisional government to maintain civil order in face of mounting sectarian violence by assuring that Treaty opponents would be represented in the Cabinet, and by removing the divisive issues of the Treaty and the constitution from the agenda of the election. It also had the benefit of enabling the provisional government to present a unified front on the constitutional issue in their dealings with the British.

Historians have speculated that the Collins–de Valera Pact probably also included a secret agreement on the content of the constitution.[52] The existence of a secret pact could explain Collins' preference for a cabinet model that permitted the inclusion of external ministers, as presented in Draft B of the constitutional committee. Moreover, the draft that was ultimately submitted to the British Cabinet strongly reflected Republican demands for maximal independence from Britain. The document mentioned the Treaty and the Crown in only two of its seventy-eight articles, in the section dealing with external relations. It also ignored the Treaty's provisions in several important aspects: it did not contain an oath of alliance to the Crown or acknowledge the special position of Ulster, and it

---

Detailed Account of the Period 1916–1923 (New York: Farrar, Straus and Giroux, 1965), 666–7.

[52] Akenson and Fallin, "The Irish Civil War and the Drafting of the Free State Constitution, Part III," 36–7. This was also implied by Macardle, who closely documented the events of these years: "When Republicans consented to a Pact with Michael Collins it was in the belief that his party, so strengthened, would now hold out with the utmost firmness for the widest possible interpretation of the Treaty in the interests of Ireland. Only if they did so could a coalition between pro-Treaty and Republican representatives hope to succeed. The Constitution would be the first critical test of Collins's sincerity and firmness and his party's loyalty to the pact." Macardle, *The Irish Republic*, 719.

did not refer to the right of appeal to the Judicial Committee of the Privy Council. It also contained a provision allowing for the entry into external treaties.[53]

London: imposed amendments

Under the Anglo-Irish Treaty, the Irish constitution required British approval. In order to avoid needlessly offending the British, the draft that was sent to London did not include the preamble, which was based on the nationalist Draft B.[54] Nonetheless, the draft expressed a radical statement of independence and sovereignty in the eyes of the British.

Collins hoped that the pact with de Valera, which provided him with support at home, would strengthen his bargaining position vis-à-vis the British. But the cooperation between Collins and the extreme Republicans increased British suspicions that the Irish did not intend to comply with the conditions set down by the Treaty. British intelligence in Dublin reported to the Cabinet in London on May 21, 1922 that "Collins has agreed with de Valera to establish a government after the election of a character contrary to the term of the Treaty."[55] When the Irish delegation arrived in London at the end of May 1922 they received an angry reception.[56]

The British rejected the argument that there was no need to repeat the terms of the Treaty in the constitution, and insisted on explicit reference to the provisions regarding Ireland's relations with the commonwealth in the Free State constitution.[57]

---

[53] The full text of the draft constitution submitted to the British is available in Akenson and Fallin, "The Irish Civil War and the Drafting of the Free State Constitution, Part III," 41–53. Not all members of the pro-Treaty leadership supported the independent constitutional draft presented to the British. Arthur Griffith, for example, strongly disapproved of the Collins–de Valera Pact, fearing a rift with England. On the disagreements among the Free State leaders see Akenson and Fallin, "The Irish Civil War and the Drafting of the Free State Constitution, Part II," 37. For detailed description of the negotiations with the British see Joseph M. Curran, *The Birth of the Irish Free State 1921–1923* (Tuscaloosa: The University of Alabama Press, 1980), ch. 14.

[54] Curran, *The Birth of the Irish Free State*, 201.

[55] Akenson and Fallin, "The Irish Civil War and the Drafting of the Free State Constitution, Part III," 39.

[56] On May 25, 1922, Eamon Duggan, Arthur Griffith and Hugh Kennedy went to London in reply to British summons. Collins was called by the British the next day.

[57] For a detailed account of the negotiations between the Irish leaders and the British Cabinet, held in London between May 27 and June 2, see Curran, *The Birth of the Irish Free State*, 204–16.

The British insistence on entrenching the terms of the Treaty and on exact definitions regarding the status of Irish dominion should be understood in the historical context of 1920s British Commonwealth. The beginning of this decade was marked by the general undermining of the imperial status quo in its four existing dominions: Canada, Australia, New Zealand and South Africa. The negotiations between Ireland and Britain occurred at the same time as some of the dominions – notably Canada – were struggling to increase their independence.

Until the early 1920s, legally, the dominions were subservient to Great Britain. Under the Colonial Laws Validity Act 1865 and their own constitutions, the British government had the power to declare their laws *ultra vires*. Further, despite the dominions' separate representation in the League of Nations, the concept of external unity of the Empire remained. The dominions had no diplomatic existence separate from Britain and any treaties they entered into had to be co-signed by the British government. In 1922, the Canadian prime minister insisted, for the first time in the Commonwealth's history, on signing a separate treaty with the Americans without the customary British co-signature. The demand to increase the dominions' freedom of decision-making, such as to include the right to negotiate and sign treaties independently, was harshly debated during the Imperial Conferences of 1921 and 1923.[58]

The Irish Free State constitution was drafted at a time when the question of the sovereignty of the dominions had become an important political issue. This explains the vehemence of the British reaction to the draft constitution.

Under pressure from the British, the provisional government added to the draft constitution the legal constraints on the Irish Dominion delineated by the Treaty.[59] It was this document which was presented to the Irish electorate on June 16, 1922.

The results were a success for the pro-Treaty faction, which won fifty-eight out of 128 seats, whereas anti-Treaty candidates received only

---

[58] Gretchen M. MacMillan, *State, Society and Authority in Ireland: The Foundation of the Modern State* (Dublin: Gill and Macmillan, 1993), 222–3. For more on the relationship between Ireland and the Commonwealth see W. K. Hancock, *Survey of British Commonwealth Affairs, Vol. I: Problems of Nationality 1918–1936* (London and New York: Oxford University Press, 1937); D. W. Harkness, *The Restless Dominion: The Irish Free State and the British Commonwealth of Nations, 1921–31* (Dublin: Gill and Macmillan, 1969); Nicolas Mansergh, *The Commonwealth Experience*, vol. II (London: Macmillan, 1981).

[59] Thomas Jones, *Whitehall Diary, Vol. III: Ireland 1918–1925*, ed. Keith Middlemas (London: Oxford University Press, 1971), 203.

thirty-five.[60] The terms of the pact signed by Collins and de Valera were never implemented.

Four days later, at the insistence of the British, the Free State army launched an attack on anti-Treaty militants who had been occupying the Four Courts building in Dublin for two months. While the bombardment of the Four Courts led to the militants' surrender, it had the effect of triggering a bloody civil war. On August 12, Arthur Griffith, the president of the Dáil, died at the age of fifty-one as a result of heart failure, arguably caused by exhaustion, strain and disappointment. Ten days later, Michael Collins, the commander-in-chief of the Free State, was killed in an ambush. The new Irish Free State government was led by William Cosgrave and Kevin O'Higgins. They allowed military trials and reprisal executions of persons found in unauthorized possession of arms or ammunition. By the end of the war, between 11,000 and 12,000 people were in military prisons, including de Valera himself.[61]

Debating the constitution

The civil war did not stop the enactment of the constitution of the Irish Free State. On September 20, 1922, one month after Collins' death, W. T. Cosgrave, the new president, presented the draft constitution to the Dáil Éireann. The debates on the draft constitution lasted for seventeen sessions, and in many ways echoed the arguments raised ten months earlier during the debates on the Anglo-Irish Treaty. Government supporters argued that the constitution was a strict and fair interpretation of the Treaty,[62] while others stressed that it was an imposed constitution and did not reflect the real aspirations of the Irish nation.[63] The extreme anti-Treatyites, however, did not participate in these debates, since the Free State government had passed a ruling that they would be arrested if they did.[64]

Members of the Dáil criticized the dominant role of Great Britain in Irish affairs, as reflected in the constitution, and proposed various amendments regarding, for example, the role of the governor-general, the oath to the Crown and the statements regarding sovereignty. What both sides

---

[60] The rest of the seats were captured by seventeen members of the Labour Party, seven independents, seven farmers (prosperous farmers who eventually supported the Free State government) and four members of Dublin University.

[61] Lyons, *Ireland since the Famine*, 467–8.

[62] Kevin O'Higgins, *Dáil Debates* (September 21, 1922); *Dáil Debates* (September 25, 1922).

[63] Thomas Johnson, *Dáil Debates* (September 20, 1922); *Dáil Debates* (October 11, 1922).

[64] Kissane, *The Politics of the Irish Civil War*.

could agree upon was that the timing of the constitutional drafting in the midst of a civil war was problematic.[65]

This did not mean that there was agreement on the role of the constitution under such extreme conflicting conditions. Those who objected to the proposed constitution viewed the moment of constitution-writing as an opportunity for a revolutionary change, and consequently criticized the draft for not being revolutionary enough. Thomas Johnson, the leader of the Labor Party and one of the most vocal speakers against the proposed constitution, argued that the problem was that the constitution had been "arrived at through English legislation with just some little change in the political arrangements of the country and stand at that and not move forward."[66]

By contrast, the supporters of the provisional government argued for an incremental approach. Acknowledging the imperfections embodied in the constitution, they emphasized the potential flexibility of the constitution, which would enable future improvements. "There is in the constitution the principle of growth," declared Sean Milroy, a member of Sinn Féin from Belfast,[67] and Darrel Figgis, the chairman of the committee that had drafted the constitution stressed that the constitution provided the Irish people "the fundamental machinery by which we [can] exercise freedom"; and although it was clearly far from perfect, this machinery could be improved in the future:

> Future generations will realize that … the machinery was of such a kind that it could improve itself, and could extend, and it could become supple with use, in order that the nation might develop and in order that the Constitution might develop with the development of the nation.[68]

"There is a very important clause in this draft constitution," stressed Professor William Magennis,

> which enables us to alter the constitution at any time, with the consent of the people, if it be their desire in any respect to alter it. Consequentially the very nature of the constitution is that it is alterable, it is susceptible of addition, subtraction, improvement or extension.[69]

Kevin O'Higgins, who was the Free State minister of home affairs, expressed a pragmatic approach in several speeches during the Dáil

---

[65] Gavan Duffy, *Dáil Debates* (September 21, 1922). See also Cathal O'Seanain's speech, *Dáil Debates* (September 21, 1922): "the weakness that has come upon the country with the civil war that is raging [thus] this country is not at the moment able to stand up and fight for its rights, to secure the exercise of all its rights."

[66] *Dáil Debates* (September 25, 1922).   [67] Sean Milroy, *Dáil Debates* (September 25, 1922).

[68] *Dáil Debates* (October 25, 1922).   [69] *Dáil Debates* (September 21, 1922)

constitutional debates. On the one hand he declared that by approving the proposed constitution "we are launching a democratic self-governing state."[70] On the other hand, he acknowledged that

> It is a political experiment. We do not propose to mould in cast iron our country's rights, or mould anything in cast iron. We do not think that, in passing this Constitution, we are fixing the *ne plus ultra* of the Constitution of the country. Facing the facts as we know them to day, I say that the Irish people have consented to accept this Treaty, and, until it is repudiated by the majority of the people, it stands, and must stand, as the national policy.[71]

Eventually, on October 25, 1922, the *Constitution of the Saorstát Éireann Bill* was passed with minor amendments to the draft. It received British approval, and entered into effect on December 6, 1922. The following day, the Northern Ireland Parliament exercised its authority under Article 12 of the Anglo-Irish Treaty to declare that the powers of the Irish Free State should not extend to Northern Ireland.

Almost six months later, on May 24, 1923, the civil war ended with a ceasefire. And in August the first elections under the new constitution were held. The pro-Irish Free State party, Cumann na nGaedheal, headed by Cosgrave, won sixty-three seats. Sinn Féin's anti-Treaty candidates captured forty-four seats but refused to take the oath of allegiance to the king and thus could not take their seats in Parliament or serve in the Cabinet.

Symbolic ambivalence

The structure of the Irish Free State constitution reflects the complex political constraints under which it was drafted. The constitution-drafting process did not result in a compromise between the competing perspectives on the Irish state. Instead, the constitution incorporated the provisions which each side had insisted on, resulting in a document that was often contradictory and inconsistent. The British insisted on the inclusion of certain formulations related to the Irish–British relationship, but paid little attention to other provisions which had no bearing on their role in Irish affairs. The Irish, for their part, insisted on including expressions of the sovereignty of "the Irish people." In this they were successful. Although the constitution declared that the Free

---

[70] *Dáil Debates* (October 3, 1922).
[71] *Dáil Debates* (September 25, 1922).

State was a member of the British Commonwealth and that the British monarch was its head of state, it also asserted that national unity stood above political power.[72]

Thus, from the foundational perspective, symbolic ambivalence was the central characteristic of the Irish Free State constitution. The amalgam of principles of British monarchism alongside statements of national sovereignty was most evident in the preamble.[73] Its first part was taken directly from the Drafting Committee's Draft B preamble:

> Dáil Éireann, sitting as a Constituent Assembly in this Provisional Parliament, acknowledging that all lawful authority comes from God to the people and in the confidence that the National life and unity of Ireland shall thus be restored, hereby proclaims the establishment of the Irish Free State (otherwise called Saorstát Éireann) and in the exercise of undoubted right, decrees and enacts as follows.[74]

The revolutionary doctrine of popular sovereignty was restated in Article 2, which declared that "all powers of government and all authority legislative, executive and judicial in Ireland are derived from the people of Ireland."

But other provisions of the constitution referred to the British monarch as the head of state and a caveat was introduced as the second part of the preamble, stressing the subordination of the constitution to the Treaty:

> The said constitution shall be construed with reference to the Articles of Agreement for a Treaty between Great Britain and Ireland … which are hereby given the force of law, and if any provision of the said Constitution or of any amendment thereof or of any law made there under is in any respect repugnant to any of the provisions of the Scheduled Treaty, it shall to the extent only of such repugnancy, be absolutely void and inoperative and the Parliament and the Executive Council of the Irish Free State (Saorstát Éireann) shall respectively pass such further legislation and do all such other things as may be necessary to implement the Scheduled Treaty.

However, whether or not the Irish constitution was truly subordinate to the Treaty was questionable. Indeed, many legal scholars of the time noted that the Irish constitution presented a "puzzling problem," since it

---

[72] Prager, *Building Democracy in Ireland*, 89.

[73] The 1922 constitution did not include a preamble in the common constitutional sense, but the opening words of the constitution of the Irish Free State (Saorstát Éireann) Act performed a similar function.

[74] The text of the Irish Free State constitution can be found in Leo Kohn, *The Constitution of the Irish Free State* (London: G. Allen & Unwin, 1932) Appendix, 389–418.

was "both supreme and subordinate."[75] The formal authority of the constitution seems to be derived neither from the Constituent Act of a sovereign Irish legislature nor, like in other dominions, from a Statute of the British Parliament. On the one hand, the legal origin of the constitution was not based exclusively on British sovereignty, since it was enacted by an Irish parliament, acting as a Constituent Assembly. Yet on the other hand it also did not represent an act of an Irish *pouvoir constituant*, since its operation required the approval of the British Parliament. Moreover, the constitution was subject to the Treaty and constrained by its provisions. However, the constitution "appeared to be of superior rank to the Treaty, since it was only by the Constituent Act (s.2) that the latter was invested with the force of law."[76]

The confusion over the meaning of Irish sovereignty was reflected in the different news headlines which appeared on the next day after the publication of the constitution: *The Sunday Times* (London) declared, "The English victory is plain. Everything which left the question of the Imperial connection in doubt in the Irish draft has been positively and successfully resorted."[77] In keeping with this interpretation, the *Republic of Ireland* called the constitution a "shameful document."[78] Others perceived that the real victors in the struggle over the constitution were the Irish. In its June 16 issue *The Times* (London) cited A. Barridale Keith, a British expert on constitutional history and law, who stated that the Free State constitution "unquestionably … recognizes the sovereignty of the people of Ireland, while leaving utterly vague the relations of Britain and Ireland."[79] And *The New York Times* wrote on the same day: "a framework of self-government has been provided for Ireland which her sons have it

---

[75] Allan F. Saunders, "The Irish Constitution," *American Political Science Review* 18, no. 2 (1924): 340–5.

[76] Kohn, *The Constitution of the Irish Free State*, 90.

[77] Cited in Macardle, *The Irish Republic*, 724.

[78] Curran, *The Birth of the Irish Free State*, 217.

[79] Arthur Berriedale Keith, *Letters on Imperial Relations, Indian Reform, Constitutional and International Law 1916–1935* (London: Oxford University Press, 1935), 34–5. In a letter to *The Scotsman*, on June 16, 1922, Keith wrote that by the constitution's "empathic declaration of the sole sovereignty of the Irish people, it conforms with Mr. Collins's doctrine that it is impossible to set bounds to the progress of a nation … The concessions now made in Southern Ireland are such as naturally to raise the question why the Republicans carry on a struggle for what is little more than a form. On the other hand, the republicans have some right to ask: Why deny us a form which we value, when we are ready to concede all you really need as regards foreign policy and defence? Is not the Constitution of the British Commonwealth of Nations elastic enough to include a Republic?" *Ibid.*, 33–4.

in their exclusive power to fill out and make effective, if they have the practical skills and the unselfish patriotism to do it."[80]

The monarchic symbolism in the constitution helped mitigate tensions with Britain, but its domestic impact was quite different. Indeed, the formal statements about Irish independence and sovereignty included in the constitution soon became the political reality. Leo Kohn, who published in 1932 what is still the most comprehensive legal study of the Irish Free State constitution, maintained that, ultimately, the symbolic ambivalence of the 1922 constitution served the interests of the Irish.[81] The constitution, he wrote, was

> a most comprehensive and, in spirit, essentially republican constitution on most advanced Continental lines. It had the characteristic dogmatic ring of all constitutions which embody not the legislative crystallization of an organic development, but the theoretical postulates of a revolutionary upheaval. It mocked the time-honoured empiricism of the British Constitution by the enunciation of basic principles and the formulation of dogmatic definitions. It postulated fundamental rights. It defined in detail the scope and the functions of the several constitutional powers. It reduced to precise terms the conventional rules of the British Constitution. Its archaic symbols had to be introduced, but their meaninglessness for Ireland was writ large on every page. The monarchical forms paled into insignificance in the light of the formal enunciation and the consistent application of the principle of the sovereignty of the people as the fundamental and the exclusive source of all political authority.[82]

In the same vein, W. K. Hancock wrote in 1937 that despite the fact that the 1922 constitution "jostled together two symbolisms," those of monarchy with those of national sovereignty, it was clear that "popular sovereignty dominated the life of the Free State from the very beginning."[83] By that, the two scholars reinforced what O'Higgins had already claimed in 1922, when he assessed the implications of the ambivalent constitution:

> On the face of it, this Constitution is not a Republican Constitution; perhaps I would not be wrong in saying that it is as little a Republican Constitution as a British Constitution. It contains the trappings, the

---

[80] *The New York Times*, June 17, 1922.

[81] The same Leo Kohn later drafted the constitutional proposal that serves as the basis for discussions of Israel's Provisional State Council Constitutional Committee in 1948. Amihai Radzyner, "A Constitution for Israel: The Design of the Leo Kohn Proposal, 1948," *Israeli Studies* 54, no. 1 (2010): 1–24.

[82] Kohn, *The Constitution of the Irish Free State*, 80.

[83] Hancock, *Survey of British Commonwealth Affairs*, Vol. I, 158.

insignia, the fiction and the symbol of a monarchical institution, but the real power is in the hands of the people.[84]

The validity of this perspective was confirmed almost six decades later by the legal scholar J. M. Kelly: "In strong contrast to other self-government Dominions," he wrote, "the Crown here [in Ireland] was kept on the shelf, scarcely visible behind an apparent of State symbolism and practice which were entirely republican. There were no royal visits. The Army was the Army of the Irish Free State, and its officers held their commissions from the Government of the Irish Free State. The State's flag was the republican tricolor for which that of France had served as a model."[85]

The constitutional symbolic ambivalence enabled the political arena to play the decisive role in determining Ireland's future. The constitution contained the possibility of two very distinct paths – the continuation of strict British control or a break from Britain and a move toward complete independence. Events of the second and third decades of the twentieth century led to the realization of the latter. The establishment of boundary lines separating Ulster from the twenty-six counties of the Irish Free State, the electoral as well as military victory of the pro-Free-Staters, and the general weakening of the British Empire, which strengthened the autonomy of the Commonwealth's dominions, all helped usher in independence within short order. Consequently, less than a year after the constitution was enacted, in September 1923, the Irish Free State joined the League of Nations as a fully sovereign state.[86] Subsequently, in July 1924, over strong British objection, the Anglo-Irish Treaty was registered with the Treaty Registration Bureau of the League of Nations as an agreement between two states.[87] Finally, the 1931 Statute of Westminster passed by British Parliament freed dominion legislatures from the constraints of British constituent acts.

Internally, in the short term, the nascent constitution did not prevent the drifting to a civil war. Apparently, it was not sufficiently ambiguous to bridge over the disagreement regarding the viability of democracy within the limited territory of twenty-six counties. It failed to blur the distinction between the competing viewpoints of radical Irish Republicans and those that accepted the British demands, and ultimately included the most extreme positions of both sides.

---

[84] *Dáil Debates* (September 20, 1922).
[85] Hogan and Whyte, *J. M. Kelly: The Irish Constitution*, x.
[86] Harkness, *The Restless Dominion*, 36.   [87] *Ibid.*, 57–62.

The question of the effects of the constitution on the civil war and on Irish democracy in general is still a matter of debate. Scholars such as Jeffrey Prager argue that the incompatibility of British monarchism and Irish populism made the task of governing in the young Free State especially difficult. Instead of bolstering the legitimacy of the government, the constitution impeded it because it failed to represent the positions of the vast majority of the Irish population, whose views were more moderate than those incorporated in the constitution. "Support for and commitment to the new Free State would have to be won despite the Constitution, not through it ... the new government was unable to wrap itself around a symbolic flag to which the majority of the population could respond."[88]

On the other hand, one could claim that while the constitution failed to prevent a civil war, expectations that it should were perhaps unrealistic. Just as in India, constitutional deliberations could not stem the tide of violence. The Indian pre-partition Constituent Assembly did not calm the tensions between religious groups, and could not enact the constitution it finally drafted after partition. When political divisions are intense, the constitution cannot solve them but can only mirror the conflict.

But after the civil war ended, the political system and the democratic institutions that were created were able to gain stability. Many consider this to be the greatest achievement of the Irish Free State government.[89] Significantly, the Irish Free State institutions were able to facilitate the peaceful and democratic transfer of power to a party that merely a decade earlier had been violently opposed to the establishment of the state.[90]

De Valera himself acknowledged the changing political realities when he became a member of the Dáil in 1927, as the leader of his new party, Fianna Fáil. In a spin that rewarded him with the title "the constitutional Houdini of his generation," de Valera joined the Dáil despite the requirement of the oath of allegiance to which he was fervently opposed.[91] He explained how he and his party reached the conclusion that the oath was

---

[88] Prager, *Building Democracy in Ireland*, 89–90.
[89] Bill Kissane, *Explaining Irish Democracy* (University College Dublin Press, 2002).
[90] On 1926 de Valera broke with the extreme Republicans of the Sinn Féin and established the Fianna Fáil party. In the 1927 elections the party gained forty-four seats in the Dáil (compared to the forty-eight seats of Cumann na nGaedheal). In the next election, in 1932, Fianna Fáil became the largest electoral force and de Valera was nominated as prime minister.
[91] Lyons, *Ireland since the Famine*, 449.

simply an empty political formula which, being so regarded even by their opponents, could be taken by Fianna Fáil "without becoming involved, or without involving their nation, in obligations of loyalty to the English Crown."[92] In other words, it was the political circumstances and not the constitutional symbolism that prevailed.

The Irish constitution's ambivalence, thus, allowed it to be sufficiently flexible so as to accommodate changes in both internal and external circumstances. Within a decade and a half after its enactment, all the monarchic symbolism in the constitution was eliminated. The radical alteration of the constitution was made possible by the Cosgrave government, which during the civil war declared a "transitional period" during which the constitution could be amended without a referendum, by ordinary legislation. When de Valera's party, Fianna Fáil, formed the government in 1932, it introduced a set of amendments which gradually disconnected the constitution from the British Commonwealth. The amendment to remove the oath of allegiance was passed in 1933. In the same year the limited right to appeal to the Privy Council was abolished. By 1936 all references to the Crown in terms of domestic arrangements, and the office of governor-general, were deleted from the constitution.[93]

In sum, the Irish Free State constitution accommodated the conflicting circumstances at the time of its drafting by employing a strategy of constitutional incrementalism and by suspending clear-cut choices between the rival visions of the Irish state. The goal of the Irish leaders was clear – a complete independence of the thirty-two counties in a united Irish republic. Yet the political realities of the time prevented the immediate realization of such an objective. Thus, it incorporated instead all competing positions in the conflict in an ambivalent constitution, hoping that in the future Irish sovereignty would be more pronounced. In the long run, the impact of the Irish constitutional ambivalence was similar to that of the Israeli strategy of avoidance and that of Indian ambiguity. In all three cases, these strategies were in essence coping mechanisms which made possible the enactment of popularly supported constitutions despite deep ideological divisions. In doing so, they enabled the development of stable and strong political institutions in which the consensus regarding the state's underlying norms and values could evolve.

---

[92] Cited in *ibid.*

[93] Brian Farrell, "From First Dail through Irish Free State," in Brian Farrell, ed., *De Valera's Constitution and Ours* (Goldenbridge, Dublin: Published for Radio Telefís Éireann by Gill and Macmillan, 1988), 30.

However, the drafting of the Irish Free State constitution was particularly complex due to the fact that it involved not only an internal ideological struggle but also an external struggle against British dominance. Hence, the provisional government of the Free State had to conduct the complicated negotiations over the constitution with the Republicans at home as well as with the British Cabinet in London. All three sides were determined to use the constitution to promote their agendas. Britain and the extreme Republicans, in particular, persistently demanded greater clarification of the constitutional formulations. Both rejected all compromise formulas presented by the Free State leaders.

These triangular negotiations meant in fact that the authority to frame the Free State constitution was not entirely in Irish hands. As opposed to Israel and India, the Irish Free state constitution was not drafted by an independent Constituent Assembly but was modified by direct involvement of an external force. This difference was responsible for the use of a strategy of ambivalence rather than avoidance or ambiguity.

The struggle against the British meant that avoidance of writing a constitution, as was done in Israel, was not a strategy ever considered by the provisional government. The Irish leadership had never seriously debated the necessity of framing a written constitution, although some, such as the legal scholar Leo Kohn, have argued that the issue could have become a matter of dispute. Pro-Treatyites could have claimed that the Treaty itself should be regarded as the organic law of the new state, and that within its framework an unwritten constitution should be allowed to develop on the evolutionary lines of the British system. Anti-Treatyites could have been swayed by their concern that a rigid constitution would perpetuate the features of British imperial system to which they objected within the internal organization of the new state. The provisional government realized that "the enactment of a written constitution by an Irish Parliament would not only give emphatic expression to the new constitutional status of Ireland, but that so far from stereotyping the obsolescent features of 'dominion status' it might indeed offer an opportunity for carrying further its re-interpretation and implementation in accordance with Irish national aspirations."[94] Thus, in other words, the risks involved in drafting a formal constitution were perceived as minor compared to the opportunities the new constitution presented for the realization of Irish national objectives.

[94] Kohn, *The Constitution of the Irish Free State*, 77.

Similarly, the British insistence on inclusion of certain formulations in the Treaty precluded the use of a strategy of ambiguity as in India, forcing the adoption of an inconsistent and ambivalent constitution. By contrast to Indian framers, who deliberately chose to defer controversial decisions regarding foundational elements of the constitution, the Irish drafters were compelled by the British Cabinet to explicitly address the issues at stake.

To be clear, ambiguity and ambivalence are two different strategies. *Ambiguous* is defined in the Oxford English dictionary as "indistinct, obscure, not clearly defined ... of double meaning or of several possible meanings."[95] *Ambivalent* means "having either or both of two contrary or parallel values, qualities or meanings ... acting on or arguing for sometimes one and sometimes the other of two opposites."[96] The inconsistency of the Indian constitution stemmed from the framers' intention to leave some of the arrangements deliberately ambiguous, allowing for later interpretation and decision-making by the political system. By contrast, the ambivalence of the Irish Free State constitution represents a coexistence of contradictory positions and principles. In the Irish case, inconsistency did not result from a deliberate choice intended to circumvent conflict but, rather, was the outcome of external imposition.

However, despite these differences, a similar logic underlined both constitutions: the logic of suspension of critical choices and decisions – whether willingly or unwillingly – while allowing political and social circumstances to evolve and to make these choices easier in the future. That was the core of Collins' "stepping stone" doctrine of constitutional incrementalism. I will elaborate more about the theoretical significance of the incrementalist constitutional strategy in the next chapter. In the meantime, in the last section of this chapter I would like to suggest that the constitutional developments which addressed the question of Irish nationalism, namely the enactment of the new constitution in 1937 and the amendment of Articles 2 and 3 of the constitution in 1998 as part of the Good Friday Agreement, can be seen as a reaction against (the 1937 constitution) or as a returning to (1998 amendment) this "stepping stone" strategy.[97]

---

[95] *Oxford English Dictionary* (Oxford University Press, 2002).
[96] *Ibid.*
[97] I focus on these two events since in both cases the meaning of Irish nationalism and sovereignty – which was the core issues of the civil war – was addressed through constitutional means, i.e. through constitutional enactment and amendment.

Table 5.1 *Timeline: the making of the Irish Free State constitution and the constitution of Ireland*

April 8, 1886	First Home Rule bill.
1905	Arthur Griffith founds the Sinn Féin Party.
1918	Sinn Féin wins sixty-nine out of seventy-three seats in Westminster. Forty-seven still in prison.
January 21, 1919	First public session of Dáil Éireann (parliament) of the Irish Republic in Mansion House, Dublin.
September 12, 1919	The Dáil Éireann was proscribed. Until 1921 held twelve secret meetings.
May 1921	Elections of second Dáil Éireann: 125 representatives (124 south, 1 north).
June 1921	Northern Ireland home rule Parliament opened.
December 6, 1921	Articles of Agreement for a Treaty between Great Britain and Ireland (Anglo-Irish Treaty) signed.
January 7, 1922	Dáil Éireann approves the Anglo-Irish Treaty.
January 9, 1922	De Valera submits his resignation from presidency.
January 10, 1922	Arthur Griffith elected president of the Dáil after anti-Treaty members left the Dáil.
January 16, 1922	Transfer of executive powers to the provisional government of the Irish Free State, chaired by Michael Collins.
January 25, 1922	First meeting of the constitutional drafting committee in Dublin.
March 8, 1922	The committee submits three drafts.
March 31, 1922	The Irish Free State (Agreement) Bill enacted by the British.
April 13, 1922	Anti-Treaty members of the Irish Republican Army seize the Four Courts.
May 20, 1922	Collins and de Valera sign the election pact (the "Collins–de Valera pact").
June 5, 1922	Negotiations over the constitution in London.
June 16, 1922	The final constitutional draft is published for the first time on the morning of election day.
June 28, 1922	The Provisional Government of the Irish Free State orders forces to fire on the Four Courts occupiers. The civil war begins.
August 1922	Collins and Griffith die.
October 25, 1922	The constitution draft approved by Dáil Éireann.
December 4, 1922	The constitution accepted by British Parliament.
December 5, 1922	The constitution signed by King George V.
December 6, 1922	The constitution of the Irish Free State goes into effect.

Table 5.1 (cont.)

December 7, 1922	Northern Ireland Parliament uses its authority under Article 12 of Anglo-Irish Treaty to declare that the powers of the Irish Free State should not extend to Northern Ireland (i.e. complete formal partition).
May 24, 1923	End of civil war.
August 1923	First elections to the Dáil Éireann.
May 1926	De Valera breaks with Sinn Féin and founds the Fianna Fáil party.
December 11, 1931	UK enacts the Statute of Westminster. By repealing the Colonial Laws Validity Act, Britain had no legal power over the dominions of the Commonwealth.
February 1932	Fianna Fáil wins the elections and forms a government headed by de Valera.
December 29, 1937	The Constitution of Ireland (Bunreacht na hÉireann) comes into force.
April 18, 1949	Ireland declared a Republic. No longer part of the Commonwealth.
May 1998	Articles 2 and 3 of the Irish constitution amended as part of the Good Friday Agreement, which aimed at ending the conflict in Northern Ireland.

1937–98: the return of constitutional incrementalism

The political differences between Collins and de Valera were also reflected in their approach to constitution-making under the conditions of deep ideological polarization that characterized Ireland at the time. For both, constitution-making was a political instrument, but they differed in the strategy by which they believed this instrument could help them achieve their political goals. Collins espoused a pragmatic approach to constitution-drafting. Between January and May 1922 he hoped to use the writing of the Free State constitution as a tool to repair the shortcomings of the Treaty. By drafting a Republican constitution, he wished to restore the principles of sovereignty and independence that were undermined by the Treaty. Yet when he realized that the British would not retreat from their demands for Irish subordination, he switched to advocating an incrementalist approach, viewing the constitution, in his words, as a stepping stone. Constitutions, according to him, could be crafted over time, gradually, and did not necessarily require a dramatic, revolutionary moment for their creation; their texts were not necessarily permanent and etched in stone. Under particularly difficult political conditions, a constitution should be constructed in an ambivalent and flexible enough fashion to enable, rather than to obstruct, subsequent political development, which, hopefully, would be in the desired direction. This approach involved some risk, the greatest being that the aspirations of the Irish drafters would not be fulfilled. That is, that Britain, as a world power, would prevent Ireland from achieving equal status and perpetuate the subjection of Ireland to its sovereignty. The recognition in this risk underpinned the anti-Treatyites' vehement objection to Collins' constitution.

De Valera, by contrast, held not only a more essentialist version of Irish nationalism but also a much stronger belief in the symbolic importance of constitutional formulations as necessary for the realization of Irish national aspirations. This perception underpinned his resistance to the ambivalent symbolism of the 1922 constitution, and in particular the inclusion of the oath of allegiance to the Crown. It also explains his insistence on rewriting the Irish constitution in 1937. The image of the 1922 constitution as an imposed document was the primary basis of de Valera's decision to draft a new constitution, which would rest solely on the sovereign authority of the Irish people.

The enactment of a new constitution in 1937 followed five years in which de Valera displayed an incrementalist attitude to constitutional amendment. Immediately after his election as president of the Executive Council, he began pursuing his aim of an independent Irish republic. But at this early stage, aware of the potential domestic and external risks that involved, he preferred to promote Irish sovereignty through gradual revision of the existing constitution. On April 1933 he revealed his method:

> Let it be made clear that we yield no willing assent to any form or symbol that is out of keeping with Ireland's right as a sovereign nation. Let us remove these forms one by one, so that this State that we control may be a Republic in fact; and then, when the time comes, the proclaiming of the Republic may involve no more than a ceremony, the formal confirmation of a status already attained.[98]

Between 1933 and 1936 the Dáil passed a set of constitutional amendments aimed at reducing and eventually eliminating Irish dependence on Britain. Indeed, in 1936, when the British were distracted by the crisis of King Edward's abdication, the final references to the Crown were removed.

---

[98] *Irish Press*, April 24, 1933. Cited in Longford and O'Neill, *Eamon De Valera*, 289.

By that time, virtually every provision of the constitution had been subject to deletions or additions: forty-one of its eighty-three articles had been
altered. But this was not the central reason for the constitutional revolution initiated by de Valera. For him, a new constitution was needed since
the amendment of the existing constitution was not enough to achieve
what he had been struggling for since 1921: a fundamental break from the
Anglo-Irish Treaty which was still considered as, at least partially, the legal
basis for the Free State constitution. Therefore, in 1937 de Valera initiated
a constitutional revolution, by the enactment of Bunreacht na hÉireann
(the constitution of Ireland). Unlike the 1922 constitution, which was
passed by the Dáil Éireann "sitting as a constituent assembly," the 1937
constitution was enacted by the authority of "the people of Éire."[99] During
the Dáil debates over the new constitution de Valera stressed:

> What we are doing is, we are going back to the sovereign authority to the
> Irish people, or that section of the Irish people whom we can consult on
> that matter. We go back to them and ask them to enact it. It is they who
> will enact it.[100]

The draft constitution was adopted by a referendum.[101] The Dáil's role
was confined to merely "approving" the draft before it was submitted to a
popular vote.[102] By this process, de Valera replaced the 1922 constitution
and made irrelevant the question of whether its validity depended on the
act of the Irish Constituent Assembly or on that of the Parliament of the
United Kingdom.[103] Ultimately, the enactment of the new Irish constitution amounted, in the words of J. M. Kelly, to "a break in legal continuity;
to a supplementing of one *Grundnorm* (albeit a disputed one) by another;
and thus, legally speaking, to a revolution."[104]

Nevertheless, while the new constitution represented a legal break from
that of 1922, in essence, the two documents should be regarded as existing
on a continuum:

> It is quite possible that the State might have developed within the 1922
> framework, in much the same way as it ultimately did within that of
> 1937 … The basic law of 1937 can be fairly presented as a stabilizing and

---

[99] The Preamble of the Constitution explicitly states: "We the people of Éire … do hereby
adopt, enact and give to ourselves this Constitution."

[100] Cited in Hogan and Whyte, *J. M. Kelly: The Irish Constitution*, 51, n. 9.

[101] Having been approved, it automatically came into effect on December 29, 1937.

[102] The Dáil (lower house) was at the time the sole legislative house, since the abolishment of
the Seanad (the senate) in 1936 by the Constitution (Amendment No 24) Act.

[103] Hogan and Whyte, *J. M. Kelly: The Irish Constitution*, 51.   [104] *Ibid.*, 52.

reforming continuation of that of 1922. Indeed, it would be misleading to present it in any other way. A great number of articles and sections of the later document are copied virtually, and often literally, word for word from the earlier one. And the case law of the years 1922–37 in the constitutional field has often been relevant to the interpretation of the 1937 Constitution. It seems to me, accordingly, that in attempting a statement of Irish constitutional law … the right approach is to regard the State as one which had been substantially the same polity since 1922.[105]

Only in one respect, Kelly emphasized, had the Irish state moved away from its 1922 origins, namely in its status in the law of nations and its relationship to the British Crown, which occupied a formal place in the 1922 constitution.[106] This distinction, however, was merely a symbolic one, since, as we have noticed above, the existence of the Crown in the Irish constitution had no practical implications. For this reason, de Valera's constitutional revolution represents first and foremost a revolution on the symbolic level.

The constitution of the Irish Free State was written in the context of intense internal tensions and undefined state borders, was a product of a negotiated treaty, and reflected a compromise between Republican nationalist demands and the constitutional principles of the British Commonwealth. By contrast, the 1937 constitution of Ireland was drafted in a context of defined borders, for a society much more homogenous religiously – 95 percent of the population in the twenty-six counties was Catholic. Consequentially, as opposed to the ambivalent nature of the 1922 constitution, which reflected the conflicts existing between the constitution's authors, the 1937 constitution "mirrored quite well the traditions, culture and aspirations of the great majority of the people of the twenty six counties."[107] The cultural homogeneity of "the people of Éire," who were supposedly the authors of the constitution, is reflected in several provisions, such as the new name of the state, Éire (Ireland), the recognition of Gaelic as the national language (English was a second official language),[108]

---

[105] *Ibid.*, Preface to First Edition, ix.   [106] *Ibid.*, x.

[107] Basil Chubb, *The Politics of the Irish Constitution* (Dublin: The Institute of Public Administration, 1991), 7.

[108] Article 8. Gaelic was also the official language of the constitution, and in any conflict between the Gaelic and English translation of the constitution the former prevails (Article 25.5). A decade later, de Valera admitted to Nehru, India's first prime minister, that the Irish had found Gaelic "hard going" and were reverting more and more to English. Nehru used de Valera's advice to persuade the Constituent Assembly to write the Indian Constitution in English rather than in Hindu. See Granville Austin, *The Indian Constitution: Cornerstone of a Nation* (Oxford and New York: Oxford University Press, 1999), 286.

and the incorporation of Roman Catholic social teachings.[109] Most importantly, Articles 2 and 3 of the constitution expressed the nationalist aspirations of reunification of Ireland. They read:

> *Article 2*:
> The national territory consists of the whole island of Ireland, its islands
> and the territorial seas.
>
> *Article 3*:
> Pending the re-integration of the national territory, and without preju-
> dice to the right of the Parliament and Government established by this
> Constitution to exercise jurisdiction over the whole of that territory, the
> laws enacted by that Parliament shall have the like area and extent of
> application as the law of Saorstát Éireann and the like extra-territorial
> effect.

Articles 2 and 3 represent de Valera's attempt to replace the ambivalence
of the Free State constitution, which represented an involuntary compromise, with a clear and explicit declaration of Ireland's nationalistic
aspirations. The document he constructed more closely resembled the
ideal of a nation-state constitution, and more fully and coherently aimed
at realizing the right of the Irish people to unfettered sovereignty over the
entire national territory of Ireland.

However, a full realization of de Valera's nationalist constitutional
ideal could not yet be achieved in Ireland in 1937 (nor, for that matter, six
decades later). The constitution embodied a set of objectives which were
in fact "contradictory and even mutually exclusive. To look for a Gaelic,

---

[109] For example, the preamble included direct reference to "the Divine Lord Jesus Christ"
and the Social and Fundamental Rights section contained principles such as the importance of the institution of the family and marriage. During the Dáil debates on the draft
constitution, feminist criticism was raised against the provision which recognized the
economic value of women's work in the home. Although the draft which was eventually
adopted acknowledged the equal rights of women, it did not change the fundamental
positions regarding the central role of women as mothers and wives. Article 41.2.1–2
reads: "the State recognises that by her life within the home, woman gives to the State
a support without which the common good cannot be achieved. The State shall, therefore, endeavour to ensure that mothers shall not be obliged by economic necessity to
engage in labour to the neglect of their duties in the home." On de Valera's negotiations with the Vatican over the constitution see Dermot Keogh, "The Constitutional
Revolution: An Analysis of the Making of the Constitution," in Frank Litton, ed.,
The Constitution of Ireland 1937–1987 (Dublin: Institute of Public Administration,
1988). On the relations between church and state in Ireland see also the study of John
Henry Whyte, *Church and State in Modern Ireland, 1923–1970* (Dublin: Gill and
Macmillan, 1971).

Catholic, thirty-two county republic was to ask for the impossible given the presence of Northern Unionists."[110]

Clearly, de Valera was aware of the gap between the declaratory and the practical implications of Articles 2 and 3. On the one hand, his acknowledgment of the fact that the separation between Ireland and Britain was not yet fully accomplished is evident in his avoidance of proclaiming the Irish state as a republic.[111] Moreover, the constitution maintained the loose and vaguely defined ties between Ireland and the British Commonwealth through the provisions on "external relations," which stipulated diplomatic coordination between the two states (Article 29). On the other hand, while accepting that little could be done in the short term to end partition, de Valera was utterly convinced that the right of the Irish people to exercise full sovereignty over all of the "national territory" had to be solemnly declared in the constitution. His justification for this rested on tactical reasoning, perceiving this claim to be a vital card in any future negotiations with the British – the de facto sovereign in the north – over the end of partition.[112]

De Valera's insistence on including in the constitution the impractical declarations of national rights over Northern Ireland, despite their incompatibility with the political reality of British control and Unionist opposition to Irish unification, is consistent with his constitutional philosophy: "You may sneer at words, but I say words mean," he contended in 1922, "they have meanings and they have facts, great realities that you cannot close your eyes to."[113] Fifteen years later he introduced "words" into the constitution, hoping that they would facilitate the "facts" he was wishing for. Indeed the constitution he drafted ultimately by himself embodied most of his dreams.[114] Articles 2 and 3 mirrored not only a wide consensus which was shared by vast majority of the population in twenty-six-county Ireland at the time of its drafting, thereby paving the way to the ratification of the 1937 constitution. They also represented de Valera's belief in the importance of constitutional symbolism for stimulating, or limiting, political developments.

---

[110] Chubb, *The Politics of the Irish Constitution*, 26.
[111] Ireland was declared a republic and formally left the Commonwealth in 1948, under the coalition government led by John Costello.
[112] Gearoid O Tuathaigh, "Irish Nation-State in the Constitution," in Brian Farrell, ed., *De Valera's Constitution and Ours* (Dublin: Gearoid O Tuathaigh, 1988), 52.
[113] Moynihan, *Speeches and Statements by Eamon De Valera 1917–1973*, 91.
[114] Mary C. Bromage, *De Valera and the March of a Nation* (Westport: Greenwood Press, 1975 [1956]), 256.

In the next decades, de Valera's constitutional dogmatism was challenged by political necessities and eventually replaced by what seems to be a return to the pragmatic incrementalist constitutional path first introduced in 1922.

In May 1998 Articles 2 and 3 of the Irish constitution were amended as part of the Good Friday Agreement (known also as the Belfast Agreement, or the British–Irish Agreement), which was aimed at ending the conflict in Northern Ireland. Fifty-six percent of the electorate of the Irish Republic participated in the referendum which approved the amendment with 94.4 percent of the votes for and 5.6 percent against.[115] The new Articles 2 and 3 abandoned the claim for territorial unity of the island. Instead, the new provisions defined the nation by reference to its people. They emphasized the unity of the people as opposed to territory, acknowledging that this unity was conditional on obtaining the consent of the people in both jurisdictions on the island. "For the first time, the constitution now prescribes the manner in which unity is to be attained, namely, by peaceful means with the consent of a majority of the people, democratically expressed, in both jurisdictions in the island."[116]

On the one hand, the amended Irish constitution maintains the goal of territorial reunification: "The commitment to achieving a united Ireland is arguably a constitutional imperative so that it would not be open to an Irish government to repudiate, or to act in any way inconsistently with the desire for unity."[117] On the other hand, the amended constitution, which validated yet another Anglo-Irish Treaty, pursues, in many ways, the incrementalist constitutional approach initiated by Collins' "stepping stone" logic. First, the amendment replaced an explicit demand for Irish unification with a recognition of the need for mutual agreement based on democratic decisions. One of the most distinctive innovations of the Agreement is that it provides for specific *processes* of self-determination, while leaving the question of future sovereignty over Northern Ireland open-ended.[118] Second, by approving the Good Friday Agreement, the Irish recognized the ambiguity in the current status of Northern Ireland. According to Brendan O'Leary, the Agreement established an institutional apparatus which "made Northern Ireland bi-national" and reinforced

---

[115] Hogan and Whyte, *J. M. Kelly: The Irish Constitution*, 68.
[116] *Ibid.*, 75.
[117] *Ibid.*, 3.
[118] Brendan O'Duffy, "British and Irish Conflict Regulation from Sunningdale to Belfast, Part II: Playing for a Draw 1985–1999," *Nations and Nationalism* 6, no. 3 (2000).

"imaginative elements of co-sovereignty."[119] Thus, in addition to internal consociational institutions, which facilitate power-sharing mechanisms between nationalists and unionists (i.e. Catholics and Protestants), the Agreement also included confederal and federal elements which are both pan-Irish and pan-British. For example, it created an all-Ireland North/South Ministerial Council (NSMC), based on the model of the Council of Ministers of the European Union, and an East–West British–Irish Council, with no hierarchical relationship between them.[120] From the Irish nationalist perspective, the North/South Ministerial Council is seen as an "embryonic institution of a federal Ireland: first confederation, then federation after trust has been built."[121] On the other hand, the Agreement provides a parallel federalist avenue through the UK 1998 Northern Irish Act which enables Northern Ireland to expand its autonomy within the Union – an autonomy much greater than that granted to the Scottish or Welsh parliaments.[122]

The 1998 constitutional amendments of Articles 2 and 3 thus represent a return to the incrementalist approach to constitution-making. Unlike 1922, these incrementalist arrangements were not achieved under the threat of external force, but were ratified by a free and independent Irish republic. Moreover, the Good Friday Agreement does not only advocate the principle of constitutional incrementalism based on gradual change of national consensus. By the very fact of its signing, it represents an outcome of the gradual change in national consensus. Although it does not embody a "post nationalist" solution, it does reflect a gradual process of liberalization of the opposing nationalisms both in the south and in Northern Ireland.[123] It was clearly achieved due to a slow emergence of national identity which was based on a civic, rather than a territorial and cultural definition of Irish nationalism.[124] This change was reflected in an

---

[119] For example, it bolsters bi-nationalism by replacing the ministerial requirement for an "Oath of Allegiance" with a "Pledge of Office," which means that nationalist ministers do not have to swear an oath of allegiance to the Crown. Brendan O'Leary, "The Nature of the British–Irish Agreement," *New Left Review* I/233 (1999): 73. Bi-nationalism was also bolstered by the inclusion of symmetric intragovernmental devices to guarantee local protection of local communities, whether the Protestants remain a majority in the North or become a minority in a unified Ireland. *Ibid.*, 87.

[120] The Agreement left open the scope and powers of the North/South Ministerial Council and its implementation bodies. *Ibid.*, 81–3.

[121] *Ibid.*, 85.   [122] *Ibid.*   [123] O'Duffy, "British and Irish Conflict Regulation," 399.

[124] John Coakley, "The Belfast Agreement and the Republic of Ireland," in Rick Wilford, ed., *Aspects of the Belfast Agreement* (Oxford and New York: Oxford University Press, 2001), 229.

opinion poll conducted in mid-December 1999, in which 96 percent of those expressing a view on the matter claimed they would like a united Ireland "at some stage in the future."[125] Thus, the popular support which the Agreement received reflects not only a change in Irish national consensus but also the growing belief on both sides that only an incrementalist constitutional approach which makes possible the gradual emergence of national agreement will result in a solution to the conflict.

[125] *Irish Independent*, December 21, 1999, cited in *ibid.*, 223.

PART III

Arguments for and against constitutional incrementalism

6

Normative arguments for constitutional incrementalism

Israel, India and Ireland are examples of different ways to address a common problem: how to write a democratic constitution when the society is deeply divided on what norms and goals should guide the state. The circumstances under which the Irish, Indian and Israeli constitutional arrangements were arrived at explain why they do not represent one definite model but rather a creative constitutional toolbox. They differ in their level of formality (two are written and one is not) as well as in the strategy that was chosen to address the deep societal disagreements. Israel circumvented the intense tensions between the secular and orthodox sectors of the Jewish population by avoiding drafting a constitution altogether. Instead, all Israeli governments have embraced a set of informal consociational arrangements in the religious sphere. India dealt with the major concern of enhancing unity amidst vast religious, cultural and linguistic diversity by glossing over disagreements regarding fundamental norms and values (such as in issues of personal law and national language) through the use of ambiguous legal language. The Irish Free State accommodated the conflicting pressures surrounding the drafting of the constitution by employing a strategy of ambivalence, namely by incorporating both the Irish and the British positions on the meaning of Irish sovereignty and territorial unity.

As the previous three chapters have shown, the unique social and geopolitical circumstances at the time of each of the constitutional draftings generated a different range of perceptions regarding the risks and opportunities associated with the making of the constitution, and a different range of dynamics affecting the constitutional consequences. In each country, the constitution was perceived not only as an instrument for the establishment of government and the entrenchment of constitutional-democratic order, but also as an important tool for the advancement of various political objectives. In India, a written constitution was needed in order for a federal system to be established. The constitution was viewed as a facilitator of national unity and legal uniformity in a context of extraordinary diversity. Moreover, the constitution served the goal of social reconstruction of India's traditional society and as a catalyst for modernization. In Ireland, the writing of the constitution was inseparable from the struggle for independence, and consequently the drafters wanted the constitution to provide a formal expression of the Irish people's sovereignty. By contrast, Israel's internal as well as external sovereignty was not contingent on a formal constitutional document. The State of Israel was founded as a unitary state awaiting the ingathering of the majority of its future citizenry from Jewish Diaspora, and therefore, from a democratic point of view, the immediate enactment of a constitution was substantially challenged.

Notwithstanding the differences between them, the Israeli, Indian and Irish constitutional strategies of avoidance, ambiguity and ambivalence are all examples of the incrementalist approach to constitution-making. The constitutional arrangements in these societies were designed to prevent potentially explosive conflict essentially by not addressing contentious issues head on, and leaving key foundational aspects of the constitution to be decided in the future. By deferring controversial choices to future political institutions, the incrementalist constitutional arrangements broke the link so common in modern politics between constitution and revolution. Particularly, of course, democratic revolution.[1] The framers introduced an innovative understanding of the relationship between constitutions and time, attempting to "pause" the radical change usually associated with the enactment of a new constitution.

While the constitutional debates in the three countries revolved around different issues, in all three cases the political leaders of the newly independent states were the chief advocates for the adoption of the evolutionary rather than revolutionary constitutional approach in their countries. This chapter traces the great similarity between the arguments they made in the course of the respective constitutional debates in support of an incrementalist approach to constitution-writing. It will demonstrate how the principles of the incrementalist approach to constitution-making evolved throughout the constitutional deliberation.

In designing constitutional arrangements, the Indian, Israeli and Irish framers did not address the foundational components of their

---

[1] Ulrich K. Preuss, *Constitutional Revolution: The Link between Constitutionalism and Progress* (Atlantic Highlands: Humanities Press, 1995); Bruce Ackerman, *The Future of Liberal Revolution* (New Haven and London: Yale University Press, 1992); Hannah Arendt, *On Revolution* (New York: Viking Press, 1965).

constitutions with the same rigidity as they did the institutional ones. The institutional aspect of constitutions, which establishes the democratic structure and procedures of the government, was perceived in all three cases examined here as crucial, and required much clarity and precision. The structure of the legislature, executive and judiciary and the allocation of power between the branches of government (and, in the case of India, between federal and state governments) were defined in a clear manner after considerable constitutional deliberations. Indeed, agreement over the procedural provisions was relatively easy to achieve in these three countries since their governmental arrangements were rooted in the semi-autonomous institutional framework that existed before independence and which was heavily influenced by the Westminster parliamentary model.

However, when it came to the foundational components of the constitutions, a more cautious approach was taken. In each case the drafters recognized that a long time frame was required in order for a consensus around the state's shared norms and ultimate values to evolve. Thus, instead of seeing the making of the constitution as a moment of radical transformation, the framers preferred to view the process – or at least the foundational part of it – as one of gradual adjustment.

This realization was not immediate, but rather emerged as work on the constitutional draft progressed. Interestingly, despite the vast differences between the particular circumstances of the constitutional construction in India, Israel and Ireland, a close study of these processes reveals a great similarity in the evolution of the incrementalist approach among the framers. In all three cases, the process involved similar disputes over meta-constitutional questions regarding constitution-making in deeply divided societies. In particular, three central issues came up in all three constitutional deliberations, and represented turning points in the evolution of the incrementalist approach in all three countries. These three issues were, first, whether a constitution was an efficient instrument of conflict resolution, second, whether a majoritarian or consensual decision-making process was appropriate, and, third, whether the foundational aspect of the constitution should be formulated in a revolutionary or evolutionary manner.

In all three countries the framers began drafting the constitution in the hope that the process would mitigate the internal conflicts and would bridge the competing visions of the state. However, the inability to achieve consensus over the foundational and symbolic aspects of their constitutions led the framers to recognize the limitations of a constitution in resolving ideational disputes. Instead of facilitating unity by staying "above" the sphere of political disagreements, the constitutional debate became yet another arena in which political controversies could be voiced. The gravity and extreme sensitivity attached to constitutional formulations, generally perceived as entrenched and rigid law, threatened to exacerbate existing political tensions. In Israel, the Provincial Council's constitutional committee began drafting a constitution immediately after independence was declared. The committee, which included representatives of all political parties, failed to reach consensus on the relations between the state institutions and Jewish religious tradition. The debates during the first two years of independence, both within the Knesset and outside it, increased the fears that continued efforts to draft a constitution would destabilize the state.[2] As the events of the 1990s revealed, attempts to constitutionally formalize the normative basis of the state, even forty years after independence, could result in an inflammation of the religious–secular conflict.

In India, a Constituent Assembly, proportionally elected, attempted to draft a constitution for united India. But the intractable disagreements between the Congress and the Muslim League led to the partition of the country. Even after partition, religious and linguistic tensions seemed unsolvable. The fear of renewed communal riots underlay many of the concessions made by the Constituent Assembly.

In Ireland, Collins intentionally appointed an apolitical constitutional committee to overcome the polarization between supporters of and objectors to the Treaty. In the end, however, despite efforts to overcome divisions, the constitutional debate inevitably served as an arena for political dispute rather than an apolitical arena for conflict resolution. Under pressure from both the British and the Republicans, Collins soon realized that formalizing the process would likely result in bloodshed.

Arguing for consensual decision-making

In all three cases, therefore, the drafters were aware of the potentially exacerbating effect of drafting a constitution under conditions of intense

---

[2] As expressed by Yosef Lam, Knesset Member from Mapai: "Before we began thinking about it, we thought it was impossible for the Constituent Assembly not to enact a constitution, but when we saw the difficulties among us, a thought had been aroused that perhaps it is possible to live without a constitution." *Meeting of Mapai Party in the Knesset and Party Secretariat*, 14 June 1949.

ideational fragmentation. The drafters acknowledged that any unequivocal choice between the competing perceptions of the state would destabilize the fragile democratic order of the newly founded state. In addition,
the increasing awareness that prevalent tensions and social segmentation
demand complex solutions led the framers to question one of the con-
ventional elements in modern constitution-making, namely the principle of majoritarianism as the sole appropriate method of democratic
decision-making in constitutional disputes. The severe degree of polarization over certain foundational aspects of the constitution made the difficulties inherent in majoritarianism apparent.

Two types of argument were raised against majoritarian decision-
making during the Israeli and Indian constitutional debates – a pragmatic
and a consensual one. The pragmatic argument against majority votes
rested on the assumption that any imposition of the views of the majority on the minority would inflame the conflict and destabilize the democratic order.[3] The consensual argument was based on the belief that for a
constitution to be accepted as legitimate the ideals and norms entrenched
in the document should enjoy broad popular support.[4]

In Ireland, the question of majoritarian decision-making as a basis
for constitution-making was intertwined with the debate over the
Anglo-Irish Treaty and ultimately concerned the democratic validity
of a majority vote under external threat. Collins tried to secure general support for the constitution through the agreement he signed with
de Valera on the eve of the 1922 elections. But the constitution, which
was published on election day, did not meet the conditions of the agreement, and thus could not prevent the eventual outbreak of civil war in
Ireland.

Despite the differences between them, in all three cases the drafters
recognized that majoritarianism was limited in its ability to resolve conflicts over the most fundamental norms and ultimate goals of the state. In
all three cases, the framers recognized that although democracy implied
the rule of the majority, it could not exist only as majority rule, and that
for a democratic society to survive, decisions on the very definition of
the collectivity, its ultimate vision and commitments should rest on a
wide consensus. This was the position that prevailed in the constitutional
debates in India and in Israel. The debate in Ireland also reflected this

---

[3] For example Israel's *Knesset Record* 4 (1950): 812. India's *Constituent Assembly Debate*
(henceforth *CAD*), IX, 1315.
[4] For example *Knesset Record* 5 (1950) 1267; *CAD* VII, 543.

view, although eventually external pressure compelled Collins to concede to the British conditions at the price of Irish unity.

Evolutionary process versus revolutionary moment of constitution-making

Given the limits of majoritarian decision-making in resolving ideational conflicts in the constitutional arena, in all three countries a new approach was introduced to constitution-drafting, advocating the deferral of key decisions over which there was no consensus. The issue of the pace at which constitutions should be formulated was addressed directly by the framers in Ireland, Israel and India. Ultimately, the dispute was between competing perceptions of the relationship between constitution-making and time: whether the constitution represents a revolutionary moment or rather marks a beginning of an evolutionary process, linked to gradual social and political change.

In Israel, this issue became a central focus of the constitutional debate. Supporters of an immediate enactment of a formal constitution stressed the "historical commitment" of the first Knesset, which was originally elected as a Constituent Assembly, to draft a constitution at the time of the foundation of the state.[5] The establishment of a modern Jewish state after two millennia in exile was perceived as a historical opportunity to realize the "will of generations" who had aspired to and labored for this extraordinary moment.[6] In spite (or even because) of the existing disagreements over the meaning of these ideals, many felt that a formal document must be adopted in order to delineate a common direction for the state. Those who supported the idea of drafting a constitution immediately viewed the constitution as a revolutionary instrument which would promote the realization of national goals. By contrast, the opponents of immediate constitution-making regarded it as a long-term process, rather than as a revolutionary moment. Zerach Verhaftig, who was the head of the provisional government's legal department and chaired Israel's first constitutional committee, describes in his memoirs how the political disagreements surrounding the constitution did not lead to compromise but rather to an agreement to postpone the enactment of the constitution:

> Things will be resolved as they will, but we should not push for an immediate solution, since it is clear that such a solution would be negative. It has gradually become clear to me that we should not hasten the process

[5] Ben-Zion Dinburg (Mapai), *Knesset Record* 4 (1950): 742.   [6] *Ibid.*

of enacting a new constitution. This generation is not yet ready for it. One must first establish some required legislative fundamentals upon which, with time, a constitution for Israel may be built.[7]

During the Knesset debates this view was also suggested by most Mapai members, who preferred to adopt a constitution in a gradual manner through a series of Basic Laws. They called for "evolution not revolution."[8] If the time frame for enacting a constitution was extended, they believed, a solution to the religious–secular divide could be found; a legitimate constitution should be constructed "step by step [and] brick by brick" in just the same way that the small Jewish settlement in Palestine grew to be a strong, independent state.[9]

In India, the issue of timing arose in connection to one of the central functions of the Indian constitution: its role as a vehicle for social reconstruction. The reformist function of the constitution was most notably expressed in the context of caste inequality, as the president of the Constituent Assembly, Ambedkar, himself a member of the untouchable caste, pushed for the inclusion of radical provisions such as the abolishment of untouchability. During the debate over the uniform civil code, a similarly reformist demand for the reform of traditional personal law of the various religions communities in India coincided with the nationalist objective of legal uniformity. However, while there was broad consensus in the Assembly on the need to reduce caste inequality, there was considerable disagreement over the role of the constitution as a vehicle of reform when it came to the issue of religious diversity. This was particularly due to the sensitivity of minority groups after partition. As far as religious issues were concerned, using the legal powers of the constitution to promote major social reform was more contentious, and many felt that it was necessary to wait for the gradual emergence of a broader consensus. While for some members of the Indian Assembly constitutions were to "advance … the time," the prevailing view of constitutions was that, rather, they must "progress with the advance of time."[10] Similarly, in the debates over the national language, the dispute was between those who insisted that Hindi should replace English "at the earliest possible moment"[11] and those who preferred to wait until an indigenous national language would "evolve" by itself.[12]

---

[7] Zerach Vahrhaftig, *A Constitution for Israel: Religion and State* (Jerusalem: Mesilot, 1988), 61.
[8] Avraham Hertzfeld (Mapai), *Knesset Record* 5 (1950): 1277.
[9] David Bar-Rav-Hai (Mapai), *Knesset Record* 5 (1950): 727.
[10] *CAD* VII, 542–3.   [11] *CAD* IX, 1331.   [12] *Ibid.*, 1457.

During the debates over the 1922 Irish constitution, the conflicting perceptions regarding the appropriate pace of constitution-making were reflected in the positions of the provisional government, which supported an incrementalist "stepping stone" approach, and the extreme Republicans who preferred a radical approach. The latter view was expressed by de Valera, who viewed the constitution as an idealistic statement of national aspirations which can bring about their political realization. For de Valera, it was the symbolic dimension of the constitution that mattered above all. De Valera's constitutional approach was manifested in the poignant nationalistic declarations of Articles 2 and 3 in his 1937 constitution. Collins, by contrast, advocated a more realistic and pragmatic model of constitution-making, which recognized the political obstacles blocking the way to the constitutional realization of the Irish national ideals. A constitution, he contended, should be perceived as a "stepping stone" in a long-term process of constitutional and national evolvement. It should mark the beginning of a revolution, not its conclusion. Indeed, this "stepping stone" approach was revived in Ireland through the 1998 amendments of de Valera's Articles 2 and 3, as part of the Good Friday Agreement with Northern Ireland.

In all three countries, therefore, drafters of the constitution developed an innovative understanding of the place of a constitution on a nation's historical timeline. They all adopted an incrementalist rather than a revolutionary perception of constitution-making. Not a "once in two millennia opportunity" but a "stepping stone." Not "forcing the issue" but waiting patiently for the desired conditions to evolve. The introduction of a longer-term perspective into the equation of constitution-making allowed them (and the societies to which they belonged) to defer controversial decisions regarding the foundational elements of the constitution to future political institutions.

Embracing competing visions

The Israeli, Indian and Irish incrementalist constitutional arrangements are thus pragmatic but creative responses to the impossibility of designing the constitution around an exclusive, coherent system of values of one of the competing ideational factions of society. But constitutional incrementalism should not be seen as merely avoiding making decisions regarding societal and political problems. Despite the attraction of the liberal constitutional paradigm, the possibility of drafting a proceduralist constitution which would establish institutional mechanisms for conflict resolution, and provide a "thin" civic basis for shared national identity, was not proposed in any of the countries in question, and presumably was not considered a viable option.[13] In Israel, where the goal of the secular majority was the enactment of a secular-liberal constitution, a "thin" constitution that adopted no stand on religious issues would have been perceived as a victory for secular society. Similarly in India, particularly as regards the issue of a uniform civil code, aligning the constitution along principles of secular unification was exactly what the Hindu nationalist majority wished for, and what the Muslim representatives fought against. In the dispute over national language, again, there was no room for a neutral procedural solution. The core of the problem was whether English would remain an official language or would be replaced by Hindi or by a variety of other languages. A choice needed to be made. Government had to function, and the language in which it would do so had to be decided. Lastly, in Ireland, the question of sovereignty over the island could not be ignored – it was the heart of the conflict. Any constitutional formulation would imply a choice between the rival perspectives. The problem of national definition could not be overlooked.

The constitutional debates in Israel, India and Ireland reveal the impracticality of the liberal-proceduralist approach to constitution-making in deeply divided societies. This constitutional doctrine is difficult to implement in societies still struggling over the definition of their collectivity and over their most fundamental commitments and beliefs. In such societies, principles of political liberalism, particularly the distinction between private identities and the public sphere, are not accepted by all members of society. Moreover, political liberalism cannot resolve conflicts in deeply divided societies because the colliding groups define themselves in terms of their competing visions of the state as a whole. In other words, the core of the division is between rival perceptions of the collectivity in its entirety, and thus an attempt to differentiate between the private and public spheres is not only impossible but also ultimately irrelevant. Thus, instead of taking the disputes over the religious, national

---

[13] In the Israeli context this option was first suggested by Moshe Landau, the former Supreme Court Chief Justice in his article "Constitution as a Supreme Law for the State of Israel," *Hapraklit* 27 (1971). During the 2003–6 debates of the Knesset's Constitution, Law and Justice Committee on the draft *Constitution in Broad Consent* a proposal for drafting a "thin" constitution, which would not include a "principles section," was discussed briefly and rejected by the majority of the Committee members.

or linguistic character of the state "off the agenda," to use John Rawls' terminology, the incrementalist constitutional approach implies the embracing of the competing positions.

The framers of the constitutional arrangements of Israel, India and Ireland found themselves in a paradoxical situation. On the one hand, they were cognizant of the potentially destabilizing affects of any clear-cut decision on the contentious issues which polarized their societies. Yet, on the other hand, they recognized that these significant issues, which defined the lines of societal fragmentation, could not be disregarded and had to be addressed by the emerging constitutional arrangements. Instead of resolving the tensions by making a clear-cut decision in favor of one side or another of the dispute, they constructed a constitution which embraced all sides of the conflict. The incrementalist constitutional arrangements contained within them the contradictory perspectives and principles, awaiting their slow and gradual resolution over time.

Thus, while the disputes over the foundational aspect of the constitution may not have been settled, neither were they ignored. The incrementalist constitution preserves within it the competing visions and beliefs that the various factions aspire to embed in formal documents. By including a variety of competing perspectives of the state, the incrementalist constitution decreases the perception of the constitution as a high-stakes moment at which decisions that are made regarding the future of the nation are permanent.

The inclusion of contrasting visions in the constitution raises the question previously discussed in Chapter 1 regarding the foundational role of a constitution. Constitutions serve as the charter of the polity's identity. To be regarded as legitimate, constitutions are expected to reflect a societal consensus regarding the ultimate goals and underlying principles of the state. This foundational role of the constitution is easily achieved in nation-states, in which the citizens presumably share a common cultural, ethnic or religious background, and in whose constitution a "thick" identity can be expressed with little controversy. Similarly, in liberal multinational or multicultural states, a liberal constitution expresses a "thin" type of identity, based on the commitment, shared by all, to the principles of political liberalism. But neither of these situations applies in deeply divided societies, which lack neither a "thick" nor "thin" basis for shared identity. Thus, in deeply divided societies, what kind of national identity can be represented in the constitution?

The incrementalist approach to constitution-making that was adopted by Israel, India and Ireland provides an opportunity to go beyond the theoretical dichotomy between the essentialist and the proceduralist constitution, as presented in Chapter 1. The Israeli, Indian and Irish constitutions suggest that the general rule regarding a constitution's foundational aspect remains valid even in deeply divided societies that are still struggling over the vision of the state. Constitutions adopted by deeply divided societies may indeed reflect the identity of "the people" in whose name the constitution was written. They do so by representing the identity of "the people" as it exists at time of constitution-making, in other words, a *divided identity*.

The experience of Israel, Ireland and India demonstrates that complex and segmented societies are able to adopt complex and segmented constitutions. Where there is no shared vision, the accommodational constitution represents the very minimal common denominator which can guarantee popular support in the government: agreement over the fact that the polity is polarized, and the core issues around which the disagreements revolve.

The constitutional approach embraced by deeply divided societies suggests a kind of political understanding (or political disposition) which recognizes the importance of context rather than abstract principles, of gradualism rather than radicalism. The political leaders who led their nations to independence understood that the unique conditions of their societies necessitated linking the establishment of constitutional arrangements to the gradual emergence of a national consensus. They recognized the limited utility of constitution-making as a moment of conflict resolution, and thus embraced within the constitutional arrangements the competing visions of the strong, entrenched identity groups which comprised their societies.

Preparing the ground for future political decisions

By refraining from making clear-cut choices between the competing visions of the state, the incrementalist constitutional arrangements defer the decisions regarding foundational issues to the future, thus exporting the divisive issues from the constitutional back into the realm of ordinary politics. This does not imply the creation of some perpetual constitutional exclusion of the divisive issues from any political or future constitutional debate. On the contrary. In many ways, the framers of the incrementalist constitutions recognize the dangers of what Stephen

Holmes terms "gag rules" in the domain of ordinary legislation.[14] They do not wish to narrow the political agenda, but only to avoid the entrenchment of unequivocal choices with regard to sensitive issues. Recognizing that these issues require long-term public and political discussions, they channel them to what they believe is the more flexible arena of the ordinary exercise of parliamentary power.

The procedural components of the constitution regulate the institutional framework through which these decisions may be reached. However, the framers did more than merely establish a procedural structure to facilitate further deliberation. The elaboration of the clashing positions in the conflict sketched the contours and the boundaries of any future political debate. The constitution thus provides a starting point for future deliberations and sets some significant guidelines regarding possible developments and decisions regarding the nature and identity of the state.

For example, the definition of Israel in its Declaration of Independence as both a Jewish state and as a guardian of liberal rights, as well as the emergence of consociational arrangements of the religious status quo, did not resolve the debate on the meaning of Israel's Jewish character on the balance between the Jewish and the liberal-democratic nature of the state. Rather, it guarantees that any future decision on the basic principles of the state will not lean heavily toward one of the extremes, but must include some variation of the two elements. The question that the first Knesset left open for future deliberation was not whether Israel is *either* Jewish *or* democratic, but rather how these terms should be reconciled.

Similarly, in India, the Constituent Assembly avoided making a decision regarding a uniform civil code and a national language. However, these issues were not taken off the constitutional agenda. Rather, after vehement debate, they were included in the formal constitution (Articles 44 and 343). The framers recognized the tensions between the aspiration to promote a uniform secular personal law and a common national language, on the one hand, and the pragmatic obstacles to the immediate realization of these national ideals, on the other. Thus, the constitution provided guidelines for future political decisions relating to these issues: government institutions should endeavor to achieve the objectives of a uniform civil code and a national language, but not at

---

[14] Stephen Holmes, "Gag Rules or the Politics of Omission," in Jon Elster and Rune Slagstad, eds., *Constitutionalism and Democracy* (Cambridge University Press, 1988). On the drawbacks of gag rules see particularly pp. 56–8.

the expense of the cultural rights and sense of security of the minority. The various principles would have to be balanced. B. R. Ambedkar, one of the fathers of the Indian constitution, saw the Directive Principles of State Policy in this light when he explained that the provisions included in this section intended to instruct future legislatures and to guide future executives:

> Whoever captures power will not be free to do what he likes with it. In the exercise of it, he will have to respect these instruments of instructions which are called Directive Principles. He cannot ignore them. He may not have to answer for their breach in a court of law. But he will certainly have to answer for the breach before the electorate at election time. What great value these Directive Principles possess will be realized better when the forces of right contrive to capture power.[15]

The Irish case is somewhat different. The ambivalent constitutional formulation on the issue of sovereignty and political authority was not the result of a decision made by an independent Constituent Assembly. Rather, it was a forced compromise accepted by the weaker side of the conflict. Nevertheless, we can learn from the Irish example that in the long run even a constitution drafted under such conditions can have implications for how issues are subsequently resolved in the political arena. The Free State constitution contained both elements of British monarchism as well as principles of popular Irish sovereignty. It was left to the governmental institutions of the Irish Free State to continue the political struggle for complete authority over the island. Ultimately, the Irish Free State constitution was able to adapt in response new political developments within Ireland and outside it because from the beginning it incorporated both competing approaches. At the same time, it also limited the scope of possible developments. Thus, for example, British control in Ireland was permanently limited by the constitution, and Irish sovereignty, although incomplete, had been established.

The three political leaders who led their countries to independence and headed the debates over the constitutions of their respective states – David Ben-Gurion in Israel, Jawaharlal Nehru in India and Michael Collins in Ireland – were strong advocates of the incrementalist approach. Their support for the notion of deferring controversial choices seemed to rest not only on pragmatic considerations, but also on an optimistic view of politics as an arena for introducing social change based on wide consensus.

---

[15] *CAD* II, 41.

As revolutionaries and as believers in modernity, they placed their trust in the ability of political processes to bring about a new and improved social order. This optimism regarding the political order underpinned Ben-Gurion's objection to empowering judges to determine state policies,[16] which was one of his chief reasons for opposing the enactment of a written constitution. He acknowledged the deep divisions within Israeli society, and did not wish to resolve them by legal formulations, which would require drawn-out philosophical deliberations.[17] In India, Nehru saw politics at the heart of the subcontinent's passage to and experience of modernity.[18] He believed that Indian society could be reconstituted and reformed through the political actions of the state. The major social and economic reforms required for India to join the Western world could only succeed if there was broad societal collaboration, which would inevitably grow gradually. While having a clear vision for future India, Nehru acknowledged the need to adopt incrementalist constitutional arrangements in contentious issues such as uniform civil code and national language.[19] Unlike Ben-Gurion and Nehru, Collins led a guerilla struggle against the British in the pre-state era. However, after the signing of the Anglo-Irish Treaty he became the strongest supporter of the Treaty, believing that it would allow for full Irish independence and sovereignty through peaceful means, rather than through war and bloodshed. Collins the soldier became a vehement proponent of the political route to reconciliation, and to incremental achievement of political goals.[20]

---

[16] *Knesset Record* 4 (1950): 817. See also Chapter 3.

[17] During a meeting of the Mapai Party in 1949 Ben-Gurion stated: "We are an ancient people, who have lived thousands of years with no constitution – cannot we continue to live without a constitution? ... The debate over the fundamental constitution will last many years, and will involve the entire state of Israel and the Diaspora ... Rather than concerning themselves with what needs to be done, Jews around the world are able to dispute the constitution." *Meeting of Mapai Party in the Knesset and Party Secretariat*, 14 June 1949 (Beit Berl Archives).

[18] Sunil Khilnani, *The Idea of India* (New York: Farrar, Straus and Giroux, 1999), 9.

[19] In an interview in 1954, Nehru said that although the uniform civil code was inevitable, the time was not ripe at independence for including it as a constitutional principle. Cited in Donald E. Smith, *Nehru and Democracy* (Bombay: Orient Longmans, 1958), 165.

[20] During the heated Dáil debates over the Anglo-Irish Treaty Michael Collins stated: "In all countries in time of change – when countries are passing from peace to war or war for peace – they have had their most trying times on an occasion such as this. Whether we are right or whether we are wrong in the view of future generations there is this: that we now are entitled to a chance; all the responsibility will fall upon us of taking over the machinery of government from the enemy." And later during the same discussion, referring to members of the opposition within Sinn Féin: "Whatever we may say, whatever we may think, I do believe that some kind of an arrangement could be fixed

The constitutional choices and compromises advocated by the three political leaders suggest that they believed in the gradual emergence of national consensus on controversial identity issues, and accordingly, in incrementalist rather than revolutionary means for dealing with disagreements. They advocated such a constitutional approach knowing that it could lead to the preservation of institutional arrangements that conflicted with their personal world view.[21] Their approach is suggestive of a kind of "practically open and imaginatively open" Burkean philosophy that emphasized a common sense manifest in the intricate constitutional architectures of the three case studies. A person in politics, Burke wrote, must seek "the exact detail of circumstances, guided by the surest general principles that are necessary to direct experiment and inquiry, in order, again, from those details to elicit principles, firm and luminous general principles, to direct a practical legislative process."[22] This seems to be what Collins, Nehru and Ben-Gurion tried to do.

between the two sides. Even though our physical presence is so distasteful that they will not meet us, I say some kind of understanding ought to be reached to preserve the present order in the country, at any rate over the weekend." *Dáil Debates*, January 7, 1922.

[21] This was most evidently in the compromises supported by Ben Gurion and Nehru concerning religion–state relations. Ben Gurion, in his personal life, held radical anti-religious views. He did not follow any of the Jewish religious practices and visited synagogue only once in all his years in Israel. Nevertheless he rejected the adoption of a secular constitution. Zvi Zameret, "Yes to the Jewish State, No to a Clericalist State: The Mapai Leadership and its Attitude to Religion and religious Jews" in Mordechai Bar-On, ed. *On Both Sides of the Bridge: Religion and State in the Early Years of Israel* (Jerusalem: Yad Izhak Ben-Zvi Press, 2002), pp. 199–201. Similarly, Nehru, a firm believer in the power of reason, rejected any form of organized religion yet recognized the persistence of religion and the need to make political compromises. See Sunil Khilnani, "Nehru's Belief" in: Anuradha Dingwaney Needham and Rajeswari Sunder Rajan, eds., *The Crisis of Secularism in India* (Duke University Press, 2007), 89–103.

[22] Edmund Burke, *The Works of the Right Honourable Edmund Burke* (London: Printed for F. C. and J. Rivington, 1812), vol. V, 87.

7

Potential dangers

The main argument of the book has been that the adoption of incrementalist strategies with respect to foundational conflicts allows deeply divided
societies either to enact a formal democratic constitution or to function
within the framework of informal material constitutional arrangements.
While avoidance and ambiguity are useful facilitating tools, it is important to understand their difficulties. This chapter will discuss the potential
dangers that are inherent to the incrementalist approach to constitution-making: compromising basic rights, potential over-rigidity of the
material constitutional arrangement, and the risk of inter-institutional
polarization between the legislature and the judiciary. It will further seek
to demonstrate how these dangers have been displayed in the political
and legal developments in the decades since the incrementalist constitutional arrangements were put in place. The conflicts involving religious
identity that were discussed in previous chapters (India's uniform civil
code and the secular–religious conflict in Israel) have intensified significantly in recent decades, compared to the other conflicts that have been
discussed (linguistic identity in India and national identity in Ireland).[1]
A further and much larger study is required in order to identify particular links, or causal mechanisms, that trace the different affect of various
incrementalist constitutional strategies on different types of conflict. One
may even doubt that such links could be drawn at all. Nevertheless, for the
sake of this study, the increasing tensions around religious foundational
issues in Israel and India will be analyzed below as illuminating examples

---

[1] The moderation of the disagreement on the nature of national identity of Ireland, as evident in the 1998 Good Friday Agreement, was discussed in Chapter 5. The impact of the
administrative reorganization of states on the tensions between language groups in India
was discussed in Chapter 4. Nevertheless, language continues to play an important role in
Indian politics. See, for example, Bethany Lacina, "Indian Language Groups, Concession
of Sub-National Autonomy, and the Origins of Political Violence" (paper presented at the
American Political Science Association Annual Meeting, Boston, August 28–31, 2008).

of the potential dangers that are inherent to the incrementalist approach to constitution-making.

Compromising basic rights

The deferral of clear and unequivocal decisions on the fundamental norms and values of the state jeopardizes what is commonly viewed as the constitution's primary function: protecting liberal values and basic rights.[2] This is particularly true when the conflict that the framers attempt to avoid has to do with religious issues.[3] The religious traditions that are being defended in such cases tend to be patriarchal in nature. Thus, accommodating them within the constitutional framework as part of the strategy of incrementalism is most likely to infringe upon women's fundamental rights and legal personhood.

The violations of basic rights in India and Israel have stood at the center of intense public, legal and political disputes for decades, and in both countries the constitutional arrangements that evolved in the early years of the state are criticized by many as missed opportunities.[4] As the next sections of this chapter will show, the non-justiciability of the constitutional provision regarding India's uniform civil code and the decision not to apply it to all religious communities meant that certain communities

[2] Carl J. Friedrich, *Constitutional Government and Democracy: Theory and Practice in Europe and America*, rev. edn (Boston: Ginn, 1950); Jon Elster and Rune Slagstad, eds., *Constitutionalism and Democracy* (Cambridge and New York: Cambridge University Press, 1988).

[3] The chapter will focus on risks involved with the incrementalist approach particularly in the context of conflicts over religious issues. As discussed in Chapter 3, it is difficult to foresee whether incrementalist constitutional arrangement may restrict or rather allow for protection of minority rights. Whether the protection of rights of Arabs in Israel has been increased over the years is a question intensely debated by legal, public and academic circles.

[4] In India this line of criticism is voiced by both proponents and opponents of the uniform civil code. For example this was part of the Hindi-nationalist BJP's campaign for national elections in 1996 and 1998. Sunil Khilnani, *The Idea of India* (New York: Farrar, Straus and Giroux, 1999). See also Seval Yildirim, "Expanding Secularism's Scope: An Indian Case Study," *American Journal of Comparative Law* 52 (2004); Rajkumari Agrawala, ed., "Uniform Civil Code: A Formula Not Solution," in Tahir Mahmood, ed., *Family Law and Social Change* (Bombay: MN Tripathy, 1975); Tahir Mahmood, *Personal Law in Crisis* (New Delhi: Manohar, 1986). In Israel, legal scholars Amnon Rubinstein and Barak Medina claim that Israeli leadership "missed an opportunity to enact a constitution at the 'revolutionary moment' of the establishment of the state." Amnon Rubinstein and Barak Medina, *Constitutional Law of the State of Israel*, 6th edn. (Tel Aviv: Schocken, 2005), vol. I, 76 (Hebrew).

are governed by family law that is often patriarchal and inegalitarian in its nature. And in Israel, the emergence of an ambiguous "religious status quo" has led to the non-separation between religion and state in personal law, thereby infringing upon the basic liberties of hundreds of thousands of citizens who are barred from marriage (and occasionally divorce) by religious authorities.

Over-rigidity of a material constitution

The constitutional framers in deeply divided societies may have believed that by avoiding making decisions in controversial issues they can transfer decisions in these issues to the more flexible arena of ordinary politics. In the political sphere, it was argued during the constitutional debates in Israel, India and Ireland, choices would evolve gradually as societal consensus changes. However, as events proved, this was not always the case. In some cases, the arrangements that many of the framers assumed would be provisional lasted for many decades and turned out to be difficult to alter through ordinary legislation. The ambiguous constitutional formulations in fact allowed the emergence of a material constitutional arrangements – either unwritten or in the form of ordinary legislation – which in many ways appear to be more rigid than a formal constitutional would have been. The emergence of a "material" constitution in the absence of a "formal" constitution on the character of the state raises an interesting question with regard to their rigidity. Unlike formal ones, material constitutions do not include clear mechanisms of amendment. This is particularly true when some constitutional principles are unwritten (for example the prohibition on public transportation on the Sabbath in Israel). But ambiguous constitutional formulations may also allow for the enactment of ordinary laws that over time appear to be very difficult to change, for various political reasons.[5] As such, incrementalist constitutional formulations open the door to a material entrenchment of the status quo, and, consequentially, to entrenched conservatism.

The danger of over-rigidity is a standard criticism of accommodational arrangements in divided societies, such as the consociational arrangements that have emerged in Israel in the religious sphere in the absence of a written constitution. Consociational solutions to conflicts between

---

[5] Hanna Lerner, "Constitutional Ambiguity as a Critical Juncture in the Evolution of Religion–State Relations: Lessons from Israel and India" (unpublished paper).

identity groups, it is argued, tend to build "systematic constraints" to rapid societal change.[6] When the accommodational arrangements are informal, the question of rigidity may be even more acute. The failure to implement a uniform civil code in India in the six decades since the constitution was enacted, despite the Constituent Assembly's explicit direction to do so, as well as the inability to enact a bill of rights or to draft a comprehensive constitution in Israel sixty years after independence, are revealing examples of the danger of potential over-rigidity of material constitutional arrangements that have evolved in the absence of a formal decision regarding foundational issues.

Increasing tensions between legislature and judiciary

The prolonged public controversies over foundational issues left unresolved by incrementalist constitutional arrangements can lead to another danger that may weaken democratic governments, namely to increasing tensions between the legislature and the judiciary. The inability of the political system to settle the controversies around the fundamental norms or ultimate goals of the state may lead to the growing involvement of the judiciary, and primarily the Supreme Court, which may result in a conflict between the two branches of government. This problem was illustrated in the legislation that was passed in India following the *Shah Bano* case.[7] Similarly, it was demonstrated in Israel in 1996 when the Knesset overrode the Supreme Court's decision in *Meatrael* and amended Basic Law: Freedom of Occupation.[8]

---

[6] Alfred Stepan, "Paths toward Redemocratization: Theoretical and Comparative Considerations," in Guillermo O'Donnell, Philippe C. Schmitter and Laurence Whitehead, eds., *Transitions from Authoritarian Rule: Comparative Perspectives* (Baltimore and London: The Johns Hopkins University Press, 1988), 80.

[7] See below in this chapter.

[8] On *Meatrael* see Chapter 3. Another recent clash between the Knesset and the Supreme Court revolves around the issue of core curriculum in state-funded Jewish Orthodox schools. In 2004, the court ruled in favor of imposing the duty to teach core curriculum (including math, English and sciences) in all state-funded schools, according to the State Education Law in HCJ 10296/02 *Secondary School Teachers' Association* v. *Minister of Education*, IsrSC 59(3) 224. However, in 2008, the Knesset passed The Unique Cultural Educational Institutions Law; which allowed for the exemption of state-funded Orthodox schools from implementing the requirement of core curriculum. Yossi Dahan and Yoav Hammer, "Democracy, the Educational Autonomy of Cultural Minorities and the Law: The Case of the Ultra-Orthodox Minority in Israel" (unpublished paper). In May 2010 the constitutionality of this law was challenged by a new appeal to the High Court of Justice (*Amnon Rubinstein* v. *The Knesset*).

The tension between the legislature and the judiciary is inherent to any democratic system. However, lack of constitutional clarity on contentious foundational issues can lead to lack of clarity with regard to which branch of government should take the lead in dealing with such issues. This is particularly problematic if the court and the parliament hold opposing views regarding the foundational issues at stake. Supreme Courts are generally expected to serve as the chief protectors of individual rights. Parliaments, by contrast, as representative bodies, are more responsive to particular demands of interest groups. Consequently, the judiciary and the legislature may attempt to advance competing visions of the state. The danger is that this difference between the worldviews will result in a direct clash between the two institutions, and may undermine both their legitimacy and public support. The court may lose its legitimacy as a neutral arbitrator in legal issues and the parliament may lose its legitimacy as a representative body of the various interests in society.

As the following sections will demonstrate, the level of polarization between the branches of government depends on various factors, among them the level of judicial intervention played out by the Supreme Court. The Israeli and the Indian Supreme Courts, for example, differed in their attempt to alter various aspects of the "material" constitutional arrangements pertaining to religious issues. While the Israeli Supreme Court clearly identified with the secular side in the religious–secular conflict over the character of the state, the Indian Supreme Court was more ambivalent in its call for the implementation of the uniform civil code. This explains the difference in the intensity of the inter-institutional tensions in the two countries. The political reaction to the Supreme Court in Israel was much more vigorous than in India, and included not only regressive parliamentary legislation (as in India) but also stark public condemnation of the Court by religious leaders.

The next two sections will illustrate how these three risks became apparent in recent developments in Israel and India, where the controversies over the vision of the state still stir intense political and legal debates. In particular, it will focus on the debates regarding the secularization of personal law, which stands at the heart of the intense internal conflict over the place of religion in Israeli and in Indian identity.

Israel: constitutional impasse

As discussed in Chapter 3, the consociational arrangements that have emerged in Israel in the absence of a written constitution, commonly referred to as "the religious status quo," effectively determine the non-separation between religion and state in certain areas, such as observance of the Sabbath, observance of *kashruth* (dietary laws) in governmental institutions, autonomy of religious educational institutions and exclusive jurisdiction of religious courts in matters of personal law. The latter issue, particularly the regulation of marriage and divorce, is considered one of the most divisive issues in the religious–secular divide, as the existing arrangements infringe on basic liberties and violate the principle of equality for hundreds of thousands of Israeli citizens.

The monopoly of the Orthodox stream of Judaism over matters of marriage and divorce pertain to the Jewish population is a key element of the religious status quo.[9] It is based on the decision of the Provisional Council, taken four days after the establishment of the state, to preserve the authority of religious institutions in the area of personal law as they existed prior to the foundation of the state.[10] This decision was formalized by Knesset legislation in 1953 with the Rabbinical Courts Jurisdiction (Marriage and Divorce) Law, which provides that "matters of marriage and divorce of Jews in Israel, being nationals or residents of the state, shall be under the exclusive jurisdiction of rabbinical courts," and that "marriage and divorce of Jews shall be performed in Israel in accordance with Jewish religious law." Consequently, the institution of civil marriage does not exist in Israel. Anyone who wishes to marry or divorce must do so in a religious ceremony, even if they are atheists.[11] Women in particular are discriminated against by the patriarchal religious legal system, since Jewish law effectively grants the husband veto power over the divorce.[12] Israel's Women's Equal Rights Law

---

[9] The religious monopoly on matters of marriage and divorce also applies to non-Jewish minorities in Israel. See Michael Karayanni, "The 'Other' Religion and State Conflict in Israel: On the Nature of Religious Accommodations for the Palestinian-Arab Minority," in Winfried Brugger and Michael Karayanni, eds., *Religion in the Public Sphere: A Comparative Analysis of German, Israeli, American and International Law* (Berlin: Springer, 2007); Aharon Layish, *Women and Islamic Law in a Non-Muslim State: A Study Based on Sharia Courts in Israel* (New Brunswick: Transaction Publishers 2006).

[10] Based on the Palestine Order in Council 1922, Paragraph 83 in Robert Harry Drayton, *The Laws of Palestine: In Force on the 31st Day of December 1933*, rev. edn. (London, Jerusalem and Palestine: Printed by Waterlow and Sons, 1934), vol. III, 2587.

[11] The state does recognize civil marriage outside of Israel. HCJ 143/62 *Schlezinger v. Ministry of Internal Affairs*.

[12] According to recent estimates, around 100,000 women in Israel have been either denied a divorce or have had to comply with conditions set by the husband in order to get a divorce. See Orit Lotan, "'Mesoravot Get' (Denied of Divorce) in Israel" (Report Presented to the Knesset Committee on the Status of Women, 2005). See also Michael Corinaldi, *Personal, Family and Inheritance Law – between Religion and State: New Trends* (Jerusalem: Nevo,

(1951) explicitly specifies that the law is not valid with regard to matters of marriage and divorce. Israel even added two reservations addressing this issue when it signed the UN Convention on the Elimination of All Forms of Discrimination against Women in 1991.[13] In addition, the Orthodox monopoly on marriage and divorce means that the state does not recognize marriage performed by Reform or Conservative rabbis in Israel. Interfaith marriage in Israel is also impossible. Finally, marriage is denied for people who are defined by the rabbinical authorities as "barred from marriage" (*psuley chitun*) for various religious reasons.[14] The right to marry is limited, for example, for an estimated 300,000 immigrants from the former Soviet Union, who are not considered Jews by the Halacha yet are not associated with any other religion.[15] While a limited civil marriage bill passed by the Knesset in May 2010 aimed to make it possible for those defined as "lacking a religion" to formally register as couples and to have same legal rights and obligations as a married couple, the bill only applies to couples who are *both* considered as not being members of any religion.[16]

2004), 173–209 (Hebrew); Frances Raday, C. Shalev and Michal Liban-Kooby, eds., *Women's Status in Israeli Society and Law* (Jerusalem: Shocken, 1995) (Hebrew); Barbara Swirski and M. P. Safir, *Calling the Equality Bluff: Woman in Israel* (New York: Pergamon Press, 1991).

[13] See: www2.ohchr.org/english/bodies/ratification/8.htm.

[14] For example, the Rabbinical courts do not recognize the marriage of children born to women who, under religious law (but not civil law) are still considered married to their former husbands (*mamzerim*). Nor do they permit marriage between a man from a priestly family (Cohen) and a divorcee. The two common arguments for preserving religious monopoly on personal law concern the attempts, first, to block intermarriage (between Jews and non-Jews) and second, to prevent the division among the Jewish people between two separate groups that cannot marry since only one group (the religious) follows all religious regulations, particularly those related to *mamzerim* (children of women who might be regarded as divorced under civil law but not under religious law). Amnon Rubinstein, "The Right to Marry," *Iunei Mishpat* 3 (1973/4) (Hebrew).

[15] According to the 2008 report of the Israeli Central Bureau of Statistics, 319,000 people in Israel (4.3 percent of the population) are defined as "others." The definition includes "immigrants who are not registered as Jews by the Ministry of Internal Affairs (non-Arab Christians and residents whose religion is not defined)." See also Pinchas Shiffman, *Civil or Sacred: Civil Marriage and Divorce Alternatives in Israel* (Jerusalem: The Association for Civil Rights in Israel, 2001).

[16] Couplehood Union (Brit Zugiut) for Lacking a Religion Bill 2010 was initiated by the Israel Beitenu Party, a right-wing party supported by former immigrants from the Soviet Union. The law does not allow for interfaith marriage and does not apply if only one partner had no religion. According to critics of the bill, the law would be helpful for only 170 couples a year, less than 4 percent of all those currently unable to marry. Tomer Zarchin, "Controversial Civil Union Bill Up for Discussion," *Haartetz*, March 9, 2010.

Over the years, the Israeli legal system developed several alternatives to circumvent limitations set by formal religious marriage, such as the institution of "common-law relationships" (*yeduim betzibur*).[17] Additionally, many Israelis travel abroad to get married in civil ceremonies. Nevertheless, while mitigating some of the effects of basic rights violations caused by religious law, these alternative arrangements have not resolved all difficulties resulting from Orthodox monopoly over formal marriage in Israel.[18] Moreover, the separation between the religious and secular court systems often results in a clash of authorities, typically when the Rabbinical Court refuses to accept the authority of the Supreme Court.[19]

An additional aspect of religious discrimination resulting from the status quo arrangements is the issue of non-Orthodox conversions and the legal definitions of "who is a Jew?" affecting not only marriage but also citizenship rights. When the Law of Return was enacted in 1950, it did not provide a clear legal definition of who is considered as Jewish, and therefore entitled to automatic citizenship upon arrival in Israel. It was not clear whether the definition should be essentially national-cultural or follow the religious definition provided by Orthodox Judaism. This question of "who is a Jew?" soon became a matter of intense public debate, and has remained so to this day.[20] Another related issue is the controversy over conversion, which touches upon the conflict between Orthodox and non-Orthodox Jewish movements – the Conservative and Reform movements.[21] The issue of conversion is particularly acute with regard to the

---

[17] On the institute of "reputed wife" see Corinaldi, *Personal, Family and Inheritance Law – between Religion and State*; Daniel Friedman, "The 'Unmarried Wife' in Israeli Law," in *Israeli Yearbook on Human Rights* (Tel Aviv: Faculty of Law, Tel Aviv University, 1972).

[18] For a comprehensive discussion of the various alterative solutions see Shachar Lifschitz, "Spousal Registration – Preliminary Design," in Aharon Barak and Daniel Friedman, eds., *Book in Memory of Prof. Shava* (Tel Aviv: Ramot-Tel Aviv University Press, 2006).

[19] Anat Scolnicov, "Religious Law, Religious Courts and Human Rights within Israeli Constitutional Structure," *International Journal of Constitutional Law* 4, no. 4 (2006).

[20] For the sake of population registry, the Israeli government adopted a religious-Orthodox definition of Jewishness. In 1970 the Knesset amended the Law of Return to define a Jew as "one who was born to a Jewish mother or was converted and is not a member of another religion." The 1970 amendment also expanded the categories of family members entitled to immigrate to Israel to include grandchildren of Jews and their spouses. Nevertheless, this definition left much ambiguity concerning what would count as a proper conversion.

[21] While there is no law granting Orthodox exclusiveness in conversion (as opposed to matters of marriage and divorce), the status quo has become that the state would recognize any type of conversion made abroad – even Reform and Conservative – while conversion in Israel would be recognized only if it were Orthodox. Since the 1990, the Reform and Conservative movements have repeatedly petitioned the courts to recognize their

estimated 300,000 immigrants from the former Soviet Union who are not recognized as Jews by the rabbinical establishment and hence deprived of various basic rights, such as the ability to marry in Israel.

Despite continuing public protest against the inegalitarian aspects of the religious status quo arrangements, and particularly those relating to personal law, these arrangements have never been altered by the Knesset. Moreover, the Knesset has failed to entrench the principle of equality in a Basic Law, due to the fear of the religious parties that legislating this principle would conflict with the existing religious monopoly over personal law.[22] The continuing parliamentary failure to reform the inegalitarian religious status quo arrangements despite the considerable legislative efforts of the liberal-secular camp demonstrates the second potential danger inherent in the incrementalist approach to constitution-making, that of the potential over-rigidity of material constitutional arrangements that evolved in the absence of a formal constitution.

Part of the failure to legislate additional Basic Laws that enhance egalitarianism and the protection of individual rights is related to the increasing tensions between the Knesset and the Supreme Court over the authority to determine the nature of the relations between religion and state in Israel. Although the status quo was recognized as a political principle for accommodating the religious–secular divide, it was never recognized as a legal principle by the Supreme Court in its decisions. To the contrary, over the years the Court has attempted to alter the status quo arrangements, when certain aspects of these arrangements conflicted with basic human rights as stated in the Declaration of Independence, in Basic Law: Freedom of Occupation or in Basic Law: Human Dignity and Liberty.[23] In face of the growing parliamentary power of the religious camp, particularly since the

---

conversions in Israel. In a series of rulings, the Supreme Court deviated from the status quo, and held that for administrative purposes non-Orthodox conversions should be recognized regardless of where they took place. HCJ 1031\93 *Pesaro (Goldstein)* v. *Minister of Interior* [1995] 49 (4) PD 661; HCJ 5070\95 *Na'amat* v. *Minister of the Interior* [2002] 56 (2) PD 721; and HCJ 2597\99 *Rodriguez-Tushbeim* v. *Minister of Interior* [2005] IsrSC 58(5) 412.

[22] Yehudit Karp, "Basic Law: Human Liberty and Dignity – a Biography of Power Struggles," *Mishpat Umimshal* 1 (1993). For more on the principle of equality see Frances Raday, "Religion, Multiculturalism and Equality: The Israeli Case," *Israel Yearbook on Human Rights* 25 (1995).

[23] On judicial intervention in religious issues in Israel see Ofrit Liviatan, "Judicial Activism and Religion-Based Tensions: The Case of India and Israel," *Arizona Journal of International and Comparative Law* 26, no. 3 (2009); Patricia J. Wood, *Judicial Power and National Politics: Courts and Gender in the Religious–Secular Conflict in Israel* (Albany: State University of New York Press, 2008).

1980s, the liberal-secular population found support in the increasingly activist Supreme Court. The increasing tensions between the Israeli legislature and the judiciary, particularly following the 1995 "constitutional revolution," were discussed at length in Chapter 3. A good example of the linkage between these tensions and the material entrenchment of the existing religious arrangements can be found in the recent debates regarding the future constitution for the State of Israel.

In the early 2000s, the debate over Israel's constitution has returned to the center of the public agenda. In 2005–6 the Knesset Constitution, Law and Justice Committee, as well as two research institutions, published complete constitutional drafts, which included proposals for constitutional solutions to the religious–secular dispute.[24] These drafts represented the most ambitious attempts – inside and outside the legislature – to draft a constitution since the 1950 Knesset decision to defer the writing of the constitution. While the various solutions for addressing the religious–secular conflict were proposed by advocates of different ideologies, none of the constitutional proposals attempted to reform the existing inegalitarian arrangements of the religious status quo.[25] Moreover, all three drafts contain provisions limiting the ability of the Supreme Court to alter the religious status quo in the future, thus preserving the supremacy of the Knesset in regulating controversial issues in religion–state relations. To illustrate this general approach which is shared by all three draft constitutions, I will discuss the solution to the problem of personal law which was proposed in the draft of the Knesset Constitution, Law and Justice Committee.

During the Committee's discussions there was broad agreement among its members that the existing marriage and divorce laws in Israel

---

[24] The *Constitution by Broad Consent Report* was submitted to the Knesset by its Constitution, Law and Justice Committee in February 2006. In addition, the *Israel Democracy Institute's Proposal for a Constitution by Consensus* was published in 2005. It was drafted by a group of twelve intellectuals headed by former Supreme Court President Meir Shamgar. Finally, the *Constitution of the State of Israel Proposed by the Institute of Zionist Strategies* was published in 2006, and is associated with the Israeli right political wing. Various other covenants and vision statements have been published in recent years by political activists and intellectual groups aiming at influencing the public debate on the constitution. Tova Ilan and Batia Kahana-Dror, *Covenants in Israel* (Jerusalem: Moetzet Yahad, 2004). For the Palestinian "vision documents" see Amal Jamal, "Future Visions and Current Dilemmas: On the Political Ethos of Palestinian Citizens of Israel," *Israel Studies Forum* 23, no. 2 (2008).

[25] For a detailed analysis of the solutions proposed by constitutional drafts regarding religious–secular conflicts in Israel see Hanna Lerner, "Entrenching the Status Quo: Religion and State in Israel's Constitutional Proposals," *Constellations* 16, no. 3 (2009).

must be changed.[26] Nevertheless, the constitutional proposals included in the "Constitution in Broad Consent Report" refrain from introducing a genuine liberal reform that would end the infringement of basic rights in the area of personal law.[27] The suggestions for regulating personal law presented in the Constitution Committee Report included three alternatives: first, avoidance of any explicit reference to personal law in the constitution;[28] second, a statement recognizing that the state should "respect the family lives of its residents," while providing for marriage and divorce laws to be enacted by the Knesset according to ordinary legislative procedures;[29] and third, entrenching the status quo by allowing religious authorities to determine who can marry in Israel.[30] The first two alternatives could, in theory, allow the Court to overrule Knesset legislation that conflicted with basic rights contained in the Basic Human Rights chapter of the draft constitution, such as the principle of equality before the law, freedom of consciousness and freedom of religion. However, such judicial interpretation would be restricted by another part of the draft under a "reservation of laws" provision, which would preserve the existing legislation even if it contradicts constitutional principles.[31] In practice, therefore, all alternative versions presented by the Knesset Constitution Committee Report would limit the possibility of liberal judicial intervention in personal law arrangements, leaving decisions regarding the future regulations of marriage and divorce – whether

---

[26] The report stated that "it is inconceivable that people who cannot marry by religious law cannot marry in Israel at all." *Constitution in Broad Consent: Report of the Constitution, Law and Justice Committee Regarding Proposals for the Constitution of the State of Israel,* 2006, 16.

[27] Although the Committee's goal was to write a proposal for a *Constitution in Broad Consent,* the draft did not represent a coherent constitutional proposal. Rather, it contained several versions and suggestions for further deliberation and decision by the Knesset. In effect, it included the various positions represented in the discussions.

[28] *Constitution in Broad Consent: Report,* ch. 1: Basic Principles, Article 12: Family Law, alternative A.

[29] Article 12: Family Life, states: "(A) The State shall respect the family lives of its residents. (B) Details regarding family arrangements shall be specified by law."

[30] Version B for Article 12 includes a proposed section (C): "No one shall be married in Israel, unless he is single, according to both civil law and his religious law."

[31] The proposed "Reservation of Laws" states: "Nothing in the Constitution shall impinge on the validity of a law that was in existence immediately before its passing, unless otherwise stated therein, [Version B: however the interpretation of a law as aforesaid shall be done in the spirit of the provisions of the Constitution]." The Sixteenth Knesset Constitution, Law, and Justice Committee Sitting as The Committee for the Preparation of a Constitution by Broad Consensus, *Proposals for a Constitution,* 73. See: http://experts.cfisrael.org:81/~admin/proposals.pdf.

by constitutional amendment or by ordinary legislation – in the hands of the legislators.

The constraints imposed upon the Supreme Court by the proposed constitutional draft reflect the parliamentary concern that the judiciary would intervene in the religious arrangements. Whether or not the Israeli Supreme Court should have taken an active part in the religious–secular debate over the most fundamental norms and character of the state is a hotly disputed question among legal scholars.[32] At the same time, there are increasing reasons to worry that the continuing uncertainty as to whether the legislature or the judiciary has the ultimate authority to decide such matters may lead to the weakening of Israel's democratic institutions, and undermine the legitimacy of, and public support for, both institutions.[33] The declining legitimacy of both judiciary and legislature are reflected in ongoing polls that examine the level of public trust in these institutions (Figure 7.1).

India: the debate over a uniform civil code continues

Despite having a written constitution, India, like Israel, refrained from making a clear choice regarding the reform of personal law of all its religious communities. Article 44 of the Indian constitution, which only recommends implementation of a uniform civil code, allowed for maintenance of a diverse personal law system in India and partial perpetuation of various traditional and mostly inegalitarian religious practices. As Flavia Agnes rightfully notes, gender equality and women's rights were

---

[32] See, for example, Menachem Mautner, "The Decline of Formalism and the Rise of Values in Israeli Law," *Iyunei Mishpat 13* no. 3 (1993); Ruth Gavison, *The Constitutional Revolution: A Reality or a Self-Fulfilling Prophecy?* (Jerusalem: Israel Democracy Institute, 1998). This issue was discussed in Chapter 3.

[33] In recent years the growing tensions between the branches of government have resulted in a direct clash, involving harsh public dispute between the Minister of Justice Daniel Friedmann and the Supreme Court Chief Justice, leading to the Minister's proposal to amend Basic Law: the Judiciary to limit judicial review, allowing the Supreme Court to overturn Knesset legislation only with a two-thirds majority of a panel comprised of at least nine justices, while allowing the Knesset to override court decisions. Supreme Court Chief Justice Dorit Beinisch expressed her objection to the proposed amendment, arguing that is should be enacted only as part of a comprehensive constitution or at least as part of a comprehensive Basic Law on Legislation that would cover all aspects of the legislative process. Yuval Yoaz, "Beinisch Opposes Bill Altering Authority to Overturn Knesset Laws," *Haaretz*, November 4, 2007. See also Daniel Friedmann, "Formalism and Values – Judicial Security and Judicial Activism," *Court* (February 2006); Arik Carmon, "Restricting the Authorities of the High Court of Justice – a Black Day to the Israeli Democracy," Israel Democracy Institute (September 7, 2008) all in Hebrew.

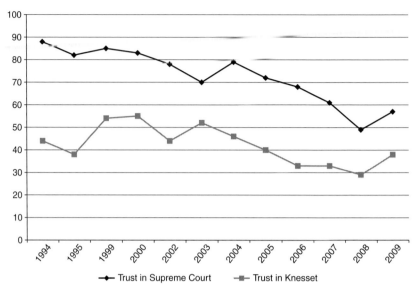

Figure 7.1   Trust in the Supreme Court and Knesset (1994–2009).*

    * Sources: for 1994–5: Yochanan Peres and Ephraim Yuchtman-Yaar, *Between Consent and Dissent: Democracy and Peace in the Israeli Mind* (Jerusalem: The Israel Democracy Institute, 1998), 244–5. For 1999–2002: Asher Arian, *Auditing Israeli Democracy* (Jerusalem: Gutman Center, 2003). For 2003–9: Asher Arian, Michael Philippov and Anna Knafelman, *Auditing Israeli Democracy 2009: Twenty Years of Immigration from the Soviet Union* (Jerusalem: The Israel Democracy Institute, 2009), 58–9.

    In 1994–5 the answer to the question "to what extent do you trust any of these institutions?" included five categories (full trust, trust, some trust, almost no trust, no trust at all). The figure shows the results for the first two categories (full trust and trust). In all other years the answer to the same question included four options (full trust, some trust, almost no trust, no trust at all). The graph shows the results for the first two categories (full trust and some trust).

    N = 1990: 1204, 1994: 1225, 1995: 1221, 1999: 1010, 2000: 1001, 2002: 1012, 2003: 1208, 2004: 1200, 2005: 1203, 2006: 1204, 2007: 1203, 2008: 1201, 2009: 1191.

not the focus of the debate in India's Constituent Assembly over a uniform civil code.[34] At independence, when the main concern of India's founding

---

[34] Flavia Agnes, "The Supreme Court, the Media and the Uniform Civil Code Debate in India," in Anuradha Dingwaney Needham and Rajeswari Sunder Rajan, eds., *The Crisis of Secularism in India* (Durham, NC and London: Duke University Press, 2007), 295.

fathers was to form a new nation-state and to ensure a smooth transfer of power, the focus of the uniform civil code debate was the authority of the state to regulate family life and the rights of minorities to maintain their religious and cultural identities. Today the non-justiciability of Article 44 and the political decision not to apply the Code to members of all religious communities are often criticized for limiting equal citizenship rights for non-Hindu women, particularly Muslims, who are subject to personal law systems that are more traditional and patriarchal. This demonstrates the first danger related to ambiguous constitutional formulations – potential infringements upon basic individual rights.

The non-justiciability of Article 44 resulted in separate personal law systems in India, which underwent some reform, inconsistently over the years that only partially changed the inegalitarian practices of religious traditions.[35] The Hindu Code Bill, debated since the 1930s, was eventually legislated by the Indian Parliament in four separate parts between 1955 and 1961.[36] The legislation substantially modified traditional Hindu practices. Among the most important modifications, the laws abolished the indissolubility of marriage and the preferential treatment of males in inheritance law. They also introduced gender equality and limited to a certain extent discrimination on the basis of caste.[37] Nevertheless, feminist commentators argue that despite the constitutional mandate to secularize Hindu family law under Article 44, during the decades that followed the enactment of the Indian constitution, "the state moved further away from its declared objective … In several instances, the vested, patriarchal and community interests of the influential sections superseded the rights of women and children."[38] The departure from the declared goal to secularize personal law for Hindus was reflected in the legal developments around issues such as marriage, succession and adoption. For example, the Special Marriage Act 1954, which originally provided for civil marriage and prohibited marriage of cousins, was amended in 1963 by subordinating the application of the law to customary patriarchal practices,

---

[35] Narendra Subramanian, "Myth of the Nation, Cultural Recognition and Personal Law in India," paper presented at the Conference of National Myths, Harvard University, May 2009. Narendra Subramanian, "Making Family and Nation: Hindu Marriage Law in Early Postcolonial India," *Journal of Asian Studies* 69, no. 3 (2010): 771–98.

[36] Hindu Marriage Act (1955), Hindu Succession Act (1956), Hindu Adoption and Maintenance Act (1956) and Dowry Prohibition Act (1961).

[37] See Marc Galanter, "The Displacement of Traditional Law in Modern India," in *Law and Society in Modern India* (Oxford University Press, 1989).

[38] Flavia Agnes, "Law and Gender Inequality: The Politics of Women's Rights in India," in *Women and Law in India* (Oxford and New York: Oxford University Press, 2004), 95.

common throughout India, that allowed for the marriage of cousins.[39] Another example is the 1976 amendment of the Special Marriage Act that affected the legal status of succession for Hindus, and consequentially ensured "that coparcenaries (and male privileges within it) are not dissolved by the contracting of civil marriage by means of the Act."[40]

While the first decades after independence witnessed extensive changes in Hindu law, the minor reforms in personal law for the non-Hindu communities were by and large postponed until the 1970s. Over the next decades, several reforms were initiated, mostly from within the religious minority groups, and led to changes of various practices (for example divorce rights for Christians and Parsis and adoption rights for Christians).[41] Nevertheless, many continued to criticize Muslim and Christian personal laws for the obstacles women have to confront in order to obtain divorce.[42]

As in the case of Israel, continuing debate over the implementation of a uniform civil code is evidence of the stagnation of some the material religious arrangements inherited from the pre-independence era, which constitutional framers refrained from reforming. As one commentator observed, India provides a classic example of the political durability of particularistic personal status laws despite "much-desired uniformity of legal reform."[43] This stagnation became particularly apparent in the *Shah Bano* case and its political and judicial ramifications. In 1985 the Indian Supreme Court affirmed the rights of a divorced Muslim woman to receive maintenance, based on section 125 of the 1973 Code of Criminal Procedures.[44] The Court rejected the husband's claim that he owed Shah Bano no maintenance since he had met his legal obligations under sharia law by having paid both a dowry prior to the marriage (*Mehr*) and the required three months' maintenance after the divorce (*Iddat*). The Court also took the opportunity of the case before it to call

---

[39] *Ibid.*, 97.   [40] *Ibid.*, 98.

[41] Subramanian, "Myths of the Nation," 21–5.

[42] Shyamla Pappu, "Women and the Law," in B. K. Pal, ed., *Problems and Concerns of Indian Women* (New Delhi: ABC Publishing, 1987); Anika Rahman, "Religious Rights Versus Women's Rights in India: A Test Case for International Human Rights Law," *Columbia Journal of Transnational Law* 28 (1990): 473; S. Raj, ed., *Quest for Gender Justice: A Critic of the Status of Women in India* (London: Sangam, 1995).

[43] Wener Menski, "The Uniform Civil Code Debate in Indian Law: New Developments and Changing Agenda," *German Law Journal* 9, no. 3 (2008): 211.

[44] Section 125 of the 1973 Code of Criminal Procedure provides that maintenance, up to maximum of 500 rupees per month, must be paid to a former spouse who would otherwise be destitute.

for the implementation of Article 44, stating that "A common civil code will help the cause of national integration by removing disparate loyalties to laws which have conflicting ideologies ... We understand the difficulties involved in bringing persons of different faiths and persuasions on a common platform. But a beginning has to be made if the Constitution is to have any meaning."[45]

The decision created a national crisis. Religious Muslim authorities claimed that the Supreme Court decision intervened in religious personal law and violated its sanctity. The ruling was criticized by Muslim religious organizations across the country as a Hindu attempt to impose legal uniformity, which could eventually lead to assimilation and to the destruction of Indian Muslim identity. At the same time, liberal Muslim and women's rights champions supported the decision claiming that there is no conflict between the Supreme Court judgment and Shari'a law.[46] Nevertheless, the religious campaign against the *Shah Bono* ruling was more vigorous. And, in an effort to appease the religious Muslim leadership, the government of Rajiv Gandhi initiated *The Muslim Women (Protection of Rights and Divorce) Act* in 1986 that nullified the precedential value of *Shah Bano* by excluding divorced Muslims from the purview of Section 125 of the Criminal Procedure Code. Zoya Hasan argued that the decision to preserve discrimination of Muslim women in issues of personal status should be seen as part of the government's effort not only to address the conservative objection to the Supreme Court verdict, but also as a "political balancing act" in the context of increasing riots against Muslims in India. More particularly, according to Hasan, it should be viewed as part of the Congress Party's strategy to pacify ruffled Muslim sentiments over the reopening of the disputed Babri mosque at Ayodhya which happened the same year.[47]

Since then the reluctance to advance the constitutional directive of uniform civil code seems to cut across political parties. Despite the fact that the Hindu-nationalist Bharatiya Janata Party (BJP) advocated the enactment of a uniform civil code as part of its national election campaigns in

[45] *Mohd Ahmed Khan* v. *Shah Bano Begum*, AIR 1985 SC 955.
[46] Zoya Hasan, "Minority Identity, Muslim Women Bill Campaign and the Political Process" *Economic and Political Weekly*, (7 January 1989) 46–47. For the various reactions to the ruling see also: Asghar Ali Engineer, ed., *The Shah Bano Controversy* (Hyderabad: Orient Longman, 1987).
[47] Hasan, "Minority Identity, Muslim Women Bill Campaign and the Political Process," 47–8. Zoya Hasan, "Minority Identity, State Policy and the Political Process," in: Zoya Hasan, ed., *Forging Identities: Gender, Communities and the state in India* (Boulder, CO: Westview Press, 1994) 59–73.

1996 and 1998, once it came into power in 1998 it avoided proposing legislation to alter the existing personal law structure in India.[48]

The *Shah Bano* controversy also mirrored the effects of ambiguous constitutional arrangements on the institutional tension between the legislature and the judiciary. One of the arguments raised against the *Shah Bano* ruling was that by calling for common civil code, the Supreme Court "arrogated to itself the function of the legislature."[49] Indeed, the Supreme Court addressed the issue of uniform civil code in a number of rulings in later years. Yet, in contrast to the Israeli Court, which appeared to take a side in the religious-secular debate, the Indian Supreme Court did not express a consistent position towards realization of the constitutional ideal of Article 44 in its various rulings.

In the first two rulings (*Ms. Jorden Diengdeh v. S. S. Chopra*[50] and *Sarla Mudgal v. India*[51]) the Court expressed its criticism of the failure of Indian governments to implement the constitutional ideal of "unified personal law for all Indians,"[52] and even singled out the Muslim community as the central obstacle for achieving this goal. But in the subsequent four rulings, the Court adopted a more reserved approach, which can be seen as a reaction to the political backlash that followed the *Shah Bano* case.[53] Thus, for example, in its 1997 *AWAG* decision, it explained that its explicit call for the enactment of a uniform civil code in *Sarla Mudgal* was "incidentally made."[54] The Court further stated that "a uniform civil law, though it is highly desirable, enactment thereof in one go perhaps may be counterproductive to unity and integrity of the nation. In a democracy governed by rule of law, gradual progressive change and order should be brought about."[55] And in its 2001 *Daniel Latifi* decision the Court upheld the constitutionality of the 1986 Muslim Women Act and remained silent on the issue of a uniform civil code.[56] By upholding different laws for different

---

[48] Jayanth Krishnan and Marc Galanter, "Personal Law and Human Rights in India and Israel," *Israel Law Review* 34 (2000): 110.

[49] Syed Shahabuffin, *Statesman*, 1 October 1985. Cited in: Hasan, "Minority Identity, Muslim Women Bill Campaign and the Political Process," 46.

[50] AIR 1985 SC 935.   [51] 3 SCC 1995 635.   [52] 3 SCC 1995 639.

[53] *Pannalal Bansilal Pitti v. State of AP* 1996 2 SCC 498; *Ahmedabad Wonen's Action Group (AWAG) v. Union of India* AIR 1997 SC 3614; *Lili Thomas v. Union of India and others* AIR 2000 SC 1650; *Daniel Latifi and other v. Union of India* 2001 7 SCC 740.

[54] *AWAG v. Union of India* 1997 SC 3614.

[55] AIR 2000 SC 1668.

[56] Nevertheless, the *Latifi* decision expanded the interpretation of "reasonable and fair provisions of maintenance" to be paid for her within the *Iddat* period by her husband, to include for example future needs, as well as her food, clothing, and residence. Thus, it

communities the ruling was viewed as belying the claim of the uniform civil code.[57]

It has been argued that the Supreme Court's expression of moderate views regarding the uniform civil code reflect its reluctance to take a leading role in bringing about any change in the situation.[58] In this respect, the Indian Supreme Court is playing a different role from its Israeli counterpart, which is more consistent in its expressions of a secular-liberal approach in the conflict over the religious character of the State of Israel. Nevertheless, the reserved approach of the Indian Supreme Court was criticized for abandoning the Court's role as the chief protector of principles of gender equality in the various communities in India.[59]

In the most recent case regarding the uniform civil code, *John Vallamattom and Anr* v. *Union of India*, the Court once again expressed support for the enactment of a uniform civil code that would "help the cause of national integration by removing the contradictions based on ideologies."[60] Predictably, this view was harshly criticized by the Indian media, which interpreted it as an expression of anti-minority sentiment.[61]

Principles versus practical necessity

Ultimately, the question of the normative implications of the incrementalist approach to constitution-making is left open for future debate. Deeply divided societies which adopt such an approach pay the price in the efficiency and ease with which the constitutional machinery is able to function. In addition, they risk the perpetuation of conservative and occasionally illiberal constitutional principles which may have been agreed upon under duress during the constitution-making process. However, it seems important to distinguish between types of foundational issues addressed by the incrementalist constitution. In this book,

---

is generally viewed as a step forward toward greater equality between men and women. Zoya Hasan, "Shah Bano Affair" *Encyclopedia of Women & Islamic Cultures*. Suad Joseph, ed. Brill, 2003.

[57] Jyoti Rattan, "Uniform Civil Code in India: A Binding Obligation under International and Domestic Law," *Journal of the Indian Law Institute* 46, no. 4 (2004): 585.

[58] *Ibid.*, 583.

[59] Rajeev Dhawan, "The Apex Court and Personal Law," *The Hindu*, March 14, 1997, cited in *ibid.*, 582.

[60] 2003(5) SCALE 284. See Virendra Kumar, "Uniform Civil Code Revisited: A Juridical Analysis of *John Vallamattom*," *Journal of the Indian Law Institute* 45, no. 3–4 (2003).

[61] Agnes, "Supreme Court, Media and Uniform Civil Code Debate in India," 303.

I have explored issues of religion and nationality without distinguishing between the two. But when thinking about the normative implications of accommodational constitutional arrangements it is worthwhile considering the two separately. The difference between the normative implications of incrementalist constitutional arrangements that address religious foundational issues and national identity issues is clearly illustrated in the Indian case, in which the making of the constitution included disputes on the national language as well as on the legal secularization of personal law. In both cases, controversial decisions were postponed to sustain pluralism. But whereas linguistic pluralism does not conflict with principles of liberalism, the preservation of a distinct traditional legal system in the area of personal law allowed for legal discrimination against Muslim women and the infringement of their basic rights. This suggests that, when it comes to the religious sphere, the incrementalist constitution could be considered as normatively inferior to the liberal-procedural constitutional ideal.

One may argue, therefore, that adopting an incrementalist approach prevents constitutions from fulfilling what is arguably their primary function– that of regulation and restriction of the exercise of governmental power and the protection of human rights.[62] In a sense, it could be claimed that this approach can lead to regression to the ancient Aristotelian model of *politeia*, which was not concerned with individual rights or limited political power, but rather, merely "the standard for its 'goodness' was its stability, or if one prefers, its durability, that is to say, its effectiveness in maintaining the particular values and beliefs intact."[63] The incrementalist constitution, it could be claimed, surrenders some of the accomplishments of Western constitutionalism by re-separating between the normative function of constitutions whereby constitutions constrain the exercise of governmental power and protect human rights, and their positive function in the formation of governmental institutions.

True, the use of incrementalist strategies does not necessarily imply a permanent surrender of liberal-democratic principles. Rather, the incrementalist constitution may sometimes be a stage on the way to the liberal ideal, when initial agreement on liberal norms is impossible. The initial constitution in a deeply divided society may be more of a stop-gap

---

[62] Carl Friedrich, *Transcendental Justice: The Religious Dimension of Constitutionalism* (Durham, NC: Duke University Press, 1964); Andrew Arato, *Civil Society, Constitution, and Legitimacy* (Lanham: Rowman & Littlefield, 2000), 230.

[63] Friedrich, *Transcendental Justice*, 7.

measure, enabling the achievement of some form of interim accommodation until a later phase when there may be broader support for liberal-
democratic norms.

However, what of cases where liberal regimes do not evolve out of
initially ambiguous constitutions? Are such constitutions normatively
inferior? Is an incrementalist constitutional approach in deeply divided
societies normatively inferior to one that imposes liberal ideals on society? Perhaps not. Perhaps, as Yael Tamir argues, drafting a constitution in
societies that are divided between liberal and illiberal worldviews should
be regarded as "a case in which practical necessity reshapes theory."

> The recognition that illiberal forces play a significant political role both
> within liberal democratic states and in the international arena, and the
> recognition consequently of the need to find ways of communicating
> with, and if necessary accommodating, these cultures, forces liberals to
> acknowledge the contextual nature of the liberal political tradition and to
> seek ways of reaching beyond it ... [This] compels liberals to re-examine
> their ideological inventory, make good use of their theoretical tools and
> expose their communal sensitivities. This re-examination allows them
> to go a long way towards respecting the needs of members of illiberal
> cultures.[64]

This ability to respect the needs of diverse groups in divided societies may
facilitate the maintenance of stable democratic societies even where deep
divisions exist. The Indian, Israeli and Irish incrementalist approaches
to constitution-formation may be seen in this light. For almost six decades India has managed to sustain the largest democracy in the world.
Israel, despite the continuing threats to its security, has maintained a stable democratic regime for almost the same period of time. And Ireland
overcame a civil war and established successful a democratic government
which avoided the European mid-century fascist wave.

It is of course impossible to say whether India and Israel could have
been as stable and as durable democracies had they adopted a more liberal
constitution. Perhaps constitution-making processes in deeply divided
societies inherently cannot produce a political solution which would be
seen as ideal by either of the parties. "Perhaps there is no right solution,
but a set of reasonable ones, which cannot be defined *a priori* but must be
the product of constant political discussions and negotiations. Perhaps
this is the moment in which philosophers ... seem to have little to say

---

[64] Yael Tamir, "Two Concepts of Multiculturalism," *Journal of Philosophy of Education* 29,
no. 2 (1995): 170.

about the nature of such agreements and should leave politicians to search for practical solutions."[65]

This lesson is also relevant to the growing discussion regarding the role of the judiciary in advancing clear-cut decisions regarding the fundamental norms and values of the state. The past few years have witnessed a worldwide shift in the pendulum of the relationship between judiciaries and legislatures in favor of the judiciary. This trend, recognized by various authors as "new constitutionalism," "global constitutionalism" or even "juristocracy," is characterized by a growing number of newly adopted or rewritten constitutions that contain a formal bill of rights and some form of judicial review, and by the increased tendency to use the judicial arena for pursuing political goals.[66] In democratic societies divided between competing visions of the state, it is often the judicial system that becomes the dominant arena for advancing principles supported by one section of the population and for attempting to change existing governmental policies. This is particularly the case when the legislature and the executive are viewed as incapable of introducing progressive change.[67]

However, as we have seen, the attempt to advance unequivocal choices between conflicting visions of the state through judicial intervention in societies that lack consensus on their fundamental values and shared norms – for example in the attempts to advance secularization in India and Israel through the courts – creates new risks that may undermine other aspects of the democratic order. The constitutional arena is thus limited in its ability to resolve foundational conflicts. Attempting to resolve conflicts between competing visions of the state within the framework of a constitution leads to a paradoxical situation. Under conditions of profound disagreement regarding the character of the state, deferring controversial choices and adopting ambiguous constitutional formulations at the foundational stage enable democratic systems to establish a stable constitutional order. However, the same ambiguous constitutional formulations may give rise to inegalitarian or illiberal constitutional arrangements which may be difficult to alter through the political system.

---

[65] *Ibid.*, 171.

[66] Ran Hirschl, *Towards Juristocracy: The Origins and Consequences of the New Constitutionalism* (Cambridge, MA: Harvard University Press, 2004); Heinz Klug, *Constituting Democracy: Law, Globalism and South Africa's Political Reconstruction* (Cambridge University Press, 2000); Alec Stone Sweet, *Governing with the Judges: Constitutional Politics in Europe* (Oxford University Press, 2000).

[67] Mark Tushnet, *Taking the Constitution Away from the Court* (Princeton University Press, 1999).

Concurrently, the empowerment of the judicial system as the chief protector of both constitutionalism and liberalism may be viewed by some
segments of the population as threatening the delicate balance of power
between the branches of government. If courts are perceived as taking
sides in the battle over the character of the state, their legitimacy may be
undermined in the eyes of the opposing camp. Thus, by their very attempt
to promote egalitarianism and liberalism through the language of constitutional law they may weaken their own basis of legitimacy as politically
neutral defenders of democratic procedures and the rule of law.

~

Conclusion

In this book I have endeavored to present an approach to constitution-making where there is severe disagreement over the shared norms and ultimate goals of the state. The book demonstrates how, by deferring controversial choices regarding the foundational aspects of the polity, an incrementalist constitutional approach enables deeply divided societies to either enact a written constitution or function with a material constitution.

At the moment of foundation, drafting a formal constitution is typically seen as a high-stakes moment in which the polity's commitments and definitions are entrenched for future generations. In the context of societal polarization between competing visions of the state, this moment is one fraught with risk. The constitutional architects in the three deeply divided societies studied here recognized this danger, and tried to circumvent it by transferring the task of making definitive choices regarding the normative and symbolic basis of the state to future political institutions. Instead of conceiving the moment of constitution-making in revolutionary terms, they introduced elements of incrementalism into the process. The constitutional arrangements they constructed included clear institutional and procedural arrangements. But when it came to contested foundational issues that touched upon the definition of "the people," the framers preferred to postpone unequivocal choices. By implementing constitutional strategies such as avoidance, legal ambiguity and symbolic ambivalence, the drafters exported contentious decisions from the formally entrenched constitutional arena to the realm of ordinary politics.

Since unequivocal choices were evaded but not ignored, the adopted constitutional arrangements encompass the competing perspectives of the state. The embrace of conflicting visions enables these arrangements to maintain constitutional legitimacy. Thus, consent, a necessary condition for meaningful and legitimate constitutions,[1] is achieved by giving the

---

[1] Daniel J. Elazar, "Constitution-Making: The Pre-Eminent Political Act," in Keith G. Banting and Richard Simeon, eds., *The Politics of Constitutional Change in Industrial Nations: Redesigning the State* (London: Macmillan, 1985), 233.

polity a sense of authorship and ownership, a sense that they are included in the constitutional "We the People." In deeply divided societies, incrementalist constitutions achieve legitimacy and consent by representing the identity of the people as it really is – a deeply divided one. In this way, the incrementalist constitutional approach goes beyond both the essentialist "nation-state" and the proceduralist "liberal" models of constitution–identity relations. On the one hand, the incrementalist constitution does not endeavor to present a homogeneous whole and recognizes that society is segmented. On the other hand, it does not attempt to "privatize" issues of identity by ignoring them and excluding them from the constitutional arena. Rather, it acknowledges the internal tensions, and uses ambiguous and vague language in an attempt to defer – not ignore – decisions regarding the foundational aspects of the constitution.

Hopefully, the constitutional experiences of Israel, India and Ireland will be of interest to societies that are trying to draft a democratic constitution while still debating their state's fundamental norms and ultimate values. For example, it could be instructive for emerging Muslim democracies such as Turkey, Indonesia, Albania and most recently Egypt, whose societies are divided over the definition of national identity in the context of conflicting demands raised by ethnic and religious minority groups. In Turkey, the recent constitutional crisis, related to the ban on religious university students wearing headscarves on campus and to the charges against the governing AKP Party that it had become a "focal point" for anti-secular political activities, represents an ongoing confrontation between the Kemalist secular establishment and political parties that are attempting to liberalize the Turkish political and constitutional order, including its relationship to expressions of religious and ethnic identity. An increasing criticism of the original model of nation-building and state formation on which the republic was constructed – based on modernization from above, directed and imposed by a military-bureaucratic establishment – is manifested in growing consensus in Turkish society that the existing 1982 constitution, which was written under supervision by the military, needs to be replaced with a civilian constitution.[2] The

---

[2] In 2007 a draft constitution was proposed by a committee of scholars, chaired by law and political science professor Ergun Özbudun. For useful analysis of the proposed draft see Zuhtu Arslan, "Turkey's Bid for a New Constitution," in *Policy Brief* (Ankara: SETA Foundation for Political, Economic and Social Research, 2007). Available at: www.ciaonet.org/pbei/seta/0001099/index.html. The need to adopt a new civilian constitution is widely discussed by Turkish commentators. For example see Bülent Keneş, "Why Is a More Civilian Constitution Needed in Turkey?" *Today's Zaman*, March 12, 2009.

incrementalist approach to constitution-making may be a helpful frame-work for addressing the constitutional challenges faced by Turkey today.[3]

Indonesia is another example of an emerging Muslim democracy struggling over the definition of its identity in a mixture of religious and secular terms. Since the beginning of the democratization reforms in 1998, following the resignation of President Soeharto, Muslim groups have repeatedly challenged the 1945 Indonesian constitution, demanding the introduction of shari'a law into the constitution and its application as the law of the land.[4] Interestingly, the constitution of Indonesia, the largest Muslim country in the world, has so far maintained a much more incrementalist attitude towards religion–state foundational questions than has the Turkish constitution. It is not clear from the constitutional text whether Indonesia should be seen as a secular or as an Islamic state. Belief in one god is the first of five fundamental pillars of the constitution (known as Pancasila) and Article 29 states that "the State is based upon belief in one supreme God." At the same time, the same Article declares that "all persons have the right to worship according to his or her own religion or belief" and the state officially recognizes six religions – Islam, Protestantism, Catholicism, Hinduism, Buddhism and Confucianism. Moreover, unlike the constitutions of Egypt, Iran and Saudi Arabia, no single word in the constitution refers to Islam as the state ideology, and the constitution does not regard Islamic law as the primary source of law.[5] Another component of an incrementalist constitutional approach represented in Indonesia is that religious legislation is decided by gov-ernmental institutions on the regional or local level and not nationally, thus allowing for differentiation and diversity of views throughout the country.

Finally, the framework of constitutional incrementalism could also be instructive in the context of the European Union, which is in the process of rethinking its constitutional future. The recent process of Treaty revi-sion that was restarted in June 2007, two years after the 2005 failure to ratify the Treaty establishing a constitution for Europe, can be viewed as

---

[3] See for example Ergun Özbudun, "New Constitution Should Be Accepted Via Consensus," *Today's Zaman*, March 5, 2008. See also Ergun Özbudun and Ömer Faruk Gençkaya, *Democratization and the Politics of Constitution Making in Turkey* (Budapest: Central European University Press, 2009).

[4] For an excellent discussion of the debates regarding the place of sharia law in the Indonesian constitution see Nadirsyah Hosen, *Shari'a and Constitutional Reform in Indonesia* (Singapore: Institute of Southeast Asian Studies, 2007).

[5] *Ibid.*

a shift toward a more incrementalist approach to constitution-making.[6] A comparison between the text of the EU constitution (which was rejected by France and the Netherlands in 2005) and that of the Treaty of Lisbon (which entered into force in 2009) shows that the Treaty of Lisbon replicates many of the provisions of the EU constitution, particularly with regard to the structure of governmental institutions and human rights. The difference lies in the attempt of the drafters of the Treaty of Lisbon to avoid "constitutional language."[7] For example, the text does not mention the term "constitution" and it avoids using the terminology of "law" and "framework law," while preserving the existing terminology of "regulations," "directives" and "decisions." Similarly, it also avoids reference to EU symbols such as the flag, anthem or motto. Nor does it include – as did the draft EU constitution – any declaratory clause expressing the primacy of EU law.[8] As one commenter argued, unlike the rejected draft of the EU constitution, the Treaty of Lisbon does not represent a "constitutional finality" but rather, provides "the institutional foundations for the European Union to move forward in the next decade."[9]

Whether a more incrementalist approach to the making of a European constitution will enhance or weaken European integration is a question which requires much wider consideration. Similarly, whether specific countries should adopt strategies of ambiguity and deference for constitution-making, and how such a strategy should be implemented, depends on the particular circumstances in each case. Nevertheless, the constitutional debates in Israel, India and Ireland, as well as the political, institutional and juridical developments that occurred in the decades that followed, may provide insight into the potential benefits and drawbacks of the incrementalist approach to constitution-making.

---

[6] The failure to ratify the Treaty establishing the constitution of Europe in 2005 generated wide academic debate regarding the reasons for, and the significance of, this failure. See for example the special issue of *Constellations* 13, no. 2, June 2006 on the "North Atlantic Divide." See also Sylvain Brouard and Vincent Tiberj, "The French Referendum: The Not So Simple Act of Saying Nay," *PS, Political Science & Politics* 39, no. 2 (2006); John E. Fossum and Agustin J. Menendez, "The Constitution's Gift? A Deliberative Democratic Analysis of Constitution Making in the European Union," *European Law Journal* 11, no. 4 (2005); Paul Hainsworth, "France Says No: The 29 May 2005 Referendum on the European Constitution," *Parliamentary Affairs* 59, no. 1 (2006).

[7] Paul Craig, "The Treaty of Lisbon: Process, Architecture and Substance," *European Law Review* 33, no. 2 (2008); Alexander Somek, "Postconstitutional Treaty," *German Law Journal* 8, no. 12 (2007).

[8] It does however include a declaration (Declaration No. 17) which recalls the European Court of Justice's existing case load.

[9] Craig, "The Treaty of Lisbon," 165.

The incrementalist approach to constitution-making rests on the recognition that the struggle over the character of the state is a political struggle which cannot be resolved through revolutionary means either at the time of constitutional drafting or later on through the courts. In this struggle, when the right solution is difficult to find, it is the politicians – and not the lawyers or the philosophers – who should lead the search for practical solutions. This is not meant to be a pessimistic conclusion, but rather to insert optimism regarding the importance of politics as the main domain for deliberating national identity and for determining the fundamental principles and shared values that underpin the state.

BIBLIOGRAPHY

Aronson, Shlomo. "Constitution for Israel: The British Model of David Ben-Gurion." *Politica: An Israeli Journal for Political Science and International Relations* 2 (1998).

Ackerman, Bruce. *The Future of Liberal Revolution.* New Haven and London: Yale University Press, 1992.

We the People: Foundations. Cambridge, MA: Belknap Press of Harvard University Press, 1991.

Aderi, Y. M. "Constitutional Revolution?" *Mishpat Umimshal: Law and Government in Israel* 3, no. 2 (1996): 453–73.

Agnes, Flavia. "Law and Gender Inequality: The Politics of Women's Rights in India." In *Women and Law in India.* Oxford and New York: Oxford University Press, 2004.

"The Supreme Court, the Media and the Uniform Civil Code Debate in India." In *The Crisis of Secularism in India*, edited by Anuradha Dingwaney Needham and Rajeswari Sunder Rajan, 294–315. Durham, NC and London: Duke University Press, 2007.

Agrawala, Rajkumari. "Uniform Civil Code: A Formula Not Solution." In *Family Law and Social Change*, edited by Tahir Mahmood. Bombay: MN Tripathy, 1975.

Ahmad, Jamil-un-Din, ed. *Speeches and Writings of Mr. Jinnah*, Vol. 1. Lahore: Shaike Muhammad Ashraf, 1960.

Akan, Murat. "The Politics of Secularization in Turkey and France: Beyond Orientalism and Occidentalism." PhD thesis, Columbia University, 2005.

Akenson, D. H. and J. F. Fallin. "The Irish Civil War and the Drafting of the Free State Constitution, Part I, II, III." *Éire-Ireland* 5, nos. 1, 2, 4 (1970).

Aloni, Shulamit. *The Arrangement: From Rule of Law to Rule of Religion.* Tel Aviv: Otpaz, 1970.

Altschul, Mark J. "Israel's Law of Return and the Debate of Altering, Repealing or Maintaining Its Present Language." *University of Illinois Law Review* 5 (2002).

Anderson, Benedict. *Imagined Communities: Reflections on the Origin and Spread of Nationalism.* London and New York: Verso, 1991.

Arato, Andrew. *Civil Society, Constitution, and Legitimacy.* Lanham: Rowman & Littlefield, 2000.

"Interim Imposition." *Ethics and International Affairs* 18, no. 3 (2004): 26–50.

Arato, Andrew. *Constitution Making Under Occupation: The Politics of Imposed Revolution in Iraq* (New York: Columbia University Press, 2009).

Arendt, Hannah. *On Revolution.* New York: Viking Press, 1965.

Arian, Asher. *Auditing Israeli Democracy.* Jerusalem: Gutmann Center, 2003.

Arian, Asher, Nir Atmor and Yael Hadar. *Auditing Israeli Democracy 2007: Cohesion in a Divided Society.* Jerusalem: The Israel Democracy Institute, 2007.

Arian, Asher, Michael Philippov and Anna Knafelman, *Auditing Israeli Democracy 2009: Twenty Years of Immigration from the Soviet Union.* Jerusalem: The Israel Democracy Institute, 2009.

Aristotle. *Politics.* Translated by Ernest Barker. Oxford University Press, 1995.

Arjomand, Said Amir, ed. *Constitutional Politics in the Middle East: With Special Reference to Turkey, Iraq, Iran and Afghanistan.* Oxford and Portland: Hart, 2007.

Arslan, Zuhtu. "Turkey's Bid for a New Constitution." In *Policy Brief.* Ankara: SETA Foundation for Political, Economic and Social Research, 2007.

Austin, Granville. *The Indian Constitution: Cornerstone of a Nation.* Oxford and New York: Oxford University Press, 1999.

Working a Democratic Constitution: The Indian Experience. New Delhi and New York: Oxford University Press, 1999.

Avnon, Dan. "'The Enlightened Public': Jewish and Democratic or Liberal and Democratic?" *Mishpat Umimshal: Law and Government in Israel* 3, no. 2 (1995).

Awad, Yaser and Ali Haider. "Representation of Arab Population in the Civil Service 2006–2007." Sikkuy, The Association for the Advancement of Civic Equality in Israel, 2008.

Azad, Maulana Abul Kalam. *India Wins Freedom: An Autobiographical Narrative.* New York: Longmans Green, 1960.

Bagehot, Walter. *The English Constitution.* Edited by R. H. S. Crossman. London: C. A. Watts, 1964.

Bailyn, Bernard. *The Ideological Origins of the American Revolution: Enlarged Edition.* Cambridge, MA and London: Belknap Press of Harvard University Press, 1992.

Banerjee, Anil Chandra. *The Making of the Indian Constitution, 1939–1947.* 2 vols. Vol. I, Documents. Calcutta: Mukherjee, 1948.

Barak, Aharon. "The Constitutional Revolution – Bath Mitzvah." *Law and Business* 1 (2004).

"The Constitutional Revolution: Protected Human Rights." *Mishpat Umimshal: Law and Government in Israel* 1, no. 1 (1992).

"The Criticism does not Affect our Considerations." *Halishka: The Israeli Bar Journal* 33 (1996)

"The Enlightened Public." In *The Landau Book*, edited by Aharon Barak and E. Mazuz, 677–98. Tel Aviv: Borsei, 1995.

"Fifty Years of Adjudication in Israel." *Aley Mishpat: The Law Review of Ramat Gan Collage of Law* 1, no. 1 (1999).

The Judge in a Democracy. Princeton: University Press, 2006.

"The Role of the Supreme Court in Democratic Society." *Tel-Aviv University Law Review* 21, no. 1 (1997).

Barry, Brian. "Political Accommodation and Consociational Democracy." *British Journal of Political Science* 5, no. 4 (1975): 477–505.

Barzilai, Gad. "Judicial Hegemony, Party Polarization and Social Change." *Politica: An Israeli Journal for Political Science and International Relations* 2 (1998).

Barzilai, Gad, Efraim Yuchtman-Yaar and Zeev Segal. *The Israeli Supreme Court and the Israeli Public*. Tel Aviv: Papirus, 1994.

Beiner, Ronald, ed. *Theorizing Citizenship*. Albany: State University of New York Press, 1995.

Bellah, Robert N. "Civil Religion in America" *Deadalus* 96 no. 1 (1976) 1–21.

Berlin, Isaiah. "The Pursuit of the Ideal." In *The Crooked Timber of Humanity: Chapters in the History of Ideas*, edited by Henry Hardy. Princeton University Press, 1990.

Bhargava, Rajeev, ed. *Politics and Ethics of the Indian Constitution*. New Delhi: Oxford University Press, 2008.

Secularism and Its Critics. Delhi and New York: Oxford University Press, 1998.

"What Is Indian Secularism and What Is It For?" *India Review* 1, no. 1 (2002).

Bhatia, K. L., ed. *Dr. B. R. Ambedkar: Social Justice and the Indian Constitution*. New Delhi: Deep and Deep Publications, 1995.

Bilgin, Mehmet Fevzi. "Constitution, Legitimacy and Democracy in Turkey." In *Constitutional Politics in the Middle East: With Special Reference to Turkey, Iraq, Iran and Afghanistan*, edited by Said Amir Arjomand. Oxford and Portland: Hart Publishing, 2007.

Blaustein, Albert P. and Gilbert H. Flanz, eds. *Constitutions of the Countries of the World*. Dobbs Ferry: Oceana Publications, 1985 and updated annually.

Bogdanor, Vernon, ed. *Constitutions in Democratic Politics*. Aldershot and Brookfield: Gower, 1988.

Bonime, Andrea R. *The Politics of Constitution-Making: Spain's Transition to Democracy*. Boulder: Westview Press, 1987.

Bose, Sarmila and Eilis Ward. "'India's Cause Is Ireland's Cause': Elite Links and Nationalist Politics." In *Ireland and India: Connections, Comparisons, Contrasts*, edited by Michael Holmes and Denis Holmes, 52–73. The Irish-Indian Business and Economic Association, and the Department of Government and Society, University of Limerick, 1997.

Bourke, Richard. *Peace in Ireland: The War of Ideas*. London: Pimlico, 2003.

Brass, Paul R. *Language, Religion and Politics in North India*. Lincoln, NE: An Authors Guild Backinprint.com, 2005.

"Elite Interests, Popular Passions, and Social Power in the Language Politics of India," in: Asha Sarangi, ed. *Language and Politics in India*. 183–217. New Delhi: Oxford University Press, 2009.

Brecher, Michael. *Nehru: A Political Biography*. London and New York: Oxford University Press, 1959.

Breslin, Beau. *The Communitarian Constitution*. Baltimore and London: The Johns Hopkins University Press, 2004.

Bromage, Mary C. *De Valera and the March of a Nation*. Westport: Greenwood Press, 1975 (1956).

Brouard, Sylvain and Vincent Tiberj. "The French Referendum: The Not So Simple Act of Saying Nay." *PS, Political Science & Politics* 39, no. 2 (2006): 261.

Brubaker, Rogers. *Citizenship and Nationhood in France and Germany*. Cambridge, MA: Harvard University Press, 1992.

Burke, Edmund. *The Works of the Right Honourable Edmund Burke*. London: Printed for F. C. and J. Rivington, 1812.

Cairns, Alan C. *Constitution, Government, and Society in Canada / Selected Essays*. Edited by Douglas E. Williams. Toronto: McClelland & Stewart, 1988.

Caldwell, Peter C. *Popular Sovereignty and the Crisis of German Constitutional Law: The Theory & Practice of Weimar Constitutionalism*. Durham, NC: Duke University Press, 1997.

Calhoun, Craig. "Imagining Solidarity: Cosmopolitanism, Constitutional Patriotism, and the Public Sphere." *Public Culture* 14, no. 1 (2002): 147–71.

Carmon, Arik. "Restricting the Authorities of the High Court of Justice – a Black Day to the Israeli Democracy." Israel Democracy Institute (September 7, 2008).

Chapman, Gerald W. *Edmund Burke: The Practical Imagination*. Cambridge, MA: Harvard University Press, 1967.

Chaube, Shibani Kinkar. *Constituent Assembly of India: Springboard of Revolution*. 2nd edn. New Delhi: Manohar Publishers & Distributors, 2000.

Census of India, Paper No. 1: Languages – 1951 Census. India (Republic) Census Commissioner, 1954.

Census of India, Paper No. 2: Religion – 1951 Census. India (Republic) Census Commissioner, 1953.

Childers, Erskine. *What the Treaty Means*. Printed from 'The Republic of Ireland', 1922.

Choudhry, Sujit, ed. *Constitutional Design for Divided Societies: Integration or Accommodation*: Oxford University Press, 2008.

Chubb, Basil. *The Politics of the Irish Constitution*. Dublin: The Institute of Public Administration, 1991.

Coakley, John. "The Belfast Agreement and the Republic of Ireland." In *Aspects of the Belfast Agreement*, edited by Rick Wilford. Oxford and New York: Oxford University Press, 2001.

Cohen, Asher and Bernard Susser. *Israel and the Politics of Jewish Identity: The Secular-Religious Impasse.* Baltimore: The Johns Hopkins University Press, 2000.

Collard, Keith. *Pakistan: A Political Study.* London: Allen and Unwin, 1957.

Collins, Michael. *The Path to Freedom.* Dublin: The Talbot Press, 1922.

Constituent Assembly Debates. New Delhi: Reprinted by Lok Sabha Secretariat, 1999.

Constitution in Broad Consent: Report of the Constitution, Law and Justice Committee Regarding Proposals for the Constitution of the State of Israel. 2006.

Corinaldi, Michael. "Freedom of Religion in Israel: What Changed in the 'Status Quo'?" *Sha'arey Mishpat* 3, no. 2 (2003).

   Personal, Family and Inheritance Law – between Religion and State: New Trends. Jerusalem: Nevo, 2004.

Coupland, Reginald. *The Indian Problem; Report on the Constitutional Problem in India.* New York and London: Oxford University Press, 1944.

Craig, Paul. "The Treaty of Lisbon: Process, Architecture and Substance." *European Law Review* 33, no. 2 (2008): 137–66.

Curran, Joseph M. *The Birth of the Irish Free State 1921–1923.* Tuscaloosa: The University of Alabama Press, 1980.

Dahan, Yossi and Yoav Hammer. "Democracy, the Educational Autonomy of Cultural Minorities and the Law: The Case of the Ultra-Orthodox Minority in Israel" (unpublished paper).

Dahrendorf, Ralf. *Reflections on the Revolution in Europe.* London: Chatto and Windus, 1990.

Dáil Debates. Díospóireachtaí Parlaiminte Parliamentary Debates. Available at: http://historical-debates.oireachtas.ie.

Dalal, Marwan. "The Guest, the House, and the Judge: A Reading in the Unread in the Qa'dan Decision." *Adalah's Review* 2 (2000).

Das Gupta, Jyotirindra, *Language Conflict and National Development: Group Politics and National Language Policy in India*, Berkley and London, University of California Press, 1970.

De Valera, Eamon. *India and Ireland.* New York: Friends of Freedom for India, 1920.

Deasy, Liam. *Brother against Brother.* Dublin and Cork: The Mercier Press, 1982.

Diamond, Larry J. and Marc F. Plattner, eds. *Electoral Systems and Democracy.* Baltimore: The Johns Hopkins University Press, 2006.

Dicey, A. V. *Introduction to the Study of the Law of the Constitution.* London: Macmillan, 1961.

Dirks, Nicholas B. *Castes of Mind: Colonialism and the Making of Modern India.* Princeton and Oxford: Princeton University Press, 2001.

Don-Yehiya, Eliezer. *Religion and Political Accommodation in Israel.* Jerusalem: Floersheimer Institute for Policy Studies, 1999.

Dotan, Yoav. "Constitution for the State of Israel? The Constitutional Dialog after the Constitutional Revolution." *Mishpatim* 28, nos. 1–2 (1997).

Drayton, Robert Harry. *The Laws of Palestine: In Force on the 31st Day of December 1933.* Rev. edn., vol. III. London, Jerusalem and Palestine: Printed by Waterlow and Sons, 1934.

Dunn, James A. "The Revision of the Constitution in Belgium: A Study in the Institutionalization of Ethnic Conflict." *Political Research Quarterly* 27, no. 1 (1974).

Dyzenhaus, David. *Legality and Legitimacy: Carl Schmitt, Hans Kelsen, and Hermann Heller in Weimar.* Oxford and New York: Clarendon Press, Oxford University Press, 1997.

Eisenstadt, S. N. *Paradoxes of Democracy: Fragility, Continuity, and Change.* Washington, DC and Baltimore: Woodrow Wilson Center Press and The Johns Hopkins University Press, 1999.

Elazar, Daniel J. "Constitution-Making: The Pre-Eminent Political Act." In *The Politics of Constitutional Change in Industrial Nations: Redesigning the State,* edited by Keith G. Banting and Richard Simeon, 232–48. London: Macmillan, 1985.

Elkins, Zachary, Tom Ginsburg and James Melon. *The Endurance of National Constitutions.* New York: Cambridge University Press, 2009.

Elon, Menachem. "The Way of Law in Constitution: The Values of Jewish and Democratic State in the Light of Basic Law: Human Dignity and Liberty." In *The Lanau Book,* edited by Aharon Barak and E. Mazuz, 641–76. Tel Aviv: Borsei, 1996.

Elster, Jon. "Forces and Mechanisms in the Constitution-Making Process." *Duke Law Journal* 45, no. 364 (1995): 363–96.

 Ulysses and the Sirens: Studies in Rationality and Irrationality. Cambridge and New York: Cambridge University Press, 1979.

Elster, Jon and Rune Slagstad, eds. *Constitutionalism and Democracy.* Cambridge and New York: Cambridge University Press, 1988.

Elster, Jon, Claus Offe and Ulrich Klaus Preuss. *Institutional Design in Post-Communist Societies: Rebuilding the Ship at Sea, Theories of Institutional Design.* Cambridge and New York: Cambridge University Press, 1998.

Engineer, Asghar Ali, ed. *Problems of Muslim Women in India.* Hyderabad: Orient Longman, 1995.

 The Shah Bano Controversy. Hyderabad: Orient Longman, 1987.

Farrell, Brian. *The Founding of Dáil Éireann: Parliament and Nation-Building.* Dublin: Gill and Macmillan, 1971.

 "From First Dail through Irish Free State." In *De Valera's Constitution and Ours,* edited by Brian Farrell. Goldenbridge, Dublin: Published for Radio Telefís Éireann by Gill and Macmillan, 1988.

Foley, Michael. *The Silence of Constitutions: Gaps, "Abeyances" and Political Temperament in the Maintenance of Government*. London and New York: Routledge, 1989.

Fossum, John E. and Agustin J. Menendez. "The Constitution's Gift? A Deliberative Democratic Analysis of Constitution Making in the European Union." *European Law Journal* 11, no. 4 (2005): 380–410.

Fraser, T. G. *Partition in Ireland, India and Palestine: Theory and Practice*. London: Macmillan, 1984.

Friedmann, Daniel. "Formalism and Values – Judicial Security and Judicial Activism." *Court* (February 2006).

"The 'Unmarried Wife' in Israeli Law." In *Israeli Yearbook on Human Rights*, 307–16. Tel Aviv: Faculty of Law, Tel Aviv University, 1972.

Friedman, Menachem. "These are the Chronicles of the Status-Quo: Religion and State in Israel." In *Brethren Dwelling Together. Orthodoxy and Non-Orthodoxy in Israel: Positions, Propositions and Accords*, edited by Uri Dromi. Jerusalem: Israel Democracy Institute, 2005.

The Haredi (Ultra-Orthodox) Society: Sources, Trends and Processes. Jerusalem: The Jerusalem Institute for Israel Studies, 1991.

Friedrich, Carl. *Constitutional Government and Democracy; Theory and Practice in Europe and America*. Rev. edn. Boston: Ginn, 1950.

Transcendental Justice: The Religious Dimension of Constitutionalism. Durham, NC: Duke University Press, 1964.

Friling, Tuvia, ed. *An Answer to a Post-Zionist Colleague*. Tel Aviv: Yediot Achronot and Sifrei Hemed, 2003.

Galanter, Marc. "The Displacement of Traditional Law in Modern India." In *Law and Society in Modern India*. Oxford University Press, 1989.

Law and Society in Modern India. Delhi and New York: Oxford University Press, 1989.

"Secularism, East and West." In *Secularism and Its Critics*, edited by Rajeev Bhargava, 234–67. Delhi: Oxford University Press, 1998.

Galanter, Marc and Jayanth Krishnan. "Personal Law and Human Rights in India and Israel." *Israel Law Review* 34 (2000).

Garvin, Tom. *1922: The Birth of Irish Democracy*. Dublin: Gill & Macmillan, 1996.

Gavison, Ruth. "Constitution for Israel: Lessons from the Constitutional Process in the 16th Knesset." In *Constitution in Broad Consent: Report of the Constitution, Law and Justice Committee Regarding Proposals for the Constitution of the State of Israel*. Jerusalem: Knesset, 2006.

The Constitutional Revolution: A Reality or a Self-Fulfilling Prophecy? Jerusalem: Israel Democracy Institute, 1998.

"Jewish and Democratic? A Rejoinder to the 'Ethnic Democracy' Debate." *Israel Studies* 4, no. 1 (1999): 44–72.

"What Belongs in a Constitution?" *Constitutional Political Economy* 13 (2002).

"Zionism in Israel? The Ka'adan Ruling." *Mishpat Umimshal: Law and Government in Israel* 6 (2001).

Gavison, Ruth, Mordechai Kremnitzer and Yoav Dotan. *Judicial Activism: For and against, the Role of the High Court of Justice in Israeli Society.* Jerusalem: Magnes, 2000.

Gellner, Ernest. *Nations and Nationalism.* Ithaca, NY: Cornell University Press, 1983.

Ghai, Yash. "A Journey around Constitution: Reflections on Contemporary Constitutions." *African Law Journal* 122 (2005): 804–31.

   ed. *Autonomy and Ethnicity: Negotiating Competing Claims in Multi-Ethnic States.* Cambridge University Press, 2000.

Ghai, Yash and Guido Galli. "Constitution Building Processes and Democratization." In *Democracy, Conflict and Human Security: Further Readings.* Stockholm: IDEA, 2006.

Ghai, Yash, Mark Lattimer and Yahia Said. "Building Democracy in Iraq." Minority Rights Group International, 2003.

Ghanem, As'ad. *The Palestinian-Arab Minority in Israel, 1948–2000.* New York: State University of New York Press, 2001.

Gloppen, Siri. *South Africa: The Battle over the Constitution.* Dartmouth: Ashgate, 1997.

Goldberg, Giora. " 'When Trees Are Planted There Is No Need for Constitution': On State Building and Constitution Making." *State, Government and International Relations* 38 (1993) (Hebrew).

Goldwin, Robert A. and Art Kaufman. *Constitution Makers on Constitution Making: The Experience of Eight Nations.* Washington, DC and Lanham: American Enterprise Institute for Public Policy Research, 1988.

Gordon, Leonard A. "Divided Bengal: Problems of Nationalism and Identity in the 1947 Partition." In *India's Partition: Process, Strategy and Mobilization*, edited by Mushirul Hasan, 279–321. Delhi and Oxford: Oxford University Press, 2001.

Gorny, Yosef. *Zionism and the Arabs 1882–1948: A Study of Ideology.* Oxford: Clarendon Press, 1987.

Government Meeting Minutes, 13 December 1949. Israel State Archive, Jerusalem.

Greenberg, Douglas, Stanley N. Katz, Melanie Beth Oliviero and Steven C. Wheatley, eds. *Constitutionalism and Democracy: Transitions in the Contemporary World.* New York: Oxford University Press, 1993.

Greenfeld, Liah. *Nationalism: Five Roads to Modernity.* Cambridge, MA: Harvard University Press, 1992.

Grey, Thomas C. "The Constitution as Scripture." *Stanford Law Review* 37, no. 1 (1984).

Griffith, Arthur. *Arguments for the Treaty.* Dublin: Martin Lester, 1922.

   The Resurrection of Hungary: A Parallel for Ireland. 3rd edn. Dublin: Whelan and Son, 1918.

Grimm, Dieter. "Integration by Constitution." *International Journal of Constitutional Law* 3, no. 2–3 (2005): 193–208.

Gupta, D. C. *Indian National Congress*. Delhi: Vikas Publications, 1970.

Gutman, Emanuel. "The Religious Cleavage." In *Israel toward 2000: Society, Politics, Culture*, edited by Moshe Lissak and Brian Kney-Paz. Jerusalem: Magnes, Hebrew University, 1996.

Habermas, Jürgen. "Citizenship and National Identity." In *Between Facts and Norms: Contributions to a Discourse Theory of Law and Democracy*, 491–515. Cambridge, MA: The MIT Press, 1996.

The Inclusion of the Other: Studies in Political Theory. Edited by Ciaran Cronin and Pablo De Greiff. Cambridge, MA: The MIT Press, 1998.

"Why Europe Needs a Constitution." *New Left Review* 11 (2nd Series) (2001): 5–26.

Hainsworth, Paul. "France Says No: The 29 May 2005 Referendum on the European Constitution." *Parliamentary Affairs* 59, no. 1 (2006): 98–117.

Hancock, W. K. *Survey of British Commonwealth Affairs, Vol. I: Problems of Nationality 1918–1936*. London and New York: Oxford University Press, 1937.

Hardgrave, Robert L. "India: The Dilemmas of Diversity." *Journal of Democracy* 4, no. 4 (October 1993).

Harkness, D. W. *The Restless Dominion: The Irish Free State and the British Commonwealth of Nations, 1921–31*. Dublin: Gill and Macmillan, 1969.

Harris, Ron. "The Israeli Judiciary." In *The First Decade: 1948–1958*, edited by Zameret Zvi and Hannah Yavlonka. Jerusalem: Yad Ben-Zvi, 1997.

Hart, Peter. *The IRA at War 1916–1923*. Oxford and New York: Oxford University Press, 2003.

Hart, Vivien. "Democratic Constitution Making." In *Special Report*. United States Institute of Peace, 2003.

Hasan, Mushirul, ed. *India's Partition: Process, Strategy and Mobilization*. Delhi and Oxford: Oxford University Press, 2001.

Hasan, Zoya. *Forging Identities: Gender, Communities, and the State in India*. Boulder: Westview Press, 1994.

Heller, Joseph. *The Stern Gang: Ideology, Politics, and Terror, 1940–1949*. London and Portland: Frank Cass, 1995.

Hirschl, Ran. *Towards Juristocracy: The Origins and Consequences of the New Constitutionalism*. Cambridge, MA: Harvard University Press, 2004.

Hirschman, Albert O. "Social Conflicts as Pillars of Democratic Market Society." *Political Theory* 22, no. 2 (1994).

Hofnung, Menachem. *Israel – Security Needs Versus the Rule of Law*. Jerusalem: Nevo, 1991.

"The Unintended Consequences of Unplanned Constitutional Reform: Constitutional Politics in Israel." *American Journal of Comparative Law* 44 (1996).

Hogan, Gerard and Gerry Whyte. *J. M. Kelly: The Irish Constitution*. 4th edn. Dublin: Lexis Nexis Butterworths, 2003.

Holmes, Stephen and Cass Sunstein. "The Politics of Constitutional Revision in Eastern Europe." In *Responding to Imperfection*, edited by Stanford Levinson, 275–305. Princeton University Press, 1995.

Holmes, Stephen. "Gag Rules or the Politics of Omission." In *Constitutionalism and Democracy*, edited by Jon Elster and Rune Slagstad, 19–58. Cambridge and New York: Cambridge University Press, 1988.

"Precommitment and the Paradox of Democracy." In *Constitutionalism and Democracy*, edited by Jon Elster and Rune Slagstad, 195–240. Cambridge and New York: Cambridge University Press, 1988.

Hopkinson, Michael. *Green against Green: The Irish Civil War*. Dublin: Gill and Macmillan, 1988.

Horowitz, Dan and Moshe Lissak. *Origins of the Israeli Polity: Palestine under the Mandate*. Chicago and London: University of Chicago Press, 1978.

Trouble in Utopia: The Overburdened Polity of Israel. Albany: State University of New York Press, 1989.

Horowitz, Donald L. *Ethnic Groups in Conflict*. Berkeley: University of California Press, 1985.

Horowitz, Neri. "The Haredim (Ultra-Orthodox) and the Supreme Court: Breaking the Tools in Historical Perspective." *Kivunim Hadashim* 5 (2001): 22–78.

"State and Religious 1993: Agenda Setting." In *State and Religion Yearbook 1993*, edited by Neri Horowitz. Tel Aviv: Center of Jewish Pluralism, 1994.

Hosen, Nadirsyah. *Shari'a and Constitutional Reform in Indonesia*. Singapore: Institute of Southeast Asian Studies, 2007.

Howard, A. E. Dick, ed. *Constitution Making in Eastern Europe*. Washington, DC: Woodrow Wilson Center Press, distributed by The Johns Hopkins University Press, 1993.

Hughes, Christopher. *The Federal Constitution of Switzerland*. London: Oxford University Press, 1954.

Hutchinson, John. *The Dynamics of Cultural Nationalism: The Gaelic Revival and the Creation of the Irish Nation State*. London: Allen & Unwin, 1987.

Hutchinson, John and Anthony Smith, eds. *Nationalism*. Oxford and New York: Oxford University Press, 1994.

Ilan, Tova and Batia Kahana-Dror. *Covenants in Israel*. Jerusalem: Moetzet Yahad, 2004.

Jabareen, Yoused T. "Constitution Building and Equality in Deeply Divided Societies: The Case of the Palestinian-Arab Minority in Israel." *Wisconsin International Law Journal* 26, no. 2 (2008): 346–401.

Jacobsohn, Gary Jeffrey. *Apple of Gold: Constitutionalism in Israel and the United States*. Princeton University Press, 1993.

Constitutional Identity. Cambridge, MA: Harvard University Press, 2010.

The Wheel of Law: India's Secularism in Comparative Constitutional Context. Princeton University Press, 2003.

Jaffrelot, Christophe. *Dr. Ambedkar and Untouchability: Fighting the Indian Caste System*. New York: Columbia University Press, 2005.

The Hindu Nationalist Movement in India. New York: Columbia University Press, 1996.

Jaffrelot, Christophe. "Composite Culture is not Multiculturalism: A Study of the Indian Constituent Assembly Debates," in: Ashutosh Varshney, India and the Politics of Developing Countries. New Delhi: Sage Publications, 2004. 126–149.

Jalal, Ayesha. *The Sole Spokesman: Jinnah, the Muslim League and the Demand for Pakistan*. Cambridge University Press, 1994.

Jamal, Amal. "The Contradictions of State–Minority Relations in Israel: The Search for Clarifications." *Constellations* 16, no. 3 (2009): 493–508.

"Future Visions and Current Dilemmas: On the Political Ethos of Palestinian Citizens of Israel." *Israel Studies Forum* 23, no. 2 (2008).

"Strategies of Minority Struggle for Equality in Ethnic States: Arab Politics in Israel." *Citizenship Studies* 11 (2007): 263–82.

Jennings, Ivor. *The Law and the Constitution*. London: University of London Press, 1959.

Jinnah, Mohammad Ali. "Forward." In M. R. T., *Nationalism in Conflict in India*. Bombay: Home Study Circle, 1942.

Jones, Thomas. *Whitehall Diary, Vol. III: Ireland 1918–1925*. Edited by Keith Middlemas. London: Oxford University Press, 1971.

Kalyvas, Andreas. *Democracy and the Politics of the Extraordinary: Max Weber, Carl Schmitt and Hanna Arendt*. Cambridge University Press, 2008.

Kalyvas, Stathis N. *The Rise of Christian Democracy in Europe*. Ithaca, NY: Cornell University Press, 1996.

Kamrava, Merhen. "Pseudo-Democratic Politics and Populist Possibilities: The Rise and Demise of Turkey's Refah Party." *British Journal of Middle Eastern Studies* 25, no. 2 (1998).

Karayanni, Michael. "The 'Other' Religion and State Conflict in Israel: On the Nature of Religious Accommodations for the Palestinian-Arab Minority." In *Religion in the Public Sphere: A Comparative Analysis of German, Israeli, American and International Law*, edited by Winfried Brugger and Michael Karayanni. Berlin: Springer, 2007.

Karp, Yehudit. "Basic Law: Human Liberty and Dignity – a Biography of Power Struggles." *Mishpat Umimshal* 1 (1993).

Karsh, Efraim. *Fabricating Israeli History: The "New Historians."* London and Portland: Frank Cass, 2000.

Kaviraj, Sudipta. "Modernity and Politics in India." *Daedalus* 129, no. 1 (2000): 137–62.

"Writing, Speaking, Being: Language and the Historical Formation of Identities in India." In *Nationalstaat Und Sprachkonflikte in Sud- Und Sudostadien*, edited by Dagmar Hellmann-Rajanayagam and Dietmar Rothernund, 25–65. Stuttgart: Franz Steiner Verlag, 1992.

Kedar, Nir. *Mamlakhtiyut: David Ben-Gurion's Civic Thought*. Jerusalem: Yad Ben-Zvi and Ben-Gurion Research Institute, Ben-Gurion University of the Negev, 2009.

Keith, Arthur Berriedale. *Letters on Imperial Relations, Indian Reform, Constitutional and International Law 1916–1935*. London: Oxford University Press, 1935.

Kelsen, Hans. *General Theory of Law and State*. New York: Russell & Russell, 1961.

Kennedy, Hugh. "Character and Sources of Constitution of the Irish Free State." *American Bar Association Journal* 14, no. 8 (1928).

Keogh, Dermot. "The Constitutional Revolution: An Analysis of the Making of the Constitution." In *The Constitution of Ireland 1937–1987*, edited by Frank Litton. Dublin: Institute of Public Administration, 1988.

Khan-Durrani, F. K. *"The Meaning of Pakistan." Lahore: Sh. Muhammad Ashraf* (1944).

Khilnani, Sunil. *The Idea of India*. New York: Farrar, Straus and Giroux, 1999.

"Nehru's Faith." In *The Crisis of Secularism in India*, edited by Anuradha Dingwaney Needham and Rajeswari Sunder Rajan, 89–103. Durham, NC and London: Duke University Press, 2007.

Kimerling, Baruch. "Religion, Nationality and Democracy in Israel." *Zemanim* 50 (1994).

King, Anthony. *The British Constitution*. Oxford University Press, 2007.

King, Robert D. *Nehru and the Language Politics of India*. Delhi: Oxford University Press, 1997.

Kissane, Bill. *Explaining Irish Democracy*. Dublin: University College Dublin Press, 2002.

The Politics of the Irish Civil War. Oxford University Press, 2005.

Klug, Heinz. *Constituting Democracy: Law, Globalism and South Africa's Political Reconstruction*. Cambridge University Press, 2000.

Knesset Records, Jerusalem, vols. 4–5 (1949–50).

Kohn, Leo. *The Constitution of the Irish Free State*. London: G. Allen & Unwin, 1932.

Kothari, Rajni. *Politics and the People: In Search of a Humane India*. Delhi: Ajanta Publications, 1989.

Kremnitzer, Mordechai. "Between Progress towards and Regression from Constitutional Liberalism: On the Need for Liberal Constitution and Judicial Review of Knesset Legislation." In *Zamir Book: On Law, Government and Society*, edited by Yoav Dotan and Ariel Bendor. Sacher Institute for Legislative Research and Comparative Law, Hebrew University of Jerusalem, 2005.

Kremnitzer, Mordechai, David Kretzmer and Avishai Benish. *The Basic Laws as a Foundation for a Constitution*. Jerusalem: Israel Democracy Institute 2002.

Kretzmer, David. *The Legal Status of the Arabs in Israel.* Boulder: Westview, 1990.
"The New Basic Laws on Human Rights: A Mini Revolution in Israeli Constitutional Law?" *Israel Law Review* 26, no. 2 (1992).

Kriesi, Hanspeter and Alexander H. Trechsel. *The Politics of Switzerland: Continuity and Change in a Consensus Democracy.* Cambridge University Press, 2008.

Kumar, Ravinder and Hari Dev Sharma, eds. *Selected Works of Motilal Nehru,* Vol. 6. New Delhi: Vikas, 1995.

Kumar, Virendra. "Uniform Civil Code Revisited: A Juridical Analysis of *John Vallamattom.*" *Journal of the Indian Law Institute* 45, no. 3–4 (2003): 315–34.

Kurrild-Klitgaard, Peter. "Blood, Baath and Beyond: The Constitutional Dilemma of Iraq." *Public Choice* 119 (2004).

Kymlicka, Will. *Multicultural Citizenship: A Liberal Theory of Minority Rights.* Oxford: Clarendon Press, 1995.

Laborde, Cecile. "From Constitutional to Civic Patriotism." *British Journal of Political Science* 32 (2002): 591–612.

Lacina, Bethany. "Indian Language Groups, Concession of Sub-National Autonomy, and the Origins of Political Violence." Paper presented at the Annual Meeting of the American Political Science Association, Boston, August 28–31, 2008.

Laffan, Michael. *The Partition of Ireland 1911–25.* Dundalk: Dundalgan Press, 1983.

Landau, Jacob M. *The Arabs in Israel: A Political Study.* Oxford University Press, 1969.

Landau, Moshe. "Constitution as a Supreme Law for the State of Israel." *Hapraklit* 27 (1971): 16–30.
"The Supreme Court as Constitution Maker for Israel." *Mishpat Umimshal: Law and Government in Israel* 3, no. 3 (1996).

Layish, Aharon. *Women and Islamic Law in a Non-Muslim State: A Study Based on Sharia Courts in Israel.* New Brunswick: Transaction Publishers, 2006.

Lerner, Hanna. "Constitutional Ambiguity as a Critical Juncture in the Evolution of Religion–State Relations: Lessons from Israel and India" (unpublished paper).
"Democracy, Constitutionalism and Identity: The Anomaly of the Israeli Case." *Constellations* 11, no. 2 (2004).
"Entrenching the Status Quo: Religion and State in Israel's Constitutional Proposals." *Constellations* 16, no. 3 (2009): 443–61.

Levinson, Sanford. *Constitutional Faith.* Princeton University Press, 1988.
ed. *Responding to Imperfection: The Theory and Practice of Constitutional Amendment.* Princeton University Press, 1995.

Lifschitz, Shachar. "Spousal Registration – Preliminary Design." In *Book in Memory of Prof. Shava,* edited by Aharon Barak and Daniel Friedman. Tel Aviv: Ramot-Tel Aviv University Press, 2006.

Lijphart, Arend. "Constitutional Design in Divided Societies." *Journal of Democracy* 15, no. 2 (2004).

Democracy in Plural Societies: A Comparative Exploration. New Haven: Yale University Press, 1977.

"Majority Rule Versus Democracy in Deeply Divided Societies." *Politikon* 4, no. 2 (1977): 113–27.

"Non-Majoritarian Democracy: A Comparison of Federal and Consociational Theories." *Publius, Federalism and Consociationalism: A Symposium* 15, no. 2 (1985): 3–15.

Patterns of Democracy: Government Forms and Performance in Thirty-Six Countries. New Haven: Yale University Press, 1999.

The Politics of Accommodation: Pluralism and Democracy in the Netherlands. Berkeley: University of California Press, 1968.

"The Puzzle of Indian Democracy: A Consociational Interpretation." *American Political Science Review* 90, no. 2 (1996): 258–68.

Linz, Juan J. and Alfred C. Stepan. *Problems of Democratic Transition and Consolidation: Southern Europe, South America, and Post-Communist Europe.* Baltimore: The Johns Hopkins University Press, 1996.

Linz, Juan J. Alfred Stepan and Yogendra Yadav. *Crafting State Nations: India and Other Multinational Democracies.* Baltimore: The Johns Hopkins University Press, 2011.

Liviatan, Ofrit. "Judicial Activism and Religion-Based Tensions: The Case of India and Israel." *Arizona Journal of International and Comparative Law* 26, no. 3 (2009).

Longford, Frank Pakenham. *Peace by Ordeal: The Negotiation of the Anglo-Irish Treaty, 1921.* London: Pimlico, 1992.

Longford, the Earl of, and Thomas P. O'Neill. *Eamon De Valera.* London: Hutchinson, 1970.

Lotan, Orit. "'Mesoravot Get' (Denied of Divorce) in Israel." Report Presented to the Knesset Committee on the Status of Women, 2005.

Ludwikowski, Rett R. *Constitution-Making in the Region of Former Soviet Dominance.* Durham, NC: Duke University Press, 1996.

Lustick, Ian. *Arabs in the Jewish State: Israel's Control of a National Minority.* Austin: University of Texas Press, 1980.

"Stability in Deeply Divided Societies: Consociationalism Versus Control." *World Politics* 31, no. 3 (1979): 325–44.

Luther, Narendra. *Hyderabad: Memoirs of a City.* Hyderabad: Orient Longman, 1995.

Lutz, Donald S. "Toward a Theory of Constitutional Amendment." *American Political Science Review* 80, no. 2 (1994): 356.

"Thinking About Constitutionalism at the Start of the Twenty-First Century." *Publius* 30, no. 4 (2000): 115–35.

Lyons, F. S. L. *Ireland since the Famine.* Glasgow: Fontana/Collins, 1975.

Macardle, Dorothy. *The Irish Republic: A Documented Chronicle of the Anglo-Irish Conflict and the Partitioning of Ireland, with a Detailed Account of the Period 1916–1923.* New York: Farrar, Straus and Giroux, 1965.

McDougall, Walter A. *Freedom Just around the Corner: A New American History 1585–1828.* New York: HarperCollins, 2004.

McGarry, John and Brendan O'Leary. "Iraq's Constitution of 2005: Liberal Consociation as Political Prescription." In *Constitutional Design for Divided Societies,* edited by Sujit Choudhry. Oxford University Press, 2008.

McGarry, John, Brendan O'Leary and Richard Simeon. "Integration or Accommodation? The Enduring Debate in Conflict Regulation." In *Constitutional Design for Divided Societies,* edited by Sujit Choudhry. Oxford University Press, 2008.

McIlwain, Charles Howard. *Constitutionalism, Ancient and Modern.* Rev. edn. Ithaca, NY: Great Seal Books, 1958.

MacMillan, Gretchen M. *State, Society and Authority in Ireland: The Foundation of the Modern State.* Dublin: Gill and Macmillan, 1993.

McWhinney, Edward. *Constitution Making: Principles, Process, Practice.* University of Toronto Press, 1981.

Mahmood, Tahir. *Personal Law in Crisis.* New Delhi: Manohar, 1986.

Mansergh, Nicholas. *The Commonwealth Experience.* 2nd edn., 2 vols. London: Macmillan, 1981.

"The Prelude to Partition: Concepts and Aims in Ireland and India." In *Nationalism and Independence: Selected Irish Papers,* edited by Diana Mansergh, xvii, 264. Cork University Press, 1997.

The Unresolved Question: The Anglo-Irish Settlement and Its Undoing, 1912–72. New Haven: Yale University Press, 1991.

Margalit, Avishai and Joseph Raz. "National Self-Determination." *Journal of Philosophy* 87, no. 9 (1990): 439–61.

Martínez-Herrera, Enric and Thomas Jeffrey Miley. "The Constitution and the Politics of National Identity in Spain." *Nations and Nationalism* 16, no. 1 (2010).

Mautner, Menachem. "The 1980s: The Years of Anxiety." *Iyunei Mishpat* 26, no. 2 (2002).

"The Decline of Formalism and the Rise of Values in Israeli Law." *Iyunei Mishpat* 13, no. 3 (1993).

Mazie, Steven V. "Importing Liberalism: *Brown* v. *Board of Education* in the Israeli Context." *Polity* 36, no. 3 (2004).

Meeting of Mapai Party in the Knesset and Party Secretariat, 14 June 1949, Tel Aviv. The Moshe Sharett Israel Labor Party Archives, Beit Berl.

Meeting of Mapai Party in the Knesset and Party Secretariat, 15 May 1949, Tel Aviv. The Moshe Sharett Israel Labor Party Archives, Beit Berl.

Mehrotra, S. R. *A History of the Indian National Congress.* New Delhi: Vikas Pub. House, 1995.

Menski, Wener. "The Uniform Civil Code Debate in Indian Law: New Developments and Changing Agenda." *German Law Journal* 9, no. 3 (2008): 211–50.

Mertens, Thomas. "Cosmopolitanism and Citizenship: Kant against Habermas." *European Journal of Philosophy* 4 (1996): 328–47.

Miller, Ronald E. "Indian Muslim Critiques of Gandhi." In *Indian Critiques of Gandhi,* edited by Harold Coward, 193–216. Albany: State University of New York Press, 2003.

Moon, Penderel. *Divide and Quit.* Berkeley: University of California Press, 1962.

Moore, R. J. "Jinnah and the Pakistan Demand." In *India's Partition: Process, Strategy and Mobilization,* edited by Mushirul Hasan, 160–97. Delhi and Oxford: Oxford University Press, 2001.

Morris, Benny. *The Birth of the Palestinian Refugee Problem Revisited.* Cambridge University Press, 2004.

Mosley, Leonard. *The Last Days of the British Raj.* 1st American edn. New York: Harcourt Brace & World, 1962.

Mouffe Chantal, ed. *The Challenge of Carl Schmitt.* London and New York: Verso, 1999.

On the Political. London: Routledge, 2005.

Moynihan, Maurice, ed. *Speeches and Statements by Eamon De Valera 1917–1973.* New York: St. Martin's Press, 1980.

Muller, Jan-Werner. *Constitutional Patriotism.* Princeton University Press, 2007.

Murphy, Brian P. "Nationalism: The Framing of the Constitution of the Irish Free State, 1922 – the Drafting Battle for the Irish Republic." In *The Irish Revolution, 1913–1923,* edited by Joost Augusteijn, xiii, 248. New York: Palgrave, 2002.

Murphy, Walter F. "Constitutions, Constitutionalism and Democracy." In *Constitutionalism and Democracy: Transitions in the Contemporary World,* edited by Douglas Greenberg, Stanley N. Katz, Melanie Beth Oliviero and Steven C. Wheatley, 3–25. New York and Oxford: Oxford University Press, 1993.

Constitutional Democracy: Creating and Maintaining a Just Political Order. Edited by Sanford Levinson and Jeffrey K. Tulis. Baltimore: The Johns Hopkins University Press, 2007.

Nanda, B. R. *Mahatma Gandhi: A Biography.* New Delhi: Oxford University Press, 1989.

Nehru, Jawaharlal. *An Autobiography.* Translated by H. Glikshtein. Merchavia, Palestine: Hakibutz Haartzi, Hashomer Hatzair, 1942.

The Discovery of India. Centenary edn. Delhi and New York: Oxford University Press, 1989.

The Unity of India: Collected Writings, 1937–1940. London: L. Drummond, 1948.

Neuberger, Benjamin. *The Constitution Debate in Israel.* Tel Aviv: Open University of Israel, 1997.

Nigam, R. C. *Language Handbook on Mother Tongues in Census*, Census of India 1971, New Delhi, 1972.

Noel, Sidney John Roderick, ed. *From Power Sharing to Democracy: Post-Conflict Institutions in Ethnically Divided Societies.* Montreal: McGill-Queen's Press, 2005.

Nordlinger, Eric A. *Conflict Regulation in Divided Societies.* Cambridge, MA: Center for International Affairs, Harvard University, 1972.

O'Duffy, Brendan. "British and Irish Conflict Regulation from Sunningdale to Belfast, Part II: Playing for a Draw 1985–1999." *Nations and Nationalism* 6, no. 3 (2000): 399–435.

O'Flynn, Ian, David Russle and Donald Horowitz, eds. *Power Sharing: New Challenges for Divided Societies.* London: Pluto Press, 2005.

O'Leary, Brendan. "The Nature of the British–Irish Agreement." *New Left Review* I/233 (1999).

Oxford English Dictionary. Oxford University Press, 2002.

Özbudun, Ergun. "Constitution Making and Democratic Consolidation in Turkey." In *Institutions and Democratic Statecraft*, edited by Metin Heper, Ali Kazancıgil and Bert A. Rockman. Boulder: Westview Press, 1997.

Özbudun, Ergun and Ömer Faruk Gençkaya. *Democratization and the Politics of Constitution Making in Turkey.* Budapest: Central European University Press, 2009.

Paine, Thomas and Gordon S. Wood. *Common Sense and Other Writings.* Modern Library pbk. edn. New York: Modern Library, 2003.

Pandey, Gyanendra. *The Construction of Communalism in Colonial North India.* Delhi: Oxford University Press, 1990.

Pappe, Ilan. *The Ethnic Cleansing of Palestine.* Oxford: Oneworld, 2006.

Pappu, Shyamla. "Women and the Law." In *Problems and Concerns of Indian Women*, edited by B. K. Pal. New Delhi: ABC Publishing, 1987.

Peled, Yoav. "Citizenship Betrayed: Israel's Emerging Immigration and Citizenship Regime." *Theoretical Inquiries in Law* 8, no. 2 (2007).

"Ethnic Democracy and the Legal Construction of Citizenship: Arab Citizens of the Jewish State." *American Political Science Review* 86, no. 2 (June 1992): 434–5.

Peres, Yochanan and Ephraim Yuchtman-Yaar. *Between Consent and Dissent: Democracy and Peace in the Israeli Mind.* Jerusalem: The Israel Democracy Institute, 1998.

Philips, C. H. and Mary Doreen Wainwright. *The Partition of India: Policies and Perspectives, 1935–1947.* Cambridge, MA: The MIT Press, 1970.

Pinto, Meital and Hillel Sommer. "From Particular Legislation to General Doctrine: The Role of the Judiciary in Entrenching Affirmative Action in Israel." In *Affirmative Action and Guarantees of Representation in Israel*, edited by Anat Maor. Tel Aviv: Ramot, Tel Aviv University Press, 2005,

Prager, Jeffrey. *Building Democracy in Ireland: Political Order and Cultural Integration in a Newly Independent Nation*. Cambridge and New York: Cambridge University Press, 1986.

Preuss, Ulrich K. "Constitutional Powermaking of the New Polity: Some Deliberations on the Relations between Constituent Power and the Constitution." In *Constitutionalism, Identity, Difference and Legitimacy*, edited by Michael Rosenfeld, 143–64. Durham, NC and London: Duke University Press, 1994.

Constitutional Revolution: The Link between Constitutionalism and Progress. Atlantic Highlands: Humanities Press, 1995.

"Political Order and Democracy." In *The Challenge of Carl Schmitt*, edited by Chantal Mouffe. London and New York: Verso, 1999.

Publius. *The Federalist Papers by Alexander Hamilton, James Madison and John Jay*. New York: Bantam Books, 1982.

Raday, Frances. "Religion, Multiculturalism and Equality: The Israeli Case." *Israel Yearbook on Human Rights* 25 (1995): 193–241.

Raday, Frances, C. Shalev and Michal Liban-Kooby, eds. *Women's Status in Israeli Society and Law*. Jerusalem: Shocken, 1995.

Radzyner, Amihai. "A Constitution for Israel: The Design of the Leo Kohn Proposal, 1948," *Israeli Studies* 54, no. 1 (2010): 1–24.

Rahman, Anika. "Religious Rights Versus Women's Rights in India: A Test Case for International Human Rights Law." *Columbia Journal of Transnational Law* 28 (1990).

Raj, S., ed. *Quest for Gender Justice: A Critic of the Status of Women in India*. London: Sangam, 1995.

Rao, B. Shiva. *The Framing of India's Constitution*. Vols. i–v. New Delhi: The Indian Institution of Public Administration, 1966.

Rattan, Jyoti. "Uniform Civil Code in India: A Binding Obligation under International and Domestic Law." *Journal of the Indian Law Institute* 46, no. 4 (2004): 577–87.

Rau, B. N. *India's Constitution in the Making*. Bombay: Orient Longmans, 1960.

Rawls, John. *Political Liberalism*. New York: Columbia University Press, 1996.

Reilly, Benjamin. *Democracy in Divided Societies: Electoral Engineering for Conflict Management*. Cambridge University Press, 2001.

Report of the Committee appointed by the All India Conference to Determine the Principles of the Constitution for India, 1928. In Ravinder Kumar and Hari Dev Sharma, eds., *Selected Works of Motilal Nehru*, Vol. 6. New Delhi: Vikas, 1995, 1–89.

Reynolds, Andrew, ed. *The Architecture of Democracy: Constitutional Design, Conflict Management, and Democracy*. New York: Oxford University Press, 2002.

Rizvi, Gowher. "Nehru and the Indo-Pakistan Rivalry over Kashmir 1947–64." *Contemporary South Asia* 4, no. 1 (1995).

Roeder, Philip G. and Donald S. Rothcild, eds. *Sustainable Peace: Power and Democracy after Civil Wars*. Ithaca, NY: Cornell University Press, 2005.

Rogan, Eugene L. and Avi Shlaim, eds. *The War for Palestine: Rewriting the History of 1948*. Cambridge University Press, 2001.

Rotenstreich, Nathan. "Constitution for Israel: Is it its Time?" *Molad* 3 (1949).

Rubin, Barnett R. "Crafting a Constitution for Afghanistan." *Journal of Democracy* 15, no. 3 (2004).

Rubinstein, Amnon. "The Right to Marry." *Iunei Mishpat* 3 (1973/4).

Rubinstein, Amnon and Barak Medina. *Constitutional Law of the State of Israel*. 6th edn. Tel Aviv: Schocken, 2005.

Ruparelia, Sanjay. "How the Politics of Recognition Enabled India's Democratic Exceptionalism." *International Journal of Politics, Culture, and Society* 21, no. 4 (2008): 39–56.

Saban, Ilan. "The Collective Rights of Arab-Palestinian Minority in Israel: The 'Is', the 'Isn't' and the Taboo." *Iyunei Mishpat* 26 (2002).

Safran, Willian and Ramon Maiz Suarez, eds. *Identity and Territorial Autonomy in Plural Societies*. London: Routledge, 2000.

Sajó, András. *Limiting Government: An Introduction to Constitutionalism*. Budapest: Central European University Press, 1999.

Sarangi, Asha, ed. *Language and Politics in India*. New Delhi: Oxford University Press, 2009.

Sartori, Giovanni. "Comparing and Miscomparing." *Journal of Theoretical Politics* 3, no. 3 (1991): 243–57.

Saunders, Allan F. "The Irish Constitution." *American Political Science Review* 18, no. 2 (1924): 340–45.

Scheuerman, William E. *Carl Schmitt: The End of Law, Twentieth Century Political Thinkers*. Lanham: Rowman & Littlefield, 1999.

Schmitt, Carl. *Constitutional Theory*. Translated by Jeffrey Seitzer. Durham, NC: Duke University Press, 2008.

   The Concept of the Political. Chicago: The University of Chicago Press, 1967.

Scolnicov, Anat. "Religious Law, Religious Courts and Human Rights within Israeli Constitutional Structure." *International Journal of Constitutional Law* 4, no. 4 (2006).

Segal, Zeev, M. Landau and Aharon Barak. "United Mizrahi Bank Decision – after Three Years: A Symposium." *Hamishpat* 5 (2000).

Segev, Yehoshua. "Why Does Israel Not Have and Will Not Have (at Least in the near Future) a Constitution? On the Advantages of 'the Decision Not to Decide.'" *Moznei Mishpat* 5 (2006).

Seitzer, Jeffrey. *Comparative History and Legal Theory: Carl Schmitt in the First German Democracy.* Westport and London: Greenwood Press, 2001.

Sen, Dhirendranath. *Revolution by Consent?* Calcutta. Saraswaty Library, 1947.

Shafir, Gershon and Yoav Peled. *Being Israeli: The Dynamics of Multiple Citizenship.* Cambridge University Press, 2002.

Shamir, Ronen. "Zionism 2000: Past, Future, and the Qa'dan Family." *Adalah's Review* 2 (2000).

Shankar, Shylashri. "The War of the Worlds: Political Equality and Religious Freedom in India and Israel." PhD dissertation, Columbia University, 2002.

Shapira, Yonathan. *Politicians as a Hegemonic Class: The Case of Israel.* Tel Aviv: Sifriat Poalim, 1996.

Sheleg, Yair. *Following the Multitude: Rabbinical Attitudes Towards Democracy in Israel,* Policy Research 67. Jerusalem: Israel Democracy Institute, 2006.

Shiffman, Pinchas. *Civil or Sacred: Civil Marriage and Divorce Alternatives in Israel.* Jerusalem: The Association for Civil Rights in Israel, 2001.

Shitrit, Shimon. "The Issues of Equality and Separate Inhabitation in Community Settlements and Villages: Was the *Ka'adan* Ruling Inevitable?" *Karka (Land): A Journal for Discussing Land Issues* 56, no. 27–65 (2003).

Sieyès, Emmanuel Joseph. *What Is the Third Estate?* New York: Praeger, 1964.

Singh, Anita Inder. *The Origins of the Partition of India, 1936–1947.* Delhi and New York: Oxford University Press, 1990.

Singh, Khushwant. *Train to Pakistan.* New York: Grove Press, 1956.

Smith, Anthony. *The Ethnic Origins of Nations.* Oxford and New York: B. Blackwell, 1986.

Smith, Donald Eugene. *India as a Secular State.* Princeton University Press, 1963.

Nehru and Democracy. Bombay: Orient Longmans, 1958.

Smooha, Sammy. "Ethnic Democracy: Israel as an Archetype." *Israel Studies* 2, no. 2 (1997) 198–241.

Index of Arab-Jewish Relations in Israel. Haifa: The Jewish-Arab Center, University of Haifa, 2004.

"Minority Status in an Ethnic Democracy: The Status of the Arab Minority in Israel." *Ethnic and Racial Studies* 13 (1990): 389–413.

Som, Reba. "Jawaharlal Nehru and the Hindu Code: A Victory of Symbol over Substance?" *Modern Asia Studies* 28, no. 1 (1994): 165–94.

Somek, Alexander. "Postconstitutional Treaty." *German Law Journal* 8, no. 12 (2007): 1121–32.

Sommer, Hillel, Tamar Waldman and Anat Yahav. "Constitutional Right of Equality." Presented to the Knesset Committee of Constitution, Law and Justice, 2005.

Sprinzak, Ehud. *Brother against Brother: Violence and Extremism in Israeli Politics from Altalena to the Rabin Assassination.* New York: The Free Press, 1999.

Stepan, Alfred. "Paths toward Redemocratization: Theoretical and Comparative Considerations." In *Transitions from Authoritarian Rule: Comparative Perspectives*, edited by Guillermo O'Donnell, Philippe C. Schmitter and Laurence Whitehead. Baltimore and London: The Johns Hopkins University Press, 1988.

"Religion, Democracy, and the 'Twin Tolerations'." *Journal of Democracy* 11, no. 4 (2000).

"Toward a New Comparative Politics of Federalism, (Multi)Nationalism, and Democracy: Beyond Rikerian Federalism." In *Arguing Comparative Politics*, 315–61. Oxford University Press, 2001.

Stepan, Alfred C. *Arguing Comparative Politics*. Oxford and New York: Oxford University Press, 2001.

Storing, Herbert J. "Slavery and the Moral Foundation of the American Revolution." In *The Moral Foundation of the American Republic*, edited by Robert H. Horowitz, 214–33. Charlottesville: University Press of Virginia, 1979.

Strum, Philippa. "The Road Not Taken: Constitutional Non-Decision Making in 1948–1950 and Its Impact on Civil Liberties in the Israeli Political Culture." In *Israel: The First Decade of Independence*, edited by S. Ilan Troen and Noah Lucas. Albany: State University of New York Press, 1995.

Subramanian, Narendra. "Making Family and Nation: Hindu Marriage Law in Early Postcolonial India," *Journal of Asian Studies* 69, no. 3 (2010): 771–98.

"Myth of the Nation, Cultural Recognition and Personal Law in India," paper presented at the Conference of National Myths, Harvard University, May 2009.

Sunstein, Cass R. *Designing Democracy: What Constitutions Do*. Oxford and New York: Oxford University Press, 2001.

Sweet, Alec Stone. *Governing with the Judges: Constitutional Politics in Europe*. Oxford University Press, 2000.

Swirski, Barbara and M. P. Safir. *Calling the Equality Bluff: Woman in Israel*. New York: Pergamon Press, 1991.

Tamir, Yael. *Liberal Nationalism, Studies in Moral, Political, and Legal Philosophy*. Princeton University Press, 1995.

"Two Concepts of Multiculturalism." *Journal of Philosophy of Education* 29, no. 2 (1995).

Tarr, George Alan, Robert Forrest Williams and Joseph Marko, eds. *Federalism, Subnational Constitutions and Minority Rights*. Santa Barbara: Greenwood Publishing Group, 2004.

Taylor, Charles and Amy Gutmann. *Multiculturalism and "The Politics of Recognition": An Essay*. Princeton University Press, 1992.

Thier, J. Alexander. "The Making of a Constitution in Afghanistan." *New York Law School Law Review* 51, no. 3 (2006).

Thomas, David M. *Whistling Past the Graveyard: Constitutional Abeyances, Quebec, and the Future of Canada.* Toronto: Oxford University Press, 1997.

Tierney, Stephen. *Constitutional Law and National Pluralism.* Oxford University Press, 2004.

Tuathaigh, Gearoid O. "Irish Nation-State in the Constitution." In *De Valera's Constitution and Ours,* edited by Brian Farrell. Dublin: Gearoid O Tuathaigh, 1988.

Tully, James. *Strange Multiplicity: Constitutionalism in an Age of Diversity.* Cambridge and New York: Cambridge University Press, 1995.

Tully, James and Alain G. Gagnon, eds. *Multinational Democracies.* Cambridge University Press, 2001.

Tushnet, Mark. *Taking the Constitution Away from the Court.* Princeton University Press, 1999.

Ugo M. Amoretti and Nancy Bermeo, eds. *Federalism and Territorial Cleavages.* Baltimore: The Johns Hopkins University Press, 2004.

Usman, Jeffrey. "Non-Justiciable Directive Principles: A Constitutional Design Defect." *Michigan State Journal of International Law* 15 (2007).

Vahrhaftig, Zerach. *A Constitution for Israel: Religion and State.* Jerusalem: Mesilot, 1988.

Varshney, Ashutosh. *Ethnic Conflict and Civic Life: Hindus and Muslims in India.* New Haven and London: Yale University Press, 2002.

"Why Democracy Survives." *Journal of Democracy* 9, no. 3 (1998).

Viroli, Maurizio. *For Love of Country: An Essay on Patriotism and Nationalism.* Oxford University Press, 1995.

Wachendorfer-Schmidt, Ute, ed. *Federalism and Political Performance.* London: Routledge, 2000.

Waldron, Jeremy. "Precommitment and Disagreement." In *Law and Disagreement.* New York: Oxford University Press, 1999.

Walker, Neil. "Europe's Constitutional Engagement." *Ratio Juris* 18 (2005): 387–99.

Walzer, Michael. *Spheres of Justice: A Defense of Pluralism and Equality.* New York: Basic Books, 1983.

Ward, Alan J. *The Irish Constitutional Tradition: Responsible Government and Modern Ireland, 1782–1992.* Washington, DC: Catholic University of America Press, 1994.

Webber, Jeremy. "Constitutional Reticence." *Australian Journal of Legal Philosophy* 25 (2000).

Reimagining Canada: Language, Culture, Community, and the Canadian Constitution. Kingston and Buffalo: McGill University Press, 1994.

Weiler, J. H. H. *The Constitution of Europe.* Cambridge University Press, 1999.

Weiler, J. H. H. and Marlene Wind, eds. *European Constitutionalism Beyond the State.* Cambridge University Press, 2003.

Weller, Marc and Stefan Wolff, eds. *Autonomy, Self-Government and Conflict Resolution: Innovative Approaches to Institutional Design in Divided Societies*. London: Routledge, 2005.

Wheare, K. C. *Modern Constitutions*. London: Oxford University Press, 1966.

Whyte, John Henry. *Church and State in Modern Ireland, 1923–1970*. Dublin: Gill and Macmillan, 1971.

Wilkinson, Steven. *Votes and Violence: Electoral Competition and Ethnic Violence in India*. Cambridge and New York: Cambridge University Press, 2004.

Wittgenstein, Ludwig. *Philosophical Investigations*. Translated by G. E. M. Anscombe. New York: Macmillan, 1968.

Wood, Gordon S. *The Creation of the American Republic, 1776–1787*. New York: Norton, 1972.

Wood, Patricia J. *Judicial Power and National Politics: Courts and Gender in the Religious–Secular Conflict in Israel*. Albany: State University of New York Press, 2008.

Yakobson, Alexander and Amnon Rubinstein. *Israel and the Family of Nations: Jewish Nation State and Human Rights*. Tel Aviv: Schocken, 2003.

Yiftachel, Oren. *Ethnocracy: Land and Identity Politics in Israel/Palestine*. Philadelphia: The University of Pennsylvania Press, 2006.

Yildirim, Seval. "Expanding Secularism's Scope: An Indian Case Study." *American Journal of Comparative Law* 52 (2004).

Zakia, Pathak and Rajeswari Sunder Rajan. "Shahbano." *Signs: Journal of Women in Culture and Sociology* 14, no. 3 (1989): 558–82.

Zaidi, A. M., ed. *Congress Presidential Addresses*, Vol. 5. New Delhi: Indian Institute of Applied Political Research, 1985.

Zameret, Zvi. "Yes to the Jewish State no to a Clericalist State: The Mapai Leadership and its Attitude to Religion and Religious Jews." in: Mordechai Bar-On and Zvi Zameret (eds.), *On Both Sides of the Bridge: Religion and State in the Early Years of Israel*. 175–245. Jerusalem: Yad Ben-Zvi Press, 2002.

Zamir, Yitzhak. "Judicial Activism: A Decision to Decide." *Iyunei Mishpat* 17, no. 3 (1993).

Zamir, Yitzhak and Moshe Sobel. "Equality before the Law." *Mishpat Umimshal: Law and Government in Israel* 5 (2000).

Ziv, Neta. "Communities, Lawyers, and Legal Strategies for Social Change – Before and After Qa'dan." *Adalah's Review* 2 (2000).

Zurcher, Eric. *Turkey: Modern History*. London: I. B. Tauris, 2005.

INDEX